Generously Donated
To Sunrise of Seal Beach
By:
Mary McBride

The Powerticians

The Powerticians

THOMAS F. X. SMITH

Lyle Stuart Inc.   Secaucus, N.J.

Second printing
Copyright © 1982 by Thomas F. X. Smith

Queries regarding rights and permissions
should be addressed to: Lyle Stuart Inc.,
120 Enterprise Ave., Secaucus, N.J. 07094

Published by Lyle Stuart Inc.
Published simultaneously in Canada by
Musson Book Company
A division of General Publishing Co. Limited
Don Mills, Ontario

Manufactured in the United States of America

Library of Congress Cataloging in Publication Data
Smith, Thomas F. X.
    The powerticians.

    1. Jersey City (N.J.)—Politics and government.
2. Hague, Frank, 1875–1956.   3. Smith, Thomas F. X.
I. Title.
F144.J557S64   1982   974.9'27043   82-10376
ISBN 0-8184-0328-4

To my mother, Mary Julia Free Smith,
and my dad, James J. Smith,
who looked, talked, thought and loved Jersey City
and the greatness of her people.

Acknowledgements

I would like to recognize the help and assistance of those who were of incalculable aid in completing the manuscript of this book.

For patient editorial suggestions: Jim Bishop, Carol Smith (my daughter), Donald H. Dunn, J. Owen Grundy, John R. Longo, Eugene Scanlon, Mary Ann Bauer, and Allan J. Wilson.

For the indefatigable political research of: Edward Hart, Helen Kozma, Mark Silver, Frank Quinn and Kenneth Quinn.

Miss Joan Doherty, Mr. Ben Grimm, Mr. Arthur Sturcke and the staff of the main branch of the Jersey City Public Library for the countless hours they spent poring over records enabling me to reconstruct decades of Jersey City history.

For offering critical evaluation of the manuscript: Paul J. Byrne, John Graham, Francis X. Hayes, Harold Krieger, Henry Przystup and Karen Quinn.

For collecting the photographs: the staff of *The Jersey Journal*, Irv Wagen, William Tremper, Wide World Photos, and, certainly, the unknown photographers who contributed other pictures.

For historical documentation: Fred W. Martin, Richard Johnson, J. Owen Grundy and John R. Longo.

For research resources: a special thanks to *The Jersey Journal* and *The Hudson Dispatch*.

And last, but certainly not least, the ladies responsible for typing the manuscript: my wife, Florence B. Smith, and my daughter, Mrs. Regina Silver, my sister, Florence C. Smith, Anna Gregory, Kerstin Trone, and my sister, Regina Quinn.

Thomas FX Smith

THOMAS F. X. SMITH

Foreword

It was over.

I knew it, the crowd of well-wishers gathered around me knew it, and even Irv Wagen, busily fussing with his cameras and lenses and film cans, had time to realize that it was over. I was not going to be the Democratic candidate in the 1981 contest for governor of New Jersey. All the votes had not been counted yet, but that much was clear. Along with 12 other hopefuls, I had been defeated.

Sitting there on that wild, exciting evening, trying to focus my attention on three different television screens filled with a blur of numbers, momentarily feeling the surge of hope and joy when the early results from my hometown, Jersey City, showed I was piling up a big lead, it was simple, easy, a pleasure to smile for Irv's ever-present camera. For some 50 years he had photographed the politicians of New Jersey, the heroic ones and the corrupt ones, and I was determined that he was going to get a shot of a Jersey City mayor who considered himself heroic at a moment of triumph.

But as more and more votes were tabulated across the state, it became more difficult to smile. Don't let anyone tell you that losing is just something that happens and you get over it. Not if you're a loser who was determined to be a winner, you don't! Of course, I'd lost before—occasionally the basketball team I'd captained at Saint Peter's College lost a game, and after I'd managed to make my way onto the All-Catholic All-American team and then onto the professional New York Knickerbockers squad—well, there were just those days sometimes when another team was better.

All right, sometimes you couldn't bring yourself to smile. But there was a special reason for it this time. Every bit of your consciousness was going into remembering where you might have made a misstep, what might have been done differently, and what would be done differently in the future, the next time around, the time when you—not them—would come out on top.

That's what was on my mind while Irv, obviously downcast, tried to get me to look like a cheerful, optimistic, *undefeated* candidate for governor. At last he got the shot he wanted.

"That's it!" he cried out, his electronic flash splashing light like a series of fireworks exploding on Fourth of July over the Hudson River. "That's the charm. That's Tommie Smith, the winner!"

Looking back on the scene now, I can tell myself that in a small way, perhaps, the elderly "official photographer" for Jersey City, the state's second largest metropolis, was right. Good Lord, for nearly four years I had served as mayor of a city with a population of some 235,000 people . . . a city with a dual identity, its own and one as a major supply depot for Manhattan and the other boroughs of New York City just across the river . . . a city whose limits enclose Liberty Island where the Statue of Liberty beckons to hundreds of thousands of yearning immigrants. What man could fail to call himself a winner after having made his way up from the tenements—from a "cold-water flat," s' help me—of a downtown section of Jersey City filled with lower- and middle-class members of the working poor, working his way up until he had a say-so not only over those citizens' destinies, but those of the city's wealthiest and most educated as well?

And if I took pride in anything, it was in the fact that I had managed to play both as a member of the team and as an individual who—in the words that were made famous by another resident of Jersey City, Frank Sinatra—"did it my way." Yes, there were those who warned me not to enter the race for the gubernatorial nomination, who told me that my record as mayor of Jersey City would ensure my reelection, so why take a major risk? Well, if I've learned anything in my political career—and in my years at Fordham where I earned a Master's in educational psychology—it's that the fellow who plays it safe is seldom looked upon as a leader. And the man who isn't considered a leader seldom gets the support that he must have from others if he is going to accomplish anything meaningful in life. And by "meaningful" I mean doing the things that help a great many others, not merely oneself.

My decision to try for a job where I thought I might be better able to help the needy people of Jersey City and Hudson County was not the first I made which the numbers later proved to be a "wrong" one. As a former professional basketball player, I had the obvious inclination to back an all-time great on the courts, Bill Bradley, in 1978 when he ran for the Democratic nomination for U.S. Senator from New Jersey. But I had publicly vowed to support Dick Leone, the choice of Governor Brendan Byrne, and—political expediency or not—I have always considered my word my bond. I worked diligently for Leone in Hudson County, where Jersey City is located, and the county came through. As it turned out, Hudson County was the only one of the state's 21 counties that supported the governor's choice—and "Dollar Bill" Bradley scored a tremendous victory.

The reader, I fervently hope, should not be left with an impression of a politician whose failures outnumber his successes. You should know, as I do, that no one man (or woman, for that matter) can succeed time and again, indefinitely. Robert Browning's "Ah, that a man's reach should exceed his grasp, or what's a heaven for?" is all too apt, in politics as in life. What is important is that the man who considers himself a leader *must* reach, must strive to grasp that which is lying just beyond his outstretched fingers—and he must be prepared to tolerate the taunts of those who prophesy failure, who see only self-gain resulting from achievement.

When I returned from a disappointing meeting with President Jimmy Carter at which I urgently proclaimed the need for more federal aid to the urban areas, and at which I felt my pleas were falling upon deaf ears, I expressed my disappointment in no uncertain terms—and earned for myself the sobriquet (that's a five-dollar word for "nickname" taught me by a Jesuit priest somewhere along the educational path) "The Mouth that Roared." Names don't bother me. No one in public life can afford to take the time to worry about that sort of thing. I've called a few people a few things in my time—usually in the heat of controversy—that I never meant for a moment but which I knew would make a point or get a laugh or otherwise bring the crowd to my side. Because of a fortunate combination of genes, a fairly forceful voice comes out of my 6'2" frame and it has been said that I could address a sold-out crowd at Giants Stadium in New Jersey's meadowlands without the benefit of a public address system.

But a voice alone isn't enough to get action when action is needed and the opposition is vigorous. I remembered, even as the gubernatorial primary vote count showed me falling farther behind, that I occasionally had had to take a seemingly unpopular stand during my tenure as mayor to accomplish my objective. One example should suffice here to make the point: The National Park Service and the Circle Line, a company that operates sightseeing boats in New York harbors, had mutually agreed that the line should cancel ferry service between Liberty State Park and the Statue of Liberty and Ellis Island, memorable sites to countless immigrants. Such action would leave the only access to these historic places via ferries from Manhattan—a situation that would require Jersey residents to travel inconveniently into New York and then return to their own state. A man of action, I acted—and threatened to cut off the water supply to both islands!

One does not have to be a very astute politician to know that threatening this kind of thing against our nation's greatest symbols of hope and freedom could produce dire results in a future election, but who can think about political expediency when the welfare of one's constituents—the people you have been elected to serve and help—is concerned? I won the "naval battle"—the ferry service was restored—and the long-range consequences were the last thing on my mind when I and a group of smiling youngsters took the inaugural voyage on a crowded ship.

"So I've had my share of victories," I mused that evening in late spring while the flashguns popped and the corks jumped out of champagne bottles and the numbers mounted ever higher on the various television screens. For only a moment, I wondered if I—if *any* mayor of Jersey City—could possibly achieve *more* had so much time not been spent trying to unravel an entangled web, an image of bossism and corruption, that has fairly shrouded the city for nearly a century.

"At least," I thought that night, "this is nothing like my earliest memory of a Jersey City election. At least no one is out to hang me."

"Did you say something?" said Dr. Vincent Krasnica, a friend and supporter who had drawn near to pass on some late voting information from another county. I suddenly realized that I had been talking half-aloud, as my mind had flashed back to a night some 30 years earlier when I and hundreds of other youngsters from my neighborhood and throughout Jersey City had gathered in front of the becolumned City Hall building to await the election results of the mayoralty race.

"No, Vinny," I said, "I was just remembering something. Something from a long time ago." I closed my eyes for a second, and I could suddenly see it all again, just as it had been that night.

May 10, 1949. A time almost before the roving red eye of the television camera was even envisioned, and certainly had not yet been freed from the confines of the downtown studio. Political parades and demonstrations of the day were organized—staged, if you will—largely by spontaneous combustion, by exciting and inciting the emotions of a gathering, a group, a mob. Yes, some participants realized that they might make good subjects for the hurrying newspaper cameramen, and occasionally a man or woman in the crowd would catch a glimpse of a radio spot news announcer lugging a microphone the size of a dinner plate and seeking to interview a citizen gone mad.

Can I take you back there, back to a time when the new Cadillac—and there were few Cadillacs in my section of Jersey City, and not many in town at all—had just sprouted tiny "fins" at the rear of each fender line . . . a time when an airplane called the Boeing Stratocruiser flew coast-to-coast at 15,000 feet and its ads boasted that the men's and ladies' dressing room and powder room, respectively, "each accomodates six comfortably" . . . a time when the young man or woman who did not use Listerine antiseptic to guard against "halitosis," or bad breath, would have little luck finding romance. It was a simpler time, then, or so it seemed. And the young men (along with a few young women with a taste for excitement) of the "rougher" sections of Jersey City figured that on election night the fun would be in front of City Hall.

Barely out of my teens, I had never seen a crowd like the one gathered in the street before that stately building. Of course, most of the people milling around knew much more about politics than I did at the time. They were quite familiar with the events leading up to this historical night. They knew that a stern, reclusive citizen named Frank Hague had ruled as mayor of Jersey City for three decades, doing what he pleased, paying off whomever he pleased, and seemingly putting what he pleased into his own pocket. Between investigations by tax men and others seeking to pinpoint the sources of his enormous wealth, Hague had managed to get the friendship of governors and presidents—and had been directly responsible for a number of them getting elected. However, after dedicating his life in service to the people of Jersey City, he retired in mid-term and announced that his nephew would serve out the remainder of his term and then run for reelection.

What he had not counted on, of course, was that one of his own lieutenants—John Kenny, an energetic and faithful worker—would turn against him. Kenny, responsible for getting voters in his Second Ward to go along with Hague's ideas, complained about the nephew's appointment. Hague, who could brook no disrespect when he was younger and who could tolerate even less at age 73, ordered Kenny out of the political structure.

The younger man promptly announced the formation of a fusion party, the "Freedom Ticket," and entered the mayoralty race against the nephew, Frank Hague Eggers. Like all the battles in Jersey City political history, it was fought hard and, frequently, with violence—and now the first voting results were trickling into City Hall to be officially counted.

Place yourself now, a bewildered young man, smack in the middle of a mob. Automobile horns blared, police cars roared by with sirens screaming, photographers' flashbulbs made popping sounds as hungry newsmen worked to capture the excitement for the morning editions. There were police everywhere—too many past elections had been investigated and frequently invalidated because boxes filled with ballots to be counted and stored away had disappeared on the short trip from polling place to City Hall. The officers in their uniforms reminded me of my father, who had been a policeman. He had urged me, warned me, not to get involved in politics. In fact, there was a prohibition on any talk on the subject while in the house. Above all, the mayor's name, Frank Hague, was not to be mentioned.

"But, Dad," I asked one day, "why can't we talk about Mayor Hague? Everybody I know, all the kids, talk about him. He built the big Medical Center, and he brought the ball club to town, and—"

My father looked slowly around the room as he raised a hand to silence me. It was as if he thought tiny microphones were hidden behind the drapes or under the table. "Not . . . in . . . this . . . house!" he said slowly, but with great force. "Never!" He dismissed me with a wave of his hand, and I could still hear the echo of his last word fading as I left the room. I recall feeling a bit hurt that the conversation ended so abruptly. From other kids whose dads were policemen, I had heard that 3 percent of my father's annual salary went directly to Frank Hague. I had tried to rationalize what I knew of such pay-offs with logical explanations: "It must be some kind of union dues . . . or a loan Dad's paying back." But in my heart I realized that my father was simply following the advice he'd given me so many times: "If you can't say something good about someone, don't say anything." He evidently had little good to say about Frank Hague, and so . . .

Suddenly, all around me, a roar went up from the crowd. John Kenny had appeared, stepping out from a big car in the street and immediately being lifted onto the shoulders of several cheering admirers. Like a triumphant fighter or baseball hero, he was literally borne aloft, riding over the multitude on a human chariot into the City Hall building. Applause swept after him as everyone in the group craned for a peek at the man who would be the new mayor of Jersey City.

Deposited safely inside the building, Kenny went into a huddle with a quartet of supporters of various backgrounds who were being swept into office along with him. There was Louis Messano, a former assistant prosecutor under the Hague administration, who had also turned against the one-time leader. Another member of the "Freedom Ticket"—Kenny had taken the name from the popular

Freedom Train rolling through America with a display of historic documents from the nation's past—was James F. Murray, a man with the courage of a lion who had fought the Hague machine for 20 years. And there were Donald Spence, an insurance executive and son of a famous local physician, and Charles S. Witkowski, an ex-football player whose name was legendary to many residents of Jersey City.

While the group inside laughed and began to help Kenny work on a victory statement, I stood outside in the growing darkness, watching as torchlights—the real, old-fashioned kind with a knot of fire pouring off oily smoke—began to illuminate parts of the crowd. There was music blaring from somewhere—whether it was a live band or just a phonograph blasting into an amplifier, I could not tell. The crowd in front of City Hall had grown so thick that I could barely move a step in any direction. A tough kid, athletically built, I suddenly felt a tremor of fear go through me. The crowd was focusing its attention on a single window in the huge governmental building behind. I twisted around, straining to see. The window was dark, curtained over—but I somehow sensed that it marked the office of the mayor. Inside, I knew, there was a huge leather chair that Mayor Eggers had sat in for the last two years and that the feared, revered Frank Hague had occupied for almost three decades previously.

The music grew louder. It was a popular World War II song—"Now Is the Hour When We Must Say Goodbye"—and the Kenny forces had used it as a campaign tune, urging voters to rid themselves of the Hague "machine." All around me, people were singing, but their eyes were fixed on the office window. Then I saw it—a group of revelers pushing their way through the crowd, from the street to the City Hall door. On their shoulders they carried an actual coffin supplied by a local undertaking establishment. A sign atop the coffin proclaimed in huge letters, "Here lies the remains of the Hague Machine, 36 years of age."

I realized a few years later, when I was wiser in the ways of crowds, that a sense of humor is sometimes needed to keep a crowd from getting out of hand and turning into a mob bent on vengeance. But at the time, my head stuffed full of such school things as *A Tale of Two Cities* and movies like *Phantom of the Opera* and the *Wolf Man* series, I assumed that the coffin was actually intended for the remains of the defeated candidates. Politics, I remember thinking, is a dangerous game. No wonder my father did not want it discussed in the house.

If ex-mayors Hague and Eggers were inside City Hall, I fervently hoped that they had a secret way to escape, a subterranean passage, perhaps, that would carry them far from the mob that seemingly was bent on their destruction. Evidently they did. Word filtered out from the City Hall building that the defeated team had slipped off into the night. Now the crowd began chanting for Kenny to appear. Long choruses of "We want Johnny, we want Johnny" rose over the sound of the music. And as each distinct cry began to fade away, one of the members of the newly elected team—except Kenny—would suddenly appear on the second floor balcony of the building. As each did so, a throaty roar of welcome welled up from the multitude.

A young man, I did not recognize the faces and barely knew the names, but I yelled myself hoarse for, one after the other, Witkowski, Murray, Messano, and Spence. Each raised his right hand, first two fingers stretched apart in the familiar "victory" sign that Winston Churchill had popularized during the war. The appearance of each victorious candidate momentarily calmed the populace, but visions of the mob storming the Bastille to tear apart Eggers and Hague continued to swim before my eyes. *What terrible things did these men do*, I wondered, even as my body was squeezed against a fence around a plot of grass so tightly that I could scarcely breathe. *What did they do?*

The band, the record, the crowd sang, over and over, "Now Is the Hour." And the hour grew later. Finally, just when I was certain a rowdy part of the assembled citizenry was going to charge City Hall like a band of revolutionary guerrillas to search out the defeated Palace Guard, there came a victory statement from the winner, John Vincent Kenny.

"This," he said, "has been the hour. Tonight Jersey City's people have had their government restored to them, after 36 years of one-man domination. My colleagues, at this hour of triumph, can never forget the citizens who rallied to our side and our gratitude to them can only be expressed in our determination to bring decent, orderly, efficient government to the people of this city. To our friends and supporters, my colleagues and I pledge our every effort to restore Jersey City to its rightful place in the economic, moral, and social life of New Jersey. Let us bid farewell to fear. Let us say goodbye to corruption.''

I feel certain, reader, that you can insert into the foregoing paragraph the cheers and applause of the multitude that I heard that evening some three decades ago. There was no way of my knowing at the time that one day I would be inside the mayor's office, looking out the same window that I looked up at that night. In fact, if any of my boyhood pals had wanted to bet that I would ever enter the political arena, I probably wouldn't have bothered to try to take his money—I would simply have taken a poke at him with a quick right hand.

But, looking back on it now, I still feel the surge of electricity and excitement that swept through me that long evening. I can still remember the music, the ringing words, the roars of applause, and perhaps, somehow, that fusion of sights and sounds fired within me the ambition to strive for public office. One cannot be sure, of course, at precisely which moment in life one's path is chosen and others are forsaken. But there must be a reason why that night refuses to fade in my memory. And if that combination of characters and events caused me to embark on the career that carried me to the mayor's office of Jersey City—and perhaps *beyond* one day—then I truly owe a debt to Kenny, Eggers, Hague, and those who preceded them.

Hence, this volume—a work recounting the fortunes and fates of Jersey City's greatest *power*ticians, many of whom were honorable, and many who were considerably less. But to all of whom I intend to pay my debt.

1

"Let us bid farewell to fear. Let us say goodbye to corruption."

Ringing words, fervently spoken by John V. Kenny on the night that he was elected—by an impressive 22,000-vote majority—over his rival for the mayoralty of Jersey City, Frank H. Eggers. I heard the words as a youngster and felt my heart swelling with pride.

And as a youngster, with all the naivete that implies, I could not foresee the day in 1971 when Kenny's career would end with a jail sentence and a charge by U.S. Attorney Frederick Lacey that Hudson County corruption paralleled that of New York's infamous Tweed Ring at its worst.

Wiser now, I think (and what man doesn't think he grows wiser as he grows older), I intend to do no moralizing. It would be simple enough to try to sum up the intent of this volume with a quote or two—perhaps Santayana's "Those who cannot remember the past are condemned to repeat it," or Friedrich A. J. Von Bernhardi's "Political morality differs from individual morality, because there is no power above the state."

But it is impossible to sum up in a pat phrase the actions of dozens of men, and one man in particular, who governed a major metropolis on the East Coast of the United States for three-quarters of the 20th century. To give the reader a picture of the times and characters, to make him or her understand how intelligent men used and abused their power over others requires more than a line or two of philosophical musings. It requires careful setting of the scene, with the sights and sounds of a forgotten day placed in perspective so that the reader—you—can make your own judgments about the individuals and their actions.

Let us provide an example. You've met John V. Kenny, and you should have no trouble picturing him as the tough-minded fighter that he was. Now meet one of his chief lieutenants, one of "Joisey" City's most beloved citizens, Barney Doyle.

Barney never would have been mistaken for a glad-handing politician. He was a poor kid of Irish immigrant stock, raised in the southern Greenville section of the city, who had followed a typical path taken by youngsters of his ilk: selling shoeshines, peddling papers, trying his skills as a club fighter (where he earned the nickname "The Barn"), and always, always, standing by to help the politicos get out the vote. His own efforts in the voting booth, it was said, bordered on promiscuity. To no one's surprise, he came out of the Navy after World War II and ascended the ranks of the Hudson County machine formed by Kenny. Committeeman, zone leader, ward chieftain—the titles were bestowed on The Barn in dazzling succession.

He wore them proudly, figuring that with the titles and flashy clothes he affected, no one would notice the nose flattened from his boxing days or the rolling, drunken gait that might have resulted from too many left hooks to his chin. Emulating the Jimmy Cagney of the gangster films of the 1930s, Barney hooked his elbows against his waist and looked directly into the eyes of much bigger men, practically daring them to challenge him or his opinions.

That attitude was well known to everyone covering the political scene in the late 1940s, which made what happened at a certain press conference all the more surprising. The conference was held by Mayor Kenny to announce that he was moving his beloved and trusted lieutenant into the higher echelons of the Democratic power structure. Sure, the mayor knew (as did everyone else) that Barney Doyle had made it only to the seventh grade—no mean achievement, considering his neighborhood—but there was a spot open for a man of The Barn's talents. And the chambers were jammed with neighbors, friends, and the press to see Barney accept the title of Commissioner of Weights and Measures for Hudson County.

The announcement was made, the applause resounded through the hall—and a young reporter from the *Jersey Journal* stunned the crowd by asking if he could fire a question—"just one"—at the new commissioner. Barney Doyle's eyes, usually glinting with an innate shrewdness, glazed over just for a second—as they sometimes had when a superior fighter drove a heavy glove into his chubby, scarred face. But he knew the crowd was watching him, certain that he would not quit, no matter how much of a beating he took.

"Aw right, kid, lemme have it," said the new commissioner.

It was a simple question, a smart-ass question: "Now that you're Commissioner of Weights and Measures for all of Hudson County, uh, could you—er—tell us how many ounces are in a pound?"

The reporter grinned, knowing that he had hit The Barn in a vital spot. He had scored a clean knockout. Almost.

Barney Doyle narrowed his eyes, looking in dismay at the young upstart. And then he swung back with his own knockdown punch. "For Christ's sake, gimme a break! I just got the job!"

The roar of laughter put the flush of defeat on the reporter's face, and the new commissioner found himself surrounded by a jovial crowd battling one another to pound congratulations on his back.

Who could fail to love a man like that, a man who—without dropping a hint—once dug deep into his pocket to buy dozens of huge floral bouquets to distribute to aged, homeless women at hospitals and nursing homes on Mother's Day. Not a man, by the way, who sent the flowers over by messenger, but who took them himself, personally handing them out and hugging each recipient, murmuring, "Here, Mom, have a kiss! It's your day!"

The Barn's gone now, but the color he put into Jersey City politics lives on in the memory of hundreds, if not thousands, of local residents. Faults? Sure, he had 'em. But who doesn't? And the people of Jersey City have always stood ready to forget a lot of faults—and forgive—if those who possessed them could provide a laugh now and then along with loyalty and friendship.

This might be the place to take a look at the people and the city itself, to start our investigation of why Jersey City has gained for itself the reputation of being "the Mecca of politics." (Put out of your mind that if politicians almost anywhere else in the U.S. face eastward, they automatically face Jersey City; they face a number of other towns of comparable size—Greenwich, Connecticut, for example—which no one ever thinks of as a Mecca for anything.)

Anyone looking at the raw numbers themselves—population of nearly 250,000, an area of 19.2 square miles, temperatures ranging from 85 degrees in July to 26 degrees in January, and so on—will learn very little. More significant in understanding the lives of the hard-working men and women who live in Jersey City and Hudson County is that each day, merely by looking eastward, they can see the Statue of Liberty at the mouth of the Hudson River. Their eyes also take in the landing place for hundreds of thousands of aspiring immigrants, Ellis Island. And, just beyond, rise the towering spires of the mystical New York skyline. "It's a view that even those people who consider themselves lucky to live in New York City cannot see," comment Jersey City residents.

With the view, the cultural and entertainment facilities of New York close at hand, and *without* the numerous well-known problems of the larger metropolis to worry about (inadequate public transport, soaring rents, racial unrest, etc.), the populace of Jersey City long has seemed content to play the role of a provider to its mammoth neighbor. It has been so almost since September 12, 1609, when Henry Hudson, an English navigator employed by the Dutch East India Company, anchored his flagship, the *Half Moon,* at a tiny inlet that later would be named Communipaw Cove. There today, on a well-manicured spread of greenery, called Liberty State Park, many New Jersey-ites relax and gaze upon the beauty of "Miss Liberty."

In his log for the journey, the *Half Moon's* mate described what he saw as "a very good land to fall in with, and a pleasant land to see." In time, the area—established as the first city in the state—grew into a factory town punctuated with smokestacks. Jersey City, as it would eventually be known, lays claim to the first government in the state, the first waterworks, school, and church. During the Revolutionary War, it held momentary fame as the strategic spot that the Americans planned to   capture   in order to launch a raid (the famous Battle of Paulus Hook) on the British who occupied New York City.

Carved out of small woodland communities, the city soon sprawled to cover an area about seven miles long and three miles wide. It was peopled at first by Dutch colonists. The British followed, and later a flood of immigrants from the troubled countries of Europe—the Irish, the Germans, the Italians, the Poles, and numerous others.

Perpetually in the shadow of Manhattan's skyscrapers—albeit at the time the skyscrapers were barely a dozen stories tall—just across the Hudson, the city took pleasure in its role as a terminus for the nation's railroads. Indeed, upon the death of Abraham Lincoln, the body of the Great Emancipator was carried by train to the local station to be ferried across the river to lie in state in New York City Hall.

But the railroads brought with them the first traces of the corruption that would grow to haunt the city and plague those men—myself included—who would try to overcome the aura of wrongdoing that seemed to float in the city's very air. By the beginning of the 20th century, nearly three dozen railroads owned mile after mile of valuable property in Jersey City. This was more property than they held in any other city in the entire United States. According to George C. Rapport, writing in *The Statesman and the Boss,* the railroad holdings "alone exceeded the entire area of most of the cities of the state."

Waterfront property facing Manhattan and the other New York City boroughs and looking toward the prospering farmlands of Long Island was considered among the choicest real estate in America. Active bidding by rival rail firms for pieces of waterfront land soon resulted in the city itself owning only about 130 feet of Hudson River property, notes Rapport. The remainder of the four-mile stretch of waterfront land was owned by the builders of docks, railroad yards, and warehouses. Buying up such select parcels not only meant that the purchasers had to come up with sizable outlays of cash—and this was no problem to the prosperous railroad magnates—but it meant they had to work through politicians who could make a good case why Jersey City should be sold off piece by piece. And, once the politicians who were willing to make deals were pinpointed, they had to be convinced to keep taxes low if the railroad owners were to realize sizable profits on their investments.

For nearly 30 years after the Civil War, a period during which a wave of Republicanism swept the country, the railroad barons paid homage—and cash—to the Democrats who tenaciously held onto control of the political reins of New Jersey. Every governor of the state, from 1869 to 1896, was a Democrat. And beneath these men, a wide-ranging and tough-minded group of political party bosses controlled the counties.

With such a history, stretching over a period of 25 years, it is easy to see where the city's reputation—and that of the state, for that matter—for corruption, skullduggery, and political legerdemain began. Asked recently by a young reporter why my hometown has been unable to shake off its aura of political chicanery, I responded with the suggestion that the questioner might as well ask why Italians are singers, Jews intellectuals, and Blacks prizefighters. Some things cannot be questioned; they simply *are*.

As the abuses became more prevalent, however, the Republicans in the state legislature banded together to order a full-scale investigation. Obviously, if things were allowed to continue the way they were going, soon the entire city would be owned by powerful monetary interests. The investigation paid off with a startling series of revelations about corruption by the Democrats at all levels. Among other things, the probers found that a number of state legislators had taken bribes from gambling interests to cast favorable votes on the legalization of racetrack betting. The publicity resulting from the investigation produced a downturn in the party's fortunes. Shortly before the turn of the century, the Republicans took over control of the state legislature, and by 1906 only seven Democrats held onto their seats in that august body.

Still, in 1901, Jersey City remained in the grip of a powerful Democratic machine. For that reason, it was all the more startling that the populace turned out to elect a Republican mayor. A year earlier, the incumbent Republican president, William McKinley, had crushed his opponent, William Jennings Bryan, and the Republicans had swept every New Jersey county with the sole exception of Hudson. Seeking to strengthen their grip, the Democrats gave up on their mayoralty candidate, man who already had served two terms, Edward Hoos; and local party boss Robert Davis nominated one George T. Smith to try to succeed him. The voter, Davis realized, might be in the mood for change.

But the people wanted more than that. The Republican candidate, Mark M. Fagan, had a serious air that impressed them. An Irish undertaker, he was lanky and wore sober, meticulously chosen clothes. A pair of pince-nez eyeglasses resting in perfect balance above his thin nose helped impress listeners who heard him vow in speeches that his election would cause the railroads to pay heavy taxes on the valuable pieces of Jersey City property they owned. And, of course, that meant the public's tax burden would be less.

Fagan had grown up in a section of the city known as the "Bloody Angle," a densely populated area where political discussion was a basic form of entertainment for many residents. A neighbor of Fagan's, Joe Tumulty, who later would become personal secretary and advisor to President Woodrow Wilson, is reported to have said, "Politics had me years before I could vote."

The people had plenty to talk about. They argued over whether the Democratic party boss really thought George T. Smith would make a good mayor—or had Davis proposed the candidate because Smith, a railroad executive, was the son-in-law of one of the area's wealthiest men, Edward F. C. Young? It was well known that Young, president of the First National Bank and a director of the Pennsylvania Railroad Company, had backed Davis during his rise in the party to the post of county sheriff, after which he was soon calling the shots on party patronage throughout the area.

Strongly partisan, the newspapers—the *Evening Journal* and the *Jersey City News*—took sides for their candidates. The *Journal* sensed an opportunity to return a member of the Grand Old Party to the head of Jersey City government and praised Fagan for his diligent door-to-door campaigning, his anti-railroad stance, and his general "magnitude." The *News* backed Smith all the way, predicting his election "by a good majority."

It was in this election that an area of Jersey City known as the "Horseshoe" served as a bellwether for the outcome. The section received its name after the state's Republican-controlled legislature decided in 1871 to attempt to concentrate all the Democratic voters in one assembly district. Consequently, the legislators had to draw up a district enclosing as many Democrats as possible, and the result was shaped like a horseshoe. Because the Democratic-inclined voters were largely working-class citizens, many of them recent immigrants, the Horseshoe contained numerous young laborers. Uneducated Irish and German workers toiled in the warehouses or railroad yards, sweated at Colgate's soap factory or the Dixon graphite facility, or spent their days in one of the area's 40 saloons—where they cursed their low fortunes and envied the primarily Protestant landlords and employers who lived in luxury "up on the hill" in the city's Bergen section.

Equating Protestantism with Republicanism, it was not difficult for some of the younger toughs to spread Republican money around whenever it became necessary to buy votes—even if those passing the money were Catholic and Democratic. Loyalty, it was known, could be bought in the Horseshoe. It could be bought so easily, and in such a large degree, that the *News* frequently quoted the expression, "As goes the Horseshoe, so goes the city."

It was evident early in the Fagan-Smith battle that things were not going well for the Democratic candidate (although magnate E. F. C. Young had plenty of money to spend to ensure his candidate's victory). True, Smith took the Horseshoe's Second Ward, but only by a margin of 316 votes. The jeers of the Davis Democrats—"We're going to send the undertaker to the morgue"—faded quickly as more returns from other wards came in. It was obvious that Republican Fagan's "reform" movement was victorious; he received 56 percent of the total vote.

As happened so frequently in American politics then (and today), the new mayor found himself bitterly opposed by a strongly entrenched machine—and there was a Republican one as well as a Democratic one. Boss Davis lost his $5,000-a-year job as city collector and was replaced by a Republican, and the state legislature shifted the primary day to a date just before Davis held his annual "Democrats Picnic." The idea was to eliminate the electioneering that typically took place when the picnic was held before the primary.

Along with these moves that helped strengthen Fagan's position, the new mayor himself was responsible for the purchase of a site for a new high school, construction of 11 temporary elementary schools, the building of a free public bath, and the lowering of the tax rate. Keeping his campaign pledge, he obtained more than $1 million in increased assessments on railroad property and more than $2.5 million on local corporations. These latter moves, as might be surmised, did not make him a favorite of either the railroads or corporations. Both began funneling new funds to the Democratic machine in Hudson County in an effort to unseat Fagan in the next election.

The efforts seemed futile. In 1903, the mayor's opponent was an Irish judge, James J. Murphy, who had the support of the continually scheming Davis. When the votes were counted and Fagan had been reelected, 21,420 to 18,398, the victorious official made a brief speech. It ended with the ominous words: "Corporations, big business, and railroads—beware!"

The threat caused corporations, big business, and railroads to increase their lobbying efforts—both openly and behind the scenes. After two years, the expenditure of time and energy seemed to begin to produce results. The *Journal,* long a Fagan supporter, suddenly began to carp in its editorials that the reform-minded mayor was actually acting like a machine all by himself: "He was rigid, unyielding, and often refused to compromise with the powers of big business that meant employment and tax money for Jersey City. Nothing less than absolute surrender," said the paper, "will please the mayor."

Fagan increased his attempts to keep the public's support. More public bathhouses, free concerts in the city's parks, free medical care for the poor—he offered them things in greater profusion, and the populace accepted them. But when the 1905 election loomed, Fagan found himself in the midst of a battle in which no holds were barred.

The idea of "dirty tricks" in American politics—an idea that reached national prominence during Nixon's heyday—probably is as old as the Grecian idea of a pure democracy, at least. But to understand how insidiously the idea was used when Fagan ran against one Archibald Henry, you should have a sense of the bitterness and distrust that existed between Catholic and Protestant voters of the time. It was not uncommon in Jersey City then for plants and shops to advertise for help with prominent signs that read "Catholics need not apply."

To take advantage of this, supporters of Democratic candidate Henry—a wealthy coal dealer—mailed out two series of letters to voters. The letters did not endorse Henry directly; in fact, they appeared to support Republican Mayor Mark M. Fagan.

Thousands of voters known to be Protestant, who had youngsters in the city's public school systems, received a letter ostensibly from "Patrick L. Callahan, Secretary of the Esoteric Order of Catholic Knighthood." It began: "Dear Sir and Brother—Knowing you to be a devout Catholic and ever ready to promote the interests and welfare of all true believers . . . we ask you to vote for Honorable Mark M. Fagan for mayor of Jersey City. In the four years this admirable young man has served our city as mayor, he has done more for the promotion of Catholicism and has placed more of our people in office than any of his predecessors." The letter went on to note that Fagan had been instrumental in getting more Catholic books into the public library and would definitely make sure that additional Catholics were named to the board of education.

Voters known to be Catholic, on the other hand, heard from "Hiram P. Pennypacker, Chairman of the Committee on Election of the American Protection Association." The letter pointed out that "Although Mark M. Fagan is a Catholic, he is *not* a member of any of their secret or church societies—and is broad-minded from the fact that his personal political advancement depends on our kind." Fagan, it was noted, had put out of office the clerk of the Board of Education, "a Knight of Columbus of high standing." In his place, Fagan had selected a Protestant, "one of our people."

Numerous Catholic voters in the Horseshoe were informed: "Among the many improvements made by Mayor Fagan, we refer to the new Jackson Avenue sewer, which has been unjustly criticized by some residents of the Horseshoe who, because they had been promised a sewer in their section of the city, objected to the appropriation being used on the Heights. The Mayor considered very properly, however, that the needs of the Heights were greater than the Horseshoe, which is composed of a different class of people.''

You doubt that such obvious and blatant appeals to prejudice would work? Ah, but you are misreading the times, the education and the make-up of the voting population. The letters did their job, but, fortunately for Fagan, they were not enough. He lost to opposition candidate Henry in the Democratic Horseshoe, but only by 377 votes. Three other wards voted against the incumbent, but Fagan swept Jersey City's eight others and defeated his rival by more than 3,500 votes in all.

Even as he adjusted his eyeglasses to read his victory statement, Fagan might have sensed his defeat down the road. His style, he knew, left no room for negotiation, and he was not about to modify it. Before the Board of Trade, he vowed that in his new term, he would strive to overcome ''the political bosses, the privileged corporations, and the daily newspaper [*Journal*] of this city.''

Making the mistake of the zealot, Fagan challenged any and all who disagreed with him—and, in the case of the *Journal*, it was a grievous error. In the early part of the century—remember, this was two decades before radio, nearly five before the introduction of television for the masses—the printed page was the primary method of disseminating information. Despite the mayor's successes, the paper began to point to evils that existed in Jersey City. They were evils that an untrained eye could spot, evils that everyone knew were part of the city's very being—but day after day the *Journal* seemed to discover them in growing numbers. More than 1,000 saloons were within the city limits, and crime was rampant in the streets. Brothels, gambling parlors, poolrooms—all with their gangs of customers, hustlers, and hangers-on—were readily accessible.

Soon, irate officials of the Catholic church journeyed to the state capital, Trenton, to ask for legislation that would help clean up the city. Then, church leaders of various faiths started to speak out against the mayor from their pulpits. Responding to murmuring from the pews and the press, Fagan dismissed police officials and replaced them with others, then dismissed the replacements and

brought in new faces. He obtained passage of an ordinance that outlawed private and hidden rooms in the backs of saloons, but penalties were seldom imposed because the police on the street—always
willing to accept a little extra cash to keep their eyes closed—
reported few violations, if any.

Working behind the scenes to undermine Fagan was a coalition of
the railroad barons, big business interests, and political bosses of
both parties who headed up strong groups of faithful supporters in
their wards. Still smarting from his previous defeats, Democratic
power broker Bob Davis was determined to put his own man into
the mayor's office once again. Backed as usual by the wealthy E. F.
C. Young's millions, Davis pointed his finger at an individual who
was relatively unknown in the political world. His name was H.
Otto Wittpenn. Young and of German descent, Wittpenn was the
owner of a small grocery store who had showed enough party loyalty to the Davis machine to earn the title of county supervisor.

Davis thought the candidate would be ideal. He was certainly in-
dustrious. His nationality would sit well with the large group of German immigrants who increasingly were making their home in Jersey
City. And he was willing to go along with principles of the "New
Idea" party that Fagan and others claimed to be trying to put into
effect. The basic idea of the party was: Equal taxes for all and strict
regulation of utilities. Few voters were aware, of course, that
Wittpenn's stance on regulation of the utilities was considerably
weaker than Fagan's.

Davis played his cards carefully. Having supported several losing
candidates, he saw that his control of the county's Democratic faction could erode drastically if his man lost again. He took the unusual step of first supporting no candidate in the party's primary,
preferring to see how much strength Wittpenn could show on his
own. The *Journal* soon began noticing that the potential candidate
was ringing doorbells and shaking hands in the Horseshoe and
throughout the city, seemingly winning friends everywhere. To no
one's surprise, the paper endorsed Wittpenn as "clean, straightfor-
ward, businesslike, and independent."

Meanwhile, voters in greater numbers were perceiving Mayor
Fagan as an honest man, but one who was not changing—or grow-

ing—with the times. There was a need for change, people felt. The reform movement that had begun in 1902 when newly elected President Theodore Roosevelt moved to break up the giant Northern Securities Company of J. Pierpont Morgan had become a force on state and local levels as well as on the national one. Roosevelt, who was certainly not a "have not" himself, looked upon big business not as an economic threat but as a moral one. For some people to be cheated out of opportunity, said the president, while others had a stranglehold on business was more than unfair; it was downright immoral.

As the populace of Jersey City peered through the shadows that fell upon them each morning as the sun rose beyond Manhattan's skyscrapers, "Good Old Teddy R." seemed to be on the right track. Others were, too. Ida Tarbell's expose of the Standard Oil Company was running in *McClure's* magazine, and Lincoln Steffens' article—the first in a series on municipal corruption—called "Tweed Days in St. Louis" had made crooked politics familiar to thousands of informed citizens. Everywhere—and especially in the state of New Jersey, where Woodrow Wilson had moved into the Governor's mansion under a banner of "democracy for all"—the cry of "Reform! Reform!" was plainly heard.

A major problem of the reformer is that he often attempts to find the one true path to reform. Joseph Tumulty, who rose to a position of importance alongside a great reformer, President Wilson, followed the reform path within organization politics. Fagan chose the unorthodox and more difficult path of the maverick. While Tumulty sought to reform the entrenched Democratic machine, Fagan looked to achieve reform everywhere—within his own Republican party and anywhere else it was needed. The man who follows the independent path—as Fagan would learn, as I have learned, and, perhaps, as you have learned—often finds himself walking alone.

The Fagan-Wittpenn election of 1907, in retrospect, seems a typical one in Jersey City's political history. That is, it was marred by fistfights, near-riots, and innumerable charges and instances of voting fraud. A few notes from the local papers will give the idea:

"The Sixth District of the First Ward . . . is in a state of siege. The police are keeping the crowds away. Democrats are in an ugly mood."

"After the arrest of Anthony J. Fay, a riot broke out at 74 York St. Democratic and Republican thugs resorted to blows and 50 men wrestled in the streets. The reserves were called out with drawn clubs. . . ."

"The first man to get hurt was hit with a blackjack by Democratic thugs. He was Sidney Welsh, a private detective brought to Jersey City to stop fraudulent voting. Welsh was hit over the head and knocked senseless. . . ."

"This morning the situation got so serious that the Board of Police Commissioners came to Police Headquarters and at once went into secret session. . . ."

There was more, much more, in the columns of cluttered newsprint. There was the tale of a Fagan supporter who came into a police station "badly battered, with his jaw dislocated." And there was the report of a well-known labor leader who was forcibly restrained from entering a polling place to cast his vote.

The same kind of criminal activity that marred election day probably reminded voters on their way to the polls of the blatant crime that seemingly had flourished under Mayor Fagan's thin nose. But there were other reasons why candidate H. Otto Wittpenn carried all 12 of Jersey City's wards, winning the election by 9,591 votes out of a total of some 43,000 that were cast. A primary cause of his victory was the opposition presented to Fagan by the powerful Public Service Company, which was dismayed by the incumbent mayor's repeated proposal that a more effective public utility commission should be established—a commission with rate-making powers. Another factor contributing to Fagan's downfall was a widening split between his "New Idea" party adherents and the old-guard Republican regulars.

In the history of politics in "the Mecca of politics," however, the 1907 election does not stand out because an erstwhile grocer, H. Otto Wittpenn, was voted in as the city's mayor. It is significant because it brought into the limelight a man who would eventually emerge as the urban political phenomenon of the century.

His name was Frank Hague.

2

To the outsider—the individual whose knowledge of politics is perhaps limited to what he learned in "civics" in elementary school—the working of the political patronage system is as mysterious as the secret rites of a Masonic lodge. Somehow, many people know, in city after city, town after town, state after state, a political boss works quietly behind the scenes, passing out well-paid jobs to those who devote time and energy to "the party." At the whim of the boss—whose name is almost unknown to the general public—anyone from the local dogcatcher up to the mayor can gain or lose position and salary. Absolute rule was maintained in earlier days (and, on occasion, even in modern times) with cash payments when necessary and brute force if such was required. And those who went along with the decisions of the boss without question—those, the party faithful, moved up the ladder most quickly.

Frank Hague was one of the fastest climbers of the day. The son of a native Irishman who had worked intermittently as a blacksmith and bank guard, Hague had been born in the Horseshoe in 1875. While his mother spent long evenings wondering when her husband would make his way home from one or another neighborhood saloon, young Frank lived the typical life of a boy "from the 'Shoe." That is, he was expelled from the sixth grade at 14, scrounged ashpits and junkyards for bits of scrap to sell, peddled newspapers and ran errands for local merchants, and occasionally made off with a drunk's wallet or watch.

One of eight children, Frank Hague joined a teenage gang along with his brothers John and Hugh. The boys' prey was the numerous fruit stands and clothing stores where loose change or loose merchandise was there for the taking. But one night after a warning blast from a policeman's whistle had sent the gang scattering, Hague hid in the shadows and whispered to a pal, "This ain't for me, Munk."

His companion raised a knowing eyebrow. "You got somethin' that's goin' to make you rich, I guess."

"Hell, I got six grades o' school behind me, and that's enough," said Hague, trying to squeeze his lanky, red-headed figure into the darkness and squinting with blue eyes at the silhouette of a policeman on the corner. "You want to know where I'm heading? Politics, that's where."

At the end of the block, the policeman strolled away. Waiting long enough to make sure it was not a ruse of some sort, the boys slipped out into the light. Hague's friend looked at him for a long moment. "Politics? What d' you know about politics?"

Young Hague twisted his wide mouth into a sneer. "Enough to know how to get dead men's ballots into a voting box."

The other knew exactly what he meant. The papers, saloons, and street-corner gossips had spread the story of one recent election in Hudson County where thousands of false ballots had been cast. Many of them bore the names of long-departed citizens who dwelled peacefully in the local cemeteries.

Hague's problem was that jobs for would-be politicians were not exactly plentiful or well paid. He began hanging around the Democratic Club in his ward, always on the ready to dash to the store for cigarettes for one of the ward heelers or handle other simple chores. Briefly, he worked as a mechanic for one of the numerous railroad lines, and he trained at a rundown gym for a possible debut as a prizefighter. Preferring to order others to fight, however, he decided to become a manager. His "boy," a boxer named Joe Craig, did only well enough to permit his manager to buy a couple of stylish suits that made him look successful—and Hague took to wearing suit, white shirt, and tie at all times, even when the summer sun blazed over Jersey City.

His apparent prosperity caught the eye of saloon keeper ''Ned'' Kenny, a political rival of boss Bob Davis in the Second Ward. ''I got a proposition for you, kid,'' Kenny said one evening. He waited, expecting an answer, but Hague only looked at him with quizzical blue eyes. ''Davis has got a candidate for constable in the election comin' up. I was thinkin' of puttin' your name up against him in the primary.''

''Yeh?'' Hague murmured. ''How come?''

Kenny provided the details. A friend of Davis's had opened a rival bar down the street, and the new competitor was pushing his own candidate for the job of constable. ''If the guy gets elected, he might put some kind o' squeeze on me. I've heard that Davis thinks I got too many customers comin' in here now, drinkin' my beer, and maybe voting the way I tell 'em to.''

Now Hague nodded. ''You don't want to take the chance of bein' closed down, right? What's in it for me?''

''Hell, it don't pay nothin'. But you don't have to do nothin' except keep an eye out for trouble and call the coppers, or maybe find a bondsman for somebody needin' bail. But it would be worth somethin' to me—say seventy-five bucks to start—just to show Davis that he can't put pressure on me.''

He looked at Hague's outstretched hand and reached to shake it. ''The money,'' Hague said coldly. ''I'll need it quick. I'll have to spread some of it around.''

The sum bought enough votes, and Hague's numerous promises to friends of better things to come bought enough others, to enable him to defeat his opponent by a three-to-one ratio in the election. Amused by the 21-year-old's easy victory, Bob Davis buttonholed ''Constable Hague'' and asked him to help get out the Democratic vote for the party in the looming 1897 Jersey City mayoralty election.

Suddenly, instead of running errands for the ward heelers, Hague was one himself. As a party lieutenant, he rang doorbells to urge voters to support the Democratic ticket, aided confused citizens in the bewildering task of voter registration, saw that a constituent's sick child got to the proper hospital, gathered clothes and furniture for victims of neighborhood fires, and handled the myriad tasks that go into arranging a successful rally, parade, fund-raising dance, or awards banquet. At such affairs, Hague never missed a chance to spend as much time as possible with his superiors in the party, both to impress those working below him and to let the bosses know he was always available for ever more important assignments.

In the elections of 1897 and 1899, Hague's efforts to get out the vote in the Second Ward paid off handsomely, and the Democratic candidate for mayor was swept into office and reelected by large margins. Where many Republican voters stayed away from the polls in both years, the Democrats—goaded by Davis and his lieutenants, including Frank Hague—showed up in huge numbers.

One of the candidates who had been elected sheriff, partly as a result of Hague's work in his behalf, appointed his young supporter as a deputy. Now Frank Hague had a salary of $25 a week, along with a job that legitimately gave him a reason to loll around the Court House. With his title and his contacts, he increasingly assumed leadership of the Second Ward's Democratic Club, and played a part in the selection of George T. Smith as the mayoralty candidate in 1901. When Smith went down to defeat under the "reform" wave that swept Mark Fagan into office, Hague's work in the Second Ward again proved fruitful. The ward was only one of two in the city that voted Democratic, and Hague himself survived the Republican tide the following year by winning a third term as constable.

His salary and position almost required him to have a home and family, but Hague had long appeared too busy making his way in the political world to pay much attention to the ladies. He proposed to a local girl, Jenny Warner, who accepted immediately. A daughter was born, only to succumb to pneumonia soon afterwards—an illness caused perhaps by the sooty, perpetually fetid air of the Horseshoe. A son, Frank Jr., came along in short time and proved strong enough to survive. His father, aware that the only escape from the oppressive perils all around him depended on having cash, was determined to acquire the power that would produce wealth. He let it be known that he could be bought—or, if he had the money, that he would just as soon do the buying.

Don't let the preceding sentence make you think that the young political leader had no sense of loyalty. He had a sense that was highly developed—to the point that he knew almost instinctively when it would do him the most good to stick up for a friend. There was a time, for example, when a tearful, elderly woman sought him out as he lounged at a table in the Democratic Club, watching a group of older men play cards.

"Mr. Hague—" the woman began.

Instantly, Hague was on his feet, pulling a chair up for the woman. "Call me Frank," he said. "And here, sit down. You look worn out."

Nodding her thanks, the woman sagged into the chair. She sniffled once or twice, almost gasping for air. "I'm Red Dugan's mother," she said. "You and he went to school togeth—"

"Of course! All the way up to—what, the fifth or sixth grade? What's Red gotten himself into now?" The youth's name was not unfamiliar to Hague. He had heard plenty about Dugan's thefts and armed robberies.

The boy's mother shook her head. After a moment, she muttered something that Hague could barely hear. Only a few words floated to the card players who were craning their necks behind him. "Jail," they heard. And "Roxbury," the name of a Massachusetts town. And something about "a check that wasn't no good."

Now Hague was patting the woman's back. "Sure," he said confidently, "I'll take care of it. I'll get 'Skidder' Madigan and we'll go up there 'n' tell them he couldn't have done it. You just go on home, and don't you worry about it."

But when he contacted his friend Skidder and said the two of them were needed to help a pal out of a scrape, Madigan was worried. "Frank, you're crazy. We can't just waltz in to the Roxbury jail and swear that we saw Red Dugan right here in town when he was passin' a bum check in Massachusetts."

Hague's eyes went wide in innocence. "No? It's the two of us—and Red himself—against one bank clerk."

Madigan swore a loud curse. "It won't work, I tell you. You're crazy to even think about tryin' it. The party's talkin' about you takin' over as ward leader, and this kind of craziness could blow the whole shootin' match.''

''I know, but I figure if a deputy sheriff puts his job on the line for somebody, that means the guy must be innocent.'' He didn't bother to tell his friend about another little problem: He was scheduled to testify in court the next day as a witness in a trial of some blacks accused of false registration. If he trekked to Massachusetts, it meant ignoring a subponea—and that could mean bigger trouble.

Hague aimed his blue eyes straight at his pal's watery grey ones. ''It might not make sense, but I got to do it, Skidder. You with me or not?''

Defeated, Madigan nodded. (He was later to win undying fame in the annals of Jersey City politics when he was elected sheriff and took lessons in public speaking to cure his habit of dropping the final ''g'' in such words as *speaking, talking,* or *running.* The lessons took so well that he soon was asking his secretary to ''get me a founting pen.'')

The journey of Hague and his friend to aid Red Dugan seemed to be a failure on every count. Their testimony at first was laughed at, and then the two were threatened with perjury charges—a threat that resulted in their hedging their story quickly. When he failed to answer the subpoena in the trial left behind him in Jersey City, Hague was found guilty of contempt of court. He was fined one hundred dollars and stripped of his deputy duties. And his chance of being made ward leader vanished in a flurry of jeering newspaper stories.

But to the residents of the Horseshoe, Frank Hague had gone out of his way to help a friend—had practically given his livelihood to aid a brother. Shortly after the first of the year, when things had quieted down, boss Davis quietly named him to help nominate candidates for the 1905 municipal election. As a county committeeman, Hague decided to run for a fourth term as constable—and won easily.

Throwing himself into the political fray (now that he had time on his hands as a result of the loss of his job as deputy), Hague worked to tie up the loose ends of the Second Ward's south-end Democratic Club. And, using his height, prizefight training, and commanding voice to its fullest, he made a modest living as a collector for a local brewery. The job was a natural for him; it kept him out on the streets and in the bars where politics was discussed continuously. Again, his skill at turning voters in the right direction—either through persuasion, wheedling, or a suggestion of physical violence—brought a reward from boss Davis. Hague was named sergeant at arms of the state assembly and officially made leader of the party in the Second Ward.

The post in the assembly let Hague rub shoulders with politicians from all over the state. The leadership title in his own ward put him in the position of being able to advise Davis on likely candidates for patronage appointments, which meant that few job seekers could gain city jobs without first catching the eye of Frank Hague.

Obviously starting to feel his own power, Hague did not hesitate to oppose Davis himself when the party boss nominated a candidate for the Street and Water Board. The man had been defeated previously as a nominee for the job of sheriff, and part of his loss was due to Hague's efforts against him—efforts made then at the instigation of Davis. Now Davis had changed his mind. Hague, however, was not about to change his, and a rift developed between him and the man to whom he owed (thought Davis) absolute allegiance. Hague looked about for a potential successor to Davis as county leader and settled on the young German grocer, H. Otto Wittpenn.

Quickly, forcefully, he threw his support behind Wittpenn in the 1907 election. Flushed with victory, the new mayor gave Hague the job of City Hall custodian—a job with much more to offer than its title might indicate. For one thing, the post put the young politician—Hague was 32 at the time—in the same building with a youthful, reform-minded mayor who would respect his advice. For another, as custodian, he had the power to appoint some two dozen janitors. For the first time, Hague tasted the power of patronage.

He also tasted something bitter, troubling. Davis, still the party leader in every respect, had proposed his own candidate for the job of custodian, but could not control Wittpenn. So he began to put pressure on Hague, threatening to relieve him of his duties as leader of the Second Ward.

To strengthen his position with Wittpenn, Hague became friendly with the mayor's secretary, 29-year-old A. Harry Moore. Moore, a

Presbyterian Sunday school teacher, lent an aura of respectability to any idea that Hague schemed up. Angered, Davis tried to replace Hague as ward leader, but the effort only split the Democratic Club into two factions. When one group met to vote to decide which candidate would head the organization, Hague's group showed up outside the meeting room. His men were armed both with clubs and the membership rolls to show that the bulk of the rival's supporters had not paid their dues and were not members in good standing—and so could not vote.

Having learned that a club in one hand and a ready paycheck in the other meant power, Hague did not fear to set up a number of "We're for Wittpenn" clubs that rivaled those of Davis's organization. At the same time, he lost no opportunity to let "the little people" of his Jersey City ward know that he was working day and night on their behalf. In one instance, the residents of the Second Ward mounted a campaign to get a viaduct that would ease congestion and make pedestrian traffic safer on a thoroughfare. City Hall agreed, but wanted the taxpayers who would benefit most from the viaduct to pay a special assessment to help defray the construction costs. Hague noisily advised his neighbors to refuse, calling the assessment illegal and unenforceable.

A worried Davis, seeing the support for Hague growing with each day, decided to compromise and announced his support for Wittpenn in the 1909 election. He had his own reasons for not wanting to battle Hague directly. Hague had already swung an ally, Harry Moore, to his side—after Davis had recruited the young man into the Democratic organization primarily because of his talent for making speeches that sounded both honest and spellbinding.

And Davis was already suffering from the first intense pain of an illness that shortly would be diagnosed as incurable cancer.

Mark Fagan had seen the split in the Democratic ranks as a chance to regain Jersey City's highest political title, but he now was confronted with the newly united opposition. He went down to defeat as Wittpenn captured all but three of the city's 12 wards. And the Second Ward, where Frank Hague promised to "get out the vote," produced the largest plurality for the victorious candidate.

If Hague, however, continually seemed to be consolidating his position as an able politician, H. Otto Wittpenn was having no more success than his predecessor with problems of crime and fair taxation. Defeated candidate Fagan won an appointment to the County Tax Board, where he promptly discovered that the Pennsylvania Railroad Company had paid no taxes for four years on a piece of property in Hudson County.

Shaken, Wittpenn sought to shift the blame for his problems to where it belonged. An obvious target was the ailing Bob Davis, whom the mayor promptly accused of "trying to block the administration in carrying out its plans in the interest of the people." Then, declaring that, "I have endured the machine as long as possible, but patience is no longer a virtue," Wittpenn announced that he would seek the nomination for the post of governor of New Jersey. At a higher level, he believed, he could clean up the political ills that affected the state's cities at the local plateau.

(It would prove to be a disastrous decision for the mayor, but he was a determined man who chose to make his own fight. Some seven decades later, when I decided to follow the same road, going against the advice of older and wiser heads who counseled that I should continue as Jersey City mayor rather than attempt to become governor, I would be called "a second H. Otto Wittpenn.")

Perhaps the Wittpenn effort, aided by Moore's inspired speeches and Hague's untiring campaigning, might have succeeded in the 1910 gubernatorial race—if an angry Davis had not come up with an almost invincible candidate. He prevailed upon Woodrow Wilson, president of Princeton University, to run. Austere, energetic, and considered brilliant, Wilson had a reputation as a true reformer.

The Wilson sweep was so overwhelming that Hague saw his own tightly controlled Second Ward turn against him. This, despite the fact that force once again was used to discourage voters from casting their ballots for Davis's candidate. Said the *Jersey Journal*: "Cops on duty were using clubs and blackjacks to assist Mayor Wittpenn and Frank Hague defeat the Davis men." And Davis told reporters, "They had the police to bat the heads off anybody not against the organization."

Bested in his try for the governor's mansion, Wittpenn set about trying to show the citizens of Jersey City that the long-awaited "reform" was at hand. It was a time, as Frederick Lewis Allen wrote in *The Big Change,* when people who had little in common "were alike in seeing the nation, not as a place where everybody went his own way regardless of the plight of others, but as a place where people had a common destiny, where their fortunes were interlocked, and where wise planning, wise statesmanship could devise new instruments of satisfaction for all men."

For the new governor, the instrument of satisfaction was a streamlined government for Jersey City. Muckrakers delving into big-city corruption of the period placed part of the blame for its presence on the physical size of large city councils, which offered innumerable opportunities for bribery and deceit as well as making it difficult to fix the blame for mistakes and wrongdoing. It would be better, reformers suggested, to have a commission system where each commissioner would have responsibility for one area of government.

It did not take long before Mayor Wittpenn came out in favor of a change in the city's charter that would permit government by commission. With the cries of "a business approach to government" echoing around him, Hague thought it over carefully. Then he decided to turn against Wittpenn.

Bob Davis's cancer had proved fatal shortly after the gubernatorial election, and the Democratic machine that he had headed was now leaderless. A quintet of minor officials known as the "big five" tried to gain control, and Hague sensed that he might grab the leadership while the others wrangled among themselves.

His first step was to try to convince the predominantly ethnic working-class population of the Horseshoe that the Wittpenn-endorsed commission system would transfer political power to the elite elements of the city. As opposition began to surface to the commission idea, Wittpenn and the men with him prevailed upon Governor Wilson to attend a last-minute rally to urge the citizens to vote in favor of the new system of government. But the "big five" gathered enough signatures on petitions to advance the date of the election to a hot day in July, rather than the September date for which it was originally scheduled. The summer heat, Hague's anti-commission crusade, and the determined efforts of the "big five" and the late Davis's forces all combined to defeat the change-of-government proposal. The dawning of commission government in Jersey City would have to wait.

Hague's idea was that it would have to wait until he himself could be assured a prominent post on the commission.

Now, however, he had to face an outraged Wittpenn. The *Jersey Journal,* which had strongly supported the commission system, also was bitter about Hague's role in defeating the measure. The paper did some muckraking of its own, noting that Hague's older brother Hugh had been on "sick leave" from his job as a battalion chief in the city's fire department for nearly three years. During that time, he had collected a monthly salary of $166.33 and had sent in regular reports of his illness from his "recuperation home" in Colorado Springs. Hague stayed out of sight for six weeks to let the furor die down, then returned to explain that his wife and child had been ill and required his full-time attention during the period.

With the idea of a commission system out of the question for the moment, Wittpenn was confronted with the task of running again for the mayoralty—against a candidate proposed by the "big five." He needed Hague's abilities to get out the vote. When Hague explained lamely, "I haven't turned against you, Mayor. Some of my enemies have lied about me," it was enough for Wittpenn. He held out his hand and the two were teamed once more.

Hague had shown a willingness to make the payoffs needed to win elections, and he was not afraid to assist the police in breaking a head or two if necessary, but he also had *ideas.* In one campaign, he had been the first to suggest filming a candidate and flashing the movie on a screen outdoors at night. Movies—even the silent ones of the period—were still a novelty, and huge crowds of voters turned out at each screening to stare in awe at the free entertainment.

Now Hague pulled out all the stops to get Wittpenn reelected. If there was an athletic event, he was on hand to toss out the first ball or act as a referee. If someone was married, Hague was waiting outside the church to be the first to congratulate the happy couple. If there was a wake, he was in the forefront of the group of mourners.

And if anyone needed something done—water turned on, garbage picked up, mail delivered to a new address—Frank Hague let it be known that he was the man to ask to handle the job.

And when Wittpenn turned back the "big five" nominee in the primary, Hague was given a plum by the voters: He was nominated to become Street and Water Commissioner for Jersey City. Just two months later, Wittpenn had another term as mayor and Hague had a new title and $3,000 a year in salary. He also had four times as many people responsible to him as he did when he was custodian of City Hall. More than a hundred people now depended on pleasing Frank Hague if they wanted to keep their jobs.

His victory was all the more savory because his rivals had gone to great lengths to try to stop him. The brilliant George L. Record, one of the Republican candidates, dug out Hague's role in attempting to get burglar Red Dugan freed six years earlier. It was also revealed that another criminal had admitted that he once paid $700 to Hague, who was a constable at the time, for his help in securing a bail bondsman.

The charges made headlines, but, as historian Mark S. Foster wrote in a study of Hague's early career, "Jersey City voters were hardened to scandal, and Hague's day-to-day helping hand at the ward level meant more to them than the remote charges of corruption by a rival politician." In addition, the Hague "scandal" had to share newspaper space with another that was uncovered at the same time: A former judge was accused of ballot box fraud. Always, of course, there was the fact that voters—particularly those in the Second Ward—liked the style of Hague, who was given to making statements like this: "The Water Board needs progressive men, men whose backbones are not of the jellyfish order, men who will fight the people's fight!"

Several days after the election, Governor Wilson invited Wittpenn to visit him at Trenton, presumably recognizing the mayor as the Hudson County leader. Hague managed to travel with Wittpenn, but Wilson—remembering an old enemy—let Hague cool his heels in an outer office.

Wittpenn fared only slightly better at the state house. Wilson met with him, but acceded to the behind-the-scenes pleading of his personal secretary, Joe Tumulty, and withheld the power of political patronage from the Jersey City mayor. Thus, Wittpenn's claim to party leadership was weakened—and Hague, never one to miss an opportunity to move ahead, decided to take advantage of the mayor's liabilities as quickly as possible.

He did not have to wait long.

Bayonne, adjacent to Jersey City, faced a serious water shortage that could be alleviated if a new main were built from one town to the other. Wittpenn invited two companies to study the situation and make proposals, then awarded a contract to one. Hague, contending that the water shortage was a temporary matter and that existing mains were adequate, refused to attend the hearings, then claimed that secret negotiations had taken place. Even when the Street and Water Board voted four to none in favor of the new main, Hague was adamant: "If my attitude . . . is to be punished by the loss of the mayor's friendship, and I am to be fought, then I will fight back."

He was embroiled in another controversy when complaints began to mount about the unclean status of many city streets. With the Department of Street Cleaners under his jurisdiction, Hague was said to be encouraging older workers to retire so that he could replace them with friends and loyal party members. If they refused, the older workers were assigned to more difficult jobs and forced to work harder by foremen. Asking for an increase of 50 percent in the department budget to do the street-cleaning job properly, Hague angrily denied that he had elevated an inordinate number of workers—nearly one-fifth of the entire complement—to the post of foreman, which meant they did no work other than supervise the laborers.

Aware that a good attack is infinitely preferable to mounting a solid defense, Hague donned the mantle of a reformer. The man he had supported for president of the Street and Water Board, Louis L. Finke, was suddenly accused by Hague of buying several thousand dollars worth of supplies without a formal contract. At a meeting of the board, Hague made a motion that the entire five-man board should be investigated by outside authorities. (The motion, not surprisingly, was defeated by a four-to-one vote.) Hague followed with a charge that Finke was awarding contracts to suppliers in small amounts that might fall under "petty cash" accounting, rather than in one large sum that would need approval from the Board of Finance. He accused another official, Superintendent of Water J. William Griffin, of embezzlement—$10,000 worth.

Such charges rapidly won Hague a reputation as a reformer—even though the charges frequently proved baseless—and when another effort to install commission government began in the spring of 1913, Hague this time accepted a part on the executive committee. It was obvious that Hague's name would draw votes if it appeared among the list of candidates for the five-man commission. His name was there, along with that of former mayor Mark Fagan, A. Harry Moore, and 90 others. H. Otto Wittpenn's name was not included, but the mayor had organized a group of five men and placed his support behind them.

Openly calling himself a "traitor" to Wittpenn—whose administration, he said, allowed the corruption and wrongdoing he had uncovered among the members of his own Street and Water Board—Hague demanded a face-to-face debate. Not wanting to give Hague any more publicity than he could, Wittpenn refused the challenge—and promptly was called a coward by his one-time ally.

Under the Walsh Act of 1911, local municipalities were to be governed by five men who each had jurisdiction over public safety, public affairs, revenue and finance, public parks and property, and streets and public improvements. When H. Otto Wittpenn's slate of candidates—except for A. Harry Moore—went down to defeat, Fagan, Moore, Hague, and two others suddenly found themselves the first members of commission government in Jersey City. They eagerly began splitting up the areas of jurisdiction.

Frank Hague leaped at the opportunity to become director of public safety.

Like the title of City Hall custodian, which had sounded innocuous but gave Hague both patronage power and close proximity to the powerticians of the era, *director of public safety* does not sound impressive. But beneath the surface, and for Hague's purposes, the job was the most important of all.

Having control of Jersey City's police and fire departments gave Hague more opportunities for patronage appointments than any other commissioner. Both departments were known to be inefficient, and Hague realized that if they could be improved, his own stature would be heightened in the eyes of the public.

Moreover, the young man who had battled his own way to eminence from a lowly life in the Horseshoe realized that it would not hurt to have at his command an armed force of uniformed officers. Within their ranks he envisioned a personal, private squad that would take orders directly from him.

At the time, Hague and no one around him could foresee the power such an elite group of policemen might have—a power that one day would cause comparisons to be drawn between the legions of Frank Hague and the SS troopers under the command of Adolf Hitler.

3

Before they are lost sight of in the chronicle of Frank Hague's continuing rise to power in "the Mecca of politics," let's pause for a moment—that's all the time it will take—to detail what happened to two of Jersey City's and our nation's finest reformers, Mark Fagan and H. Otto Wittpenn. The pause must come here, because once Hague began to flex his new-found muscle, Fagan and Wittpenn were destined to fade rapidly in the pages of history.

Neither man, of course, foresaw his political future ending with the start of commission government in Jersey City.

Ex-mayor Wittpenn still had plans to try for the gubernatorial spot, and one of the five newly elected commissioners, A. Harry Moore, was an ardent supporter of his candidacy. But Governor Wilson had given up his post to try for the presidency, and he was backing Acting Governor James F. Fielder of Jersey City (then serving out Wilson's unexpired term) in the upcoming election. For party unity, Wilson asked Wittpenn to drop out of the contest and support the acting governor's candidacy. Wittpenn, loyal to the end, did as he was asked.

The erstwhile grocer, still a force in the Democratic party, worked hard to keep at least one hand on the reins of power, but saw his authority slowly erode. More and more, he was looked upon as a relic of the past, of "the old machine" that had controlled the city's politics for so long a time. Even though Wittpenn had diligently battled against the machine, his reign as mayor was in the precommission era—and that was suddenly old-fashioned where the voters were concerned. At one point, Hague accused his fellow commissioner Moore of taking orders from Wittpenn, and Moore violently—albeit only with words—attacked Hague for making such an accusation.

Wittpenn bided his time, trying to avoid a direct confrontation with the anti-Wittpenn forces within his own party, until 1916. President Wilson ran for reelection then, and Wittpenn—who had been at the president's beck and call throughout his years of service, looked upon the Jersey gubernatorial nomination as rightfully his. To earn it, however, he knew that he would have to show Wilson that he could unite the divided Jersey City Democratic party. Hague was not about to let Wittpenn build up his own strength if he could help it—and he saw to it that he could not. The best that Wittpenn achieved was a fusion ticket made up of candidates proposed by his own supporters, the Hague faction, and a third group of independent party members. His failure as a conciliator led to Wittpenn's defeat by a Republican opponent. Worse still, President Wilson—although he won reelection—failed to carry his home state of New Jersey.

Such defeats, especially for an aging candidate who had suffered several in a row, bode grim news for future efforts, and Wittpenn's enthusiasm for the political wars rapidly drained away. Soon, he left Jersey City entirely, entering the business world once more as president of a land improvement company in Hoboken. While serving as president of First National Bank of Hoboken, he was named to the state highway commission in 1928 by the Republican governor, and held the post until his death three years later. He left behind a memory of a man concerned with fair play and honesty—qualities that were not abundant in Jersey City politics for many decades. Today, citizens driving over the Wittpenn Bridge that crosses the area known as the Jersey Meadows remember with fondness the man whose name it bears—if they are old enough, or if they have studied history in a diligent search for the rare political leaders who won respect for their integrity and honor.

Mark Fagan, the progressive Republican who was mayor and overseer of the first Jersey City commission, attempted futilely to prevent Hague from increasing his own power. But Hague had the much-admired Moore on his side at the beginning and later worked to make sure that retiring commissioners were replaced by men who would lend him a ready ear. Despite Hague's opposition, Fagan compiled an impressive list of accomplishments. He reduced the taxes of the citizenry, then increased assessments on big corporate property owners. He attempted to bring in experts from outside Jersey City to administer to institutions—preferring to select those most qualified rather than those "from the neighborhood"—and he enthusiastically supported the construction of more public schools. Unfortunately, his efforts to bring in outsiders resulted in charges by the opposition that he was not looking out for the welfare of deserving local residents, and his efforts to build public schools were seen as a threat to the local Catholic school system.

Fagan's political base dwindled steadily, and in 1917 he failed to win another post on the commission. He returned, somewhat wearily, to his funeral home business. Nearly a dozen years later, a few longtime supporters nearly prevailed on him to reenter the political wars, but he wisely shook off their pleas. (By that time, Frank Hague's grip on the sceptre of power in Jersey City was so strong that he would have crushed Fagan with little trouble.) Upon his death, Fagan was buried in Holy Name Cemetery in the city that he had hoped so fervently to reform during his tenure as mayor.

Determined to use his first years as a commissioner to benefit himself as well as the public, Hague acted at once to convince the citizens of Jersey City that they had nothing to fear from street criminals. The police, he insisted, were to be visible, competent, and plentiful.

"The 'social club' atmosphere is through around here," he told the force. "You'll patrol your beats properly, or you're finished!"

The new director of public safety took to the streets himself to check on how his orders were being followed. When a survey of twelve beats failed to find a single patrolman on duty—the police had a system that let them spend their working hours in bars while friends phoned in for them from the duty phones on the streetcorners—Hague opted for drastic action. Under the Walsh Act, which gave commissioners the power "to make such rules as may be necessary for the efficient and economical conduct of the business of the city," Hague decided that he had the right to punish the offenders.

Setting himself up as prosecutor, judge and jury, he fined one officer 60 days' pay for being found drunk on the job. Another man, caught inebriated for the second time, was dismissed on the spot. A fastidious dresser since the time he had first made enough money as a fighter's manager to buy a couple of natty suits, Hague insisted that his officers never appear in public with their uniforms dirty or unbuttoned. Because he himself usually wore a high collar and necktie, even on August days when the summer sun blazed down on Jersey City buildings that would not be air-conditioned for decades, a rule went out that policemen should dress in similar fashion. Smoking on the job was forbidden, and the cop caught with a cigarette in his mouth would swiftly find himself penalized, losing either vacation days or salary, and sometimes both, depending on how angry Hague was at the time.

There was some opposition, as might be expected, to the new commissioner's arbitrary and high-handed tactics. The Policeman's Benevolent Association—the force's union, as it were—protested angrily that if Hague continued to mete out harsh punishment, the entire complement of officers might walk off their jobs. Hague was not frightened; he knew how many wives and children depended on a cop-husband's paycheck for their survival. When the PBA pointed out that the Walsh Act required that the entire five-man commission must hear any case involving termination of employment Hague felt confident. He knew that although he had opposition on the commission, a three-to-two vote was all that was needed on any question.

Besides, he took steps to make sure that the "little people" of Jersey City were behind his every action. Almost immediately upon gaining command, he ordered that the city's numerous bars could no longer admit women—a move that appealed to church groups, temperance advocates, and the Society for the Suppression of Vice. When a police officer was killed in the line of duty, Hague grandly and loudly announced that the man was to be promoted posthumously so that his widow coud receive a larger pension. He ordered extra patrols for the city's parks, where the public enjoyed outdoor concerts on hot nights, and offered support to a group of young men (similar to the "Guardian Angels" organization of today) who promised protection from rowdies preying on Jersey City citizens on the streets.

A non-smoker who abhorred liquor, the ramrod-straight, stern-visaged commissioner mounted a crusade against the use of drugs that amounted to a personal vendetta. To get the names of suppliers, he promised to free any arrested user who turned witness for the state. Some of the citizenry was aghast at the idea of known addicts being allowed to go back on the streets, but Hague got the names he wanted—along with headlines in the local papers for his tireless efforts to solve a serious problem.

While his fellow commissioners also announced progressive changes in their areas of command, few newspaper editors could get excited about a new accounting technique in the finance department or the acquisition of additional benches for the park department. Ah, but an idea that affected the city's hordes of police and firemen—that was something else again. Keeping the pressure on for an ever-growing budget to outfit his vitally needed and hard-working officers properly with new uniforms and equipment, Hague called for a grand parade of his troops. All off-duty members of both forces were to pass in review while he surveyed them from a stand in front of City Hall. For the public, the sight of the smartly dressed men and gleaming new firetrucks proved to be a morale-booster. And Hague had an audience of thousands gathered to hear him make an impromptu speech—delivered in his forceful, bombastic style—about his remarkable and numerous achievements as a commissioner.

On the surface, it appeared that Hague had all the right aspects of a reformer concerned with the welfare of the people of Jersey City. And perhaps he did. But he also had the characteristics common to a politician with a background of little education—the use of force when it was felt necessary, and an intimate knowledge of payoffs. Because he made it a policy almost from the beginning never to put anything in writing—and probably felt quite uncomfortable with the nuances of language needed for clear, concise written communication—no records exist to prove precisely when Hague first ordered all policemen and firemen to "kick back" part of their salary in order to retain their jobs. But such orders were given, and regular payments began to filter upward through the ranks—upward until Hague himself was the ultimate beneficiary.

Undoubtedly, he felt that his efforts deserved some reward. After all, he had built up the morale of the forces themselves, and was clearly giving the Jersey City "man on the street" greater protection. And all that he had done in a few short months after his election in 1913, he knew, was just the beginning.

In July, 1914, he delighted area residents with a crusade against local grocers who began to raise their food prices in response to the war clouds gathering in Europe. Such action, Hague told the *Jersey Journal* in his typical off-the-cuff style, "causes suffering among the poorer classes and people who do it are entitled to no consideration." Because he made good copy, the *Journal* began to hang onto every move made by Hague. In the primary election that fall, both the paper and Hague stood soundly against a slate of candidates proposed by former mayor Wittpenn. Thus, when Hague's police arrested 17 "suspicious characters" who were loitering at the polls "to try to manipulate votes of the citizens," the *Journal* praised Commissioner Hague. Even after only four of the 17 were convicted—on charges of disorderly conduct—and even after that verdict was overturned on a technicality by a county court which ruled that no specific charges had been brought against the men, the paper sided with Hague: "So long as Commissioner Hague continues to arrest men who act like 'gophers' and gunmen in the vicinity of the polling places on election days and who cannot give an account of themselves, the people of Jersey City will sustain him."

Hague gave the people plenty of reasons to sustain him. When factory management in a nearby town broke a strike with the aid of thugs hired to bloody the heads of the picketing workers, Hague made himself available to the reporters. Calling "the majority of so-called 'strike breakers' " such names as "notorious gunmen" and "ex-convicts who have no regard for human life," he once again proved to his constituency that he was 100 percent on the side of the working-class "little guy." People in the Horseshoe and throughout the area nodded knowingly when they read Hague's accusation of "butchery" against those who had hired the strike breakers—although they probably knew little about the real issues of the case.

A master at reading the temper of the voter, Hague knew when to pull in his horns to avoid defeat. After a schoolhouse fire in Massachusetts killed two dozen youngsters, the Jersey City Commissioner of Public Safety began a well-publicized probe into safety conditions in local schools and theaters. The public applauded when he ordered several movie houses closed until violations were corrected, but when he ordered a large high school closed immediately, students and parents were dismayed. Hague did not like to be told that his orders were not to be carried out and insisted that the school be closed. A confrontation was avoided when he learned that the local board of education with the concurrence of the State Board of Education had responsibility for safety conditions in the schools. "The Board of Education has assumed full responsibility in the situation," he said, "and I have no objection to offer." In other words: "If there's a fire and people die, it's not *my* fault."

Effectively presenting to the public the image of a man who could do even more for the "little guy" if he were not opposed by the Patrolmen's Benevolent Association and idlers among the police and fire ranks who preferred things "the way they used to be," Hague pressured the state assembly to adopt an ingredient of the commission government regulations that had been approved for Jersey City's neighbor, Hoboken. The measure gave the public safety commissioner power to try all cases that did not involve dismissal. When he was given the nod in Jersey City, Hague promptly flexed his muscles by levying a heavy fine against the president of the PBA. The charge: "Sarcastic criticism of his superiors."

When the other commissioners refused to challenge Hague's action, perhaps thinking that it might serve as a warning to critics within their own departments, the public safety commissioner took another giant step. He accused the chief of police of being incompetent, untruthful, and a poor example to the men in the ranks. This time, the charges were not upheld in a meeting of the full commission, but Hague, although very upset, at least had shown every man on the force that he could be brought to "trial" merely on the strength of the commissioner's accusation.

With the enmity between the police chief and himself growing stronger as each week passed, Hague searched through the ranks of the force for a small group that would report directly to him. The hand-picked squad had to possess strength—a primary consideration—and each man had to show a willingness to follow the commissioner's orders blindly. Often working in plainclothes, the men were to be well paid. They had to be, Hague knew, because he wanted them to report to him on any infractions committed by their fellow officers.

Borrowing the name from the headline-making and novel mode of transportation of the day, Hague called his special force the "Zeppelin Squad." Like its namesake, the "Zepps" were to swoop down silently and without warning on the unsuspecting drunken cop, the officer napping in the back of a luncheonette, or the man who otherwise appeared to be ignoring Hague's stern regulations. And, because Hague trusted the members of the squad implicitly (after all, hadn't he chosen them personally?), the word of a Zeppelin against a fellow officer was tantamount to a conviction.

Slowly, inexorably, Hague tightened his control against the forces that opposed him both within and outside the government. And, as he did so, he managed to convince the public that everything he did was for its welfare. In early 1916, he stumbled upon the fact that the army was assembling large stores of explosives in Jersey City in preparation for a possible entry by the U.S. into the European war. Contending that area residents were frightened about the accident potential, Hague journeyed to Washington to demand that the stores be moved. "Jersey City is an appropriate port," he was told, "and they have to be put somewhere."

Angry at the rebuff by the congressmen, Hague fretted awhile, biding his time—and probably he felt a flush of joy when a few months later a munitions ship exploded at a Jersey City dock and several people were killed. Rushing to the other commissioners for approval, he won the right to stop and inspect all trains entering the city. The police promptly put barricades across the railroad tracks, and entry was refused any car loaded with explosives.

In a few days, however, reality had to be faced. Not only was Hague about to be charged with acting against the interests of the nation—in his zeal to protect "the little guy" in his own city—but railroad and dock workers whose livelihood depended on moving and storing the munitions were about to lose their jobs. A fellow commissioner, Henry Byrne, pointed to the improbability of a second, similar accident, and accused Hague of locking the barn door after the horse was stolen. Hague, who had selected Byrne to replace a commissioner who had retired earlier, was incensed at the opposition. He silently vowed to find a replacement for Byrne before the 1917 election.

Although three other commissioners stayed with him and supported the blockade, Hague eventually had to bow to the pressure. The barricades came down. But up went the headlines, making it clear that the commissioner of public safety once more had done his best to guard the interests of the citizens of Jersey City.

Undaunted, Hague mounted a new campaign. His leadership of the fire department, he said, had made it so efficient that the chance of serious fire damage was greatly reduced. Therefore, he told newsmen, the huge, trust-controlled insurance companies should reduce their rates for Jersey City residents. As might be expected, the insurance companies disagreed. But Hague won his headlines and his applause—ingredients which would add up to votes in the ballot boxes in the future.

The future—the election of 1917—quickly loomed on the horizon.

Only about half as many candidates for the five commission posts were proposed to the electorate as had been put up for the first commission four years earlier. Hague, Wittpenn, and Mark Fagan each presented a slate of candidates, and Hague had taken great care in his choices. In addition to himself, he named his convert, A. Harry Moore, and fellow commissioner George F. Brensinger, a lawyer who was also serving as a major in the Army. Instead of the antagonistic Byrne, he named City Clerk Michael I. Fagen to the slate, and he replaced independent-minded Mark Fagan (who had served as mayor) with Charles F. X. O'Brien, a police judge.

Both Fagen and O'Brien were Catholics; Moore and Brensinger were Protestant. And, while Hague himself was certainly draped in the mantle of "The Boss," the group chose for itself the slogan, "The Unbossed."

The imminence of war was on the mind of much of the electorate, which chose to ignore an investigation by accountants that showed Jersey City's finances were muddled and the taxpayers' money often was being improperly spent. Some of the money went for large newspaper ads to present Hague's nominees as "the men who get things done" and "the poor man's friends." Faced with weak opposition from the dejected H. Otto Wittpenn and Mark M. Fagan, the "Unbossed" ticket swept the election.

A. Harry Moore, with a total of just over 20,000 votes to runner-up Hague's 19,348, rightfully could have accepted the title of mayor. According to the terms of the Walsh Act, the only authority that a mayor had over and above the powers of the other members of the commission was that he could appoint the three members of the school board. Moore, aware of Hague's strength, announced that he would be satisfied just to serve as a commissioner—and Frank Hague was given the title of mayor.

He grabbed it.

4

The Mayor, as he insisted he be called at all times—or "duh Mare," as he himself pronounced it—would over the next three decades grab power considerably removed from merely naming appointees to a school board. Incredibly, at the time it appeared that his actions were in such concert with the wishes of the public that the *Jersey Journal* could easily state, "The old organization days are gone." What went unnoticed was that Jersey City was actually witnessing the birth of one of the most powerful political organizations in the history of the state of New Jersey, and perhaps in the history of the nation as well.

Hague's immediate task was to pull together the factions—most notably those led by the defeated Wittpenn and Fagan—that divided his own Democratic party. The task was not a difficult one for him. He had learned that "reform" to residents of poor neighborhoods meant that they should share in the bribes and graft doled out by corrupt politicians. Although the *Journal* had already questioned the padded payrolls of the police and fire departments under Hague's control, he increased the rolls still more. His magnanimity was not limited to those who had supported him in the past, either. Jobs were found for Wittpenn supporters, Fagan supporters—anyone who would swear allegiance to "duh Mare."

H. Otto Wittpenn himself, striving to convince his own weary mind that a united Democratic party held out the best hope for city and state in a chaotic wartime period, retired from politics. His retirement passed unto Frank Hague the reins of party leadership in Hudson County.

No sooner was it done, however, than Hague faced a problem that threatened his consolidation efforts. Commissioner Brensinger was killed in an automobile accident. By moving quickly, one or another rival factions in the party might place a man on the commission—a man who could oppose Hague. The Mayor realized that he had no time to lose. The city clerk announced, in accordance with the law, a special election. There was barely a month to choose a candidate and campaign. Backed by the *Jersey Journal,* whose publisher sought a role in Jersey City government, former police judge John Warren made a dogged effort to gain the empty seat. He managed to win four wards, but went down to defeat in the others.

It was the thrashing delivered to Warren in Hague's old Second Ward—where the vote was 1,652 for James F. Gannon, Jr., Hague's candidate, to only 72 for the rival—that precipitated the first charges of wholesale fraud against Hague's election-winning techniques. Some 56 grand jury indictments were handed down, and many members of the election board in the Second Ward were named in them. No one, however, was convicted—despite evidence that showed votes had been cast by deceased New Jersey residents and by men who were undergoing Army training at distant camps. No one went to jail—and Warren did not go to City Hall.

Now Hague moved decisively. He gave a job to the son of the president of the state Civil Service Commission, thus lessening chances of state interference with his hiring-and-firing policies. His fellow commissioners deferred to the Mayor's wishes regarding the appointments of several new magistrates: Irishmen got the jobs. He named three members to the Board of Education, enough to give his supporters a 5-4 majority on the nine-member board. Now also responsible for the Department of Public Affairs, Hague had jurisdiction of the city hospital, where he wanted to place his own man in charge. To remove the present superintendent, Hague set up a public hearing at which all those with complaints against the hospital might be heard. No one, including the supervisor, was allowed to speak about what was *right,* and the hearing ended with Hague's announcement that the plethora of complaints demanded immediate suspension of the doctor in charge of the facility. Further, he said, the man would be placed on trial before the commission for neglect of duty. Aware of what happened to policemen and firemen who had undergone such trials, the doctor resigned and was immediately supplanted by a Hague choice.

It was probably difficult for the common man, the "little people" of Jersey City, to see anything wrong with Hague's tactics. After all, this was the same man who once threatened the president of a coal company with "justice at the end of a nightstick" if needed coal were not delivered at once to needy citizens at a fraction of the cost. ("I'll see that it gets there, Your Honor," the coal company head reportedly said.) And this was the same Frank Hague who prowled Jersey City streets at night in an armored limousine, searching out the occasional patrolman who was derelict in his duty. Spotting one, Hague would order his chauffeur to stop the car and beckon the offending officer over. "Tell the precinct captain that I don't like kewpie dolls like you out on the street," he snapped at one overweight cop. "You give our city a bad image."

The following morning, the precinct captain could expect to be called to the Mayor's office, where a stiff jab to his chest by Hague's extended index finger would emphasize his warning.

And this was the same Mayor Hague who showed his concern for the citizenry by rushing to local fires to make sure the firemen responded to a call within a few minutes. On occasion, he would create an emergency call or fire alarm to test the speed of his forces. And once, when an ambulance took 45 minutes to reach an accident scene, the Mayor asked a young physician what had taken him so long. The response—"I had to put my clothes on, didn't I?"—brought the doctor a swift punch in the face, personally delivered by Hague. The intellectual, observing that few doctors called out on cold nights to aid an injured party enjoy being questioned as they set about their duties, might consider Hague's action objectionable in the extreme—but the great majority of Jersey City residents weren't concerned with intellectuals. They saw only a man concerned with making sure his people got prompt medical attention when it was needed.

Neither did the people object to Hague's look of prosperity. After all, wasn't he really one of them underneath the expensive, tailor-made suit he usually wore with a vest and stiff, high collar? That pearl stickpin, costly necktie, shining patent leather shoes, and tilted derby—weren't they only the signs of a local boy who had made good? And if Frank Hague, the kid from the Horseshoe, could make it, well, couldn't they make it, too?

A lifetime friend of Hague, John Milton, would write some years later that the Mayor "realized the strength of his organization must rest with the loyalty of the tenements, not mansions. So the poor became and remained the chief beneficiaries of his rule."

At the same time Hague reached this realization, he began to remove himself still further from the poor over whom he governed. The railroads and public utilities that had drawn the fire of socialistic-minded Mayor Fagan were willing to spend unlimited funds to combat any idea of municipal ownership, and they began to pour campaign contributions into Hague's coffers. Leading the way was banker Edward I. Edwards, who had become a close friend to Hague.

For Edwards, Hague's power presented a unique opportunity. Having succeeded Young as president of the city's First National Bank some years before, he had supported both Governor Wilson and Mayor Wittpenn and sought the position of state treasurer for himself. Wilson opposed the idea and prevailed upon Wittpenn to work with him against Edwards's appointment. The motive for Wilson's action became apparent when it was revealed that Edwards—who already held the title of comptroller for the state—had withheld Governor Wilson's pay in 1911 while the statesman was campaigning across the country for the presidential nomination. Edwards contended that the state constitution required such an action while the governor was not performing the duties of his office.

To consolidate his rise to power—a rise that had begun just 20 years previously when then-21-year-old Frank Hague had been offered the chance to run for constable by saloon keeper Ned Kenny—"duh Mare" decided to try to put his own choice in office as governor of New Jersey. His choice was Edward I. Edwards. It took little effort, other than passing the word around to the city's voters, to send Edwards to the state capital as senator from Hudson

County in 1918. The following year, Senator Edwards' name was entered in the Democratic gubernatorial primary against a man who had succeeded the reigning boss of neighboring Essex County. Again, Edwards won. And when he challenged the Republican nominee, a native of Trenton, in the general election, the strength of Hague's behind-the-scenes manipulations was evident.

The Democratic standardbearer lost 16 of the state's 21 counties. But he took Hudson County with a plurality of 36,113 votes—enough to give him a razor-thin margin of victory, 14,510 votes out of a total of 420,000. Hague, of course, was roundly applauded by the residents of Jersey City. He had helped another "local boy" get to the top.

And Edwards, knowing the source of political power, was quite willing to accept Hague's suggestions as to which men should be named to the tax board, the bench, the civil service board, and other key state positions.

Always, always, always Hague managed to convince the public that while it might look as if he were building and fueling a powerful political machine, it was not a machine in the sense that the word had traditionally been used. This was a machine that had to exist in order to maintain the gains that his reform program had achieved. Without the right men in power, he intimated, it would be impossible to keep crime off the streets of Jersey City, to see that evil-doers were punished, to provide superior fire protection and medical care, and so on. Unlike Woodrow Wilson, whose notions of reform tended to be philosophical and beyond the capacity of most people to grasp from an intellectual standpoint, Hague made things simple: "Follow my instructions, and I'll take care of you." It was language that the residents understood in the Horseshoe, and elsewhere. And "Haguey," as he was called by many of them, faced little opposition from those around him.

He was not so fortunate with those who looked upon his kingdom from outside. Although the nation's concern with World War I had lessened public interest in muckraking, as the battling wound down people began to look again at the evils of political corruption. Senator William Mackay of New Jersey's Bergen County was named to head a committee that would investigate the state of affairs in Hudson

County. The investigation was set to take place during the 1921 commission election, and the dwindling forces opposed to Hague rule looked to its findings as a spur for their own efforts to obtain power.

One of those local citizens most vocal in his demand for an investigation was Reverend J. Harvey Murphy, the pastor of the Central Avenue Reformed Church. He repeatedly demanded that "Someone must turn on the lights" to illuminate Hague's activities. Rather than answer Murphy's charges directly—which would put him in the position of a Catholic responding to a Protestant—Hague named a newcomer, John Bentley, to replace a commission member who suddenly resigned to run for a congressional post on a Hague-backed ticket. Bentley, the grandson of a former Jersey City mayor, was a distinguished lawyer and a Protestant, and it fell to him to reply to Murphy. The young pastor, Bentley noted, had "an insatiable greed for publicity."

Other opponents complained of a lack of enough school buildings to house the city's children, and said that union members were forced to march in pro-Hague parades in order to hold onto their jobs. Still others noted that the city's bonded indebtedness had increased 30 percent, or $10 million, under the Hague regime.

The Mayor sidestepped comment on most of the issues raised—noting, for example, that he had supported women's suffrage and helped bring about the registration of 38,000 first-time female voters for the coming election. But he knew that he had little to fear from the Mackay probe: Governor Edwards suddenly vetoed an appropriation of $15,000 to fund the investigation, and it came to an end.

When the final report was filed, some of the charges against Hague were so minor as to cause laughter. He had, it was said, used two nurses from the city hospital to give personal care to his son during a flu epidemic. In his amused response to the attack, Hague contended that he had personally paid the nurses for their services, and that they had worked for him during their off-duty hours. Others testified to the effect that Hague had requested the nurses' help so that he would be free to supervise medical care of flu-stricken patients at the hospital. It was brought out that the Mayor personally had carried suffering patients into the hospital and had volunteered to help empty bedpans if his aid was required.

With that sort of story gaining the attention of newspaper readers, few Jersey City residents paid much attention to the Mackay probe finding that in the November 1920 election, "a saturnalia of crime was committed in many voting districts in Hudson County." One disclosure told what happened when 125 young students from Princeton were hired at $10 per day to supervise the election. Paid by an organization known as the Honest Ballot Association, and equipped with credentials attesting to their observer status, the young men showed up at various polling places.

At one, an election board official declared the credentials invalid because they lacked a state seal. "Throw them out," said a Democratic worker, and members of the Jersey City police force followed his orders. At another polling place, officers ordered the youths to stay 100 feet away. When two students entered a tavern to use a phone and seek instructions from the county prosecutor—failing to notice that the saloon was illegally open on election day—they were set upon by a gang of local toughs. Hurrying from the site, the two jumped into a friend's car to escape—and were promptly jailed by the police and charged with various offenses, including theft of a car.

Various students testified that they had observed two people at a time in numerous polling booths, while police and election officials looked the other way. When the practice was questioned, one student was told, "It's okay, they're husband and wife." Another was told, "It's all right, they're probably sisters."

One Princeton youth noted that he had the opportunity to meet "duh Mare" face to face. Surrounded by uniformed officers and members of the Zeppelins, Hague had shown up at a polling place to check on how things were going for his favorites. The appearance of several youthful observers brought the question, "What are you fellows doing here?" When their purpose was explained, Hague glared at the young man, said he hoped he and his fellow students "aren't trying to pull anything funny," and warned them that "if you get hurt—knocked cold—it's your own hard luck."

With little concrete to say against Hague, the Mackay probe tried to sweep up as many charges and complaints as it could against those under him. A contract for $300,000 worth of building work had been given to a New York company owned by a police magistrate who was the leader of the city's Eleventh Ward, and the official admitted that his company owned no office, records, or construction equipment. A member of the city clerk's office was accused of stealing razors purchased for servicemen overseas and reselling them for $435. Hague's old friend, "Skidder" Madigan, who had accompanied him years earlier to plead Red Dugan's innocence, was asked how—as a sheriff—he rated a chauffeur-driven limousine. And a quartet of singing policemen, it was revealed, had been relieved of their duties as officers so they could devote all their time to vocalizing at "patriotic functions."

J. Arthur O'Toole, a World War veteran who headed the opposition fusion party ticket, was dismayed when the Mackay investigation failed to dampen the voters' enthusiasm for Hague and his handpicked associates. The nearness of the municipal election called for drastic measures.

Resorting to a trick previously tried in the Jersey City election of 1905, "someone" sent a letter to thousands of Catholic voters calling for the defeat of all Catholic candidates on both Hague's and O'Toole's tickets. It appeared evident that the writer was trying to use reverse psychology and boost O'Toole's chances. Quick police work—by Hague's forces, naturally—led to a trail that ended at the apartment door of a close friend of O'Toole.

Whether or not the leader of the fusion party had anything to do with the letter, he ended up at the tail-end of the list of candidates seeking office in the election. As was usual, Hague's slate—which included the Mayor—won handily, and A. Harry Moore rolled up the largest number of votes ever given one man in Jersey City history. His popularity would set the stage for his eventual try for the governor's mansion.

While crowds converged on City Hall to congratulate the victors, a groups of pranksters surrounded the home of Reverend Murphy. When he answered the doorbell, he discovered a funeral wreath hanging on his door and a solemn-looking group of mourners singing a dirge in celebration of his failure to bring Hague down. Later, the cheering residents of the Horseshoe carried a coffin through the streets, grave diggers on either side, with a banner signifying "O'Toole is dead." Overhead, fireworks (purchased at city expense) exploded to light the night sky.

Once again, Frank Hague had no doubt that his grip on the voting public could not be loosened. He had to show his gratitude to the people who supported him, he knew, and what better way than to give Jersey City residents a present? Something they could be proud of, something that would benefit them—even the poorest among them, the youngest and the oldest alike. He did not have to search far to come to a decision about what should be done.

The controversy over his use of city hospital nurses to aid his ailing son was still fresh in his mind. Why not, he mused, create a huge medical complex that would provide the finest care for Jersey City's men, women, and children?

Because Hague envisioned one of the finest medical facilities in the world, he knew that the cost of construction would far exceed anything that Jersey City taxation could provide. Therefore, he decided, the county must bear some of the cost. Initially, it was estimated that $1.6 million in bonds, and an equal amount in interest, would be required. The first building to be constructed, Hague ordered, would be a maternity hospital named for his mother, Margaret. He conferred with two members of the County Board of Freeholders, Oscar L. Auf der Heide and Mary T. Norton, who quickly supported the idea.

Hague gave the orders to begin planning the Jersey City Medical Center, a facility that would cost upwards of $30 million during Hague's years in office, that would be embroiled in numerous controversies over possibilities of graft and corruption during its construction, and which would prove to be a financial drain upon Jersey City taxpayers for decades to come.

Building the Medical Center would be a long-range project, Hague observed, Jersey City citizens deserved an *immediate* reward. Harking back to his days as a boxer and fight manager, he brought them the first prizefight in ring history to chalk up a "million-dollar gate." Jack Dempsey, the famed "Manassa Mauler," was preparing to defend his championship against Georges Carpentier, a French challenger, in New York City. Dempsey's manager, Jack Kearns, however, spoke to fight promoter Tex Rickard. "It just happens that I know Frank Hague, the political boss in Jersey," he said. "If he gives us his okay, we'll be in business, because you can bet that nobody will bother us." Hague, Kearns knew, enjoyed sports—particularly the track and the ring—and would rejoice in any event that brought gambling money and taxes on ticket sales into his close proximity.

In addition, Hague had a personal friend who was willing to rent 30 acres of property as a site for the fight. An agreement was reached that called for the construction of stands to hold a crowd of 50,000 people, but the demand for seats prompted the promoters to enlarge the flimsy wooden structures. Room was made for more than 91,000 spectators before it was decided that the swaying stands already constituted a danger to life and limb.

The initial tab for the stadium, Hague told Kearns in a phone call, was $80,000. But with each request for the addition of seats, the price shot up. The final bill came to $150,000.

The headline-making match—which saw Dempsey knock Carpentier out with a straight right in the fourth round—focussed the attention of the entire nation on Jersey City, and its mayor, Frank Hague, reveled in the attention. He prominently pointed out to anyone who would listen that Jersey City had a pretty fair boxer of its own, one of the few fighters in the annals of ring history to win two different titles in one year. Johnny Buff, from the section of the city known as Gammontown, beat one opponent in February, 1921, to take the American flyweight championship, then captured the world bantamweight championship in September.

Buff was a Polish-American scrapper who had learned his trade at a punching bag set up in a Jersey City firehouse. His *nom de ring* was derived from "Buffalo," a term used to describe volunteer fire fighters, and Buff used it because the Irish and German fire fighters who helped him train had trouble pronouncing his Polish name. During his peak years, the ferocious fighter stopped a formidable list of opponents—Abe Goldstein, Harry Mansell, Midget Smith, Joe Lynch, and Pancho Villa among them.

A devoted fan, Frank Hague was at ringside (along with an uncle of mine, Joe "Kelly" Buczkowski) when Buff, then 34 years old, lost his titles. The fighter was floored several times when the referee asked his manager, Lew Diamond, if the fight should be stopped. "Nothing doing," muttered Buff as the blood flowed from his battered mouth. "I'll kill you if you stop it." He was eventually carried to his corner, going out like a champion and proving the truth of a statement that Hague had made to Tex Rickard years before: "I have a kid in Jersey City who, pound for pound, can lick anyone in the world."

Hague, a fighter himself, knew one when he saw one.

5

If ever there was a period of time when a determined and ruthless politician had an opportunity to weld together an invincible machine, the years that followed the Armistice of 1918 made up such an era. Disillusioned by the bloody fighting, soldiers returned home—ready to think of themselves for a change, not of the country and the world. Such topics as the newly-formed League of Nations, foreign affairs, and politics became less important to the newspapers, while emphasis was put on the doings of society, human drama, sports, scandals, and other amusing subjects. Dancing became not a mere pastime, but a craze; Prohibition was a law to be flaunted; and the accumulation of wealth—for both the individual and for business—became an obsession. Perhaps the Roaring Twenties were not yet roaring, but a growl of self-indulgence was beginning to be heard.

In Jersey City, Mayor Frank Hague felt the mood of the people and decided to go along with it. Long considered almost of Puritan stock, he surprised some of his supporters by refusing to enforce Prohibition. "It's a matter of giving the people what they want," went his thoughts, and, besides, there were far more hard-drinking Irish immigrants in the city than there were voting members of the Anti-Saloon League. He even rescinded an earlier ruling that had closed movie theaters on Sunday.

The population of the city changed, too, to Hague's benefit. Former residents of the Horseshoe and other areas where newcomers had settled began moving to the suburbs and the ''Hill'' wards as they ''made it'' in America. Replacing them was a new wave of immigrants, poor and ready to vote the Democratic ticket—because, after all, wasn't that the ticket that had helped their predecessors in the dilapidated tenements and brownstones move upward? The first thing many new residents of the Horseshoe heard was that the mayor of Jersey City not long before had been one of them.

With Governor Edwards ready to overlook almost any move made by Frank Hague, the Mayor—his red hair starting to thin at a faster rate—moved with impunity to silence his critics. ''Any critic of His Honor was likely to find his tax assessment raised, his right to vote impugned, and he was lucky indeed if he wasn't arrested for fraudulent voting or gambling or any of a dozen other offenses,'' said a newsman in the Trenton *Times*.

There were few critics among women voters, Hague made sure. His stance of staunch morality, from his first crusades against saloon back rooms and prostitution when he was commissioner of public safety, endeared him to the female population of Jersey City. He had been one of the first of the nation's politicians to urge the formation of ladies' auxiliaries in each ward's Democratic club. As soon as he was in the position to do so, he picked the first female member of the state assembly from Hudson County, the first female freeholder, and, eventually, the first congresswoman. Few women served longer in the nation's House of Representatives than Mary T. Norton, whose congressional career extended from 1925 to 1951.

If the Irish came uppermost in Hague's consideration, the other diverse ethnic groups that made up Jersey City's population at the time were not far behind. Shrewd enough to recognize that the melting pot that was America attracted groups from Italy, Russia, Poland, and other troubled nations, he had sponsored classes in English for many newcomers at the time he organized ''We're for Wittpenn'' clubs a decade earlier. Most nationalities, however, were ''foreigners'' in his lexicon, while the Irish were Americans. In 1925, according to a *Jersey Journal* report, Hague was saying in a speech to a newly arrived immigrant gathering: ''The Democratic party welcomes the foreigner and offers him a chance to make good, but the Republican party ignores the strangers to our shores.''

In passing out the patronage appointments he controlled, Hague made sure that "foreigners" got their share. Michael Scatuorchio, leader of the Democratic organization in the Fifth Ward, was the recipient of the city's lucrative contract for garbage removal. "Mike Scat," as he was known, was the man whose blessing meant a job or favor for countless Italians over a period of 30 years. His counterpart was an influential Pole, John Saturniewicz—who was usually called John "Saturday-Night" by those laborers who had difficulty with the Polish name.

(As an indication of how long such men were in power, how much power they possessed, and how deeply rooted they were among members of their ethnic communities, John "Saturday-Night" ended a 30-year retirement in 1977 to lend his support to my campaign for the mayoralty of Jersey City. Polish publications, such as ardent supporter Chester Grabowski's *Post Eagle,* leaped at the opportunity to run John's picture as he endorsed my bid for the mayor's office.)

It was not hard—in a period when people were delighted with the new miracle of radio, absorbed with Babe Ruth's home runs and the triumphs of Jack Dempsey, and thrilling to the aviation feats that would be capped by Lindbergh's non-stop flight from New York to Paris in 1927—it was not hard in such a time for Hague and those around him to reap the rewards that often come to persons in power. Several scholarly writers, most notably Dayton D. McKean in *The Boss* and Ralph G. Martin in *The Bosses,* have gone into great detail about the depth of the pockets that were lined during the Hague years with taxpayers' money, under-the-table bribes, and government funds.

The Medical Center, as McKean well documents, gave Hague and his friends an opportunity to enrich themselves not in one fell swoop, but over a period of years, as each additional building was constructed and as each new city employee—doctor, nurse, maintenance man, and the like—were added to the city payroll. Starting with the Margaret Hague Maternity Hospital in 1922, the facility added a surgical building, a psychiatric hospital, a house for the staff, and other structures. Eventually, some 2,000 beds for the ill were available, making the Medical Center the third largest hospital in the world.

There is no doubt that the construction work was given to companies that Hague approved of, and that many of the companies had relations with one another and with the mayor's office. Whether or not the entire building cost came to $25 million, $30 million, or even $40 million (as Hague once claimed in an off-the-cuff remark), it appears obvious that considerable sums allocated for construction costs went into the pockets of Hague friends and associates friendly to the party. It has even been noted that the same buff-colored brick that was used on the face of the Medical Center buildings was used to construct a number of homes where Jersey City politicians dwelled.

Corruption at its most blatant? Perhaps, and yet the residents of Jersey city, and particularly the poorer ones, cheered every move Frank Hague made. The Medical Center, after all, was conceived in Hague's mind as a place where those who could not afford to pay for hospital care could receive it. When a sick man or woman who could not afford to pay was rushed to one or another of the Center's buildings, he or she was not overly concerned with how much the professional care that was received might cost other Jersey City taxpayers.

Those who worked at the Medical Center either convinced themselves or were convinced by Hague's forcefulness that his methods were thoroughly proper. One such person was Dr. Thomas White, a respected and world-famous heart specialist, who was riding one day in Hague's limousine with the Mayor and his son. As Dr. White recalls it:

"Dad, why do the papers all print such bad things about you?" the boy asked.

"Son," answered the Mayor with a shake of his head, "if reporters wrote good things about Mayor Hague, they would be fired. Their editors would say that Frank Hague bribed them."

Contending that "the real story of Frank Hague was never told," the venerable Dr. White looked back in 1970, some 14 years after Hague's death, and wrote a paper for the *Academy of Medicine of New Jersey Bulletin*. In it, he commended the Mayor for "great innate talent and a fine mind . . . large vision and great ambition." He praised "the excellent quality of medical care" offered by the Center, and said that it was all the more remarkable that the facility continued to function well under allegations of "political mismanagement and intrigue.'' Summing up, Dr. White conjectured, ''If it were possible to free one's mind from cynicism, from the acceptance of partial truth and to realize that the qualities of a complex personality are neither simply defined nor explained, it might be accepted that Frank Hague did have a sincere desire to change the conditions of medical care that he had witnessed during his impoverished youth.''

With that kind of tribute coming to a man long deceased, and from whom no one had anything to fear any longer, it was small wonder that the Jersey City population glowed with paternalistic pride when they learned that ''duh Mare'' had acquired a summer home in ''the millionaire's colony'' at Deal, New Jersey; a 14-room duplex in the city's fashionable Bergen Hill section, and a villa in Florida. How ''Haguey'' could get so much on a salary that ran to less than $8,000 annually was not a question many people thought about. The excitement of the Twenties was the important thing.

And while people looked the other way, Hague reinforced any weak points he discovered in his organization. Because the law at the time did not allow a New Jersey governor to succeed himself, Hague needed a replacement for Governor Edwards in 1922. He gave the nod to George S. Silzer, a judge in Middlesex County, and sat back to watch a familiar scene: Silzer trailed statewide in the balloting until the tally for Hudson County came in—and suddenly the candidate was victorious by a large plurality. In appreciation, Governor Silzer accepted Hague's recommendations for judgeships in Hudson County, including a Hudson County Democrat to serve as a supreme court justice.

Hague had also brought his attention to focus on the state's Democratic party mechanism. His choice for state chairman was elected, and Congresswoman Norton was named vice-chairwoman. Hague settled that year for the title of National Committeeman, but he rose to vice-chairman of the national Democratic party within two years' time.

Firmly believing that control of law enforcement was the key to real political power, he kept the pressure on for top-level appointments for his key associates. One such person was John Milton, a shrewd lawyer who had become Hague's personal attorney and adviser, and who had been named corporation counsel of Jersey City.

The Newark *Evening News* would describe Milton as "the man who made Mayor Hague what he is politically and financially; the most influential adviser in New Jersey affairs; the most active lawyer in the state with the least, proportionately, appearance of record."

It seems obvious that "Haguey" approved of Milton's ability to speak the language of the streets, as he himself did. "I ain't never been arrested," Milton once told a reporter. "I ain't never been indicted. I ain't never been convicted. Sure, I've been investigated plenty, but that's politics."

John Milton was named prosecutor for Hudson County.

Not everything went so simply for "duh Mare," however. The *Jersey Journal,* seeing its own taxes rise inexorably along with those of other businesses as Hague's payrolls and payroll-padding increased, began to question his record and his methods. Hague responded in typical fashion: The *Journal*'s tax assessment was raised from $375,000 to $550,000. Then he went further. He ordered the police and fire forces to solicit subscriptions for a rival newspaper, and requested all local theaters to pull their advertising from the *Journal.* If the theaters did not comply, he hinted, they would be subject to a fire inspection that might result in their being closed down for failing to comply with safety regulations.

And, demonstrating that he knew well that there is more than one way to skin a cat (or silence an opponent), in 1926 Hague saw to it that his friend A. Harry Moore, who had been elected governor of New Jersey a year earlier, appointed a special judge to the Court of Errors and Appeals. The new judge was Joseph A. Dear, co-owner and editor of the *Jersey Journal.*

In his post as "duh Mare," Hague had successfully moved his previous choice for governor, Edwards, into the U. S. Senate. Governor Silzer might have followed the same route if he had not annoyed Hague by breaking up a highway board that Edwards (at Hague's urging) had appointed—a board made up of five Democrats and three Republicans. Silzer, perhaps feeling the need for independence, publicly said at the time: "For years there has been graft in the paving of New Jersey highways and everybody knew it. . . . I do not cast any reflections on the members of the board. It is sufficient to say the action is in the public interest." When Silzer's term ended, he sought the Democratic nomination for the presidency, and the New Jersey convention delegation supported him for a few ballots before switching to Al Smith. Silzer faded from the political scene, and Hague put all his attention on the matter of getting the next New Jersey governor elected: A. Harry Moore.

There can be little doubt that Hague himself would have tried for the governor's office and, after getting it, for the office of president if he had not been a Catholic. There was no chance, he knew, for the Protestant voters—whose numbers were greater in state and nation—to allow a Catholic to reach the topmost rungs of power.

Moore, of course, was a solid choice. A Protestant with a silver tongue, a member of the Masons and the Elks, popular Harry rolled up huge votes in four straight commission elections. As Commissioner of Parks, he was an ardent advocate of more parks and playgrounds. He spoke frequently on the need to censure large corporations. He was in favor of stiff penalties for criminals. And he urged special educational facilities for handicapped children. (One such great facility, A. Harry Moore School, still stands in Jersey City.)

Moore had so much going for him, in fact, that his Republican opponent in the 1925 election could come up with little else to criticize than Moore's close friendship with Frank Hague. The issue of "Hagueism" was enough to win the opponent, State Senator Arthur Whitney of Morris County, a majority of the votes cast outside Hudson County. But, as usual, when the Hudson votes came in, Moore had a plurality that totalled an incredible 103,000 votes—and he was catapulted into the governor's chair.

If such statistics create wonderment, remember that this was the time of paper ballots. It was relatively easy for Hague's people manning the polls to erase ballots, change ballots, destroy ballots, miscount ballots—while Hague-controlled policeman looked the other way or pressured inspection officials to stand aside. And where other counties were lucky if as much as 60 percent of registered voters turned out on election day, Hudson County usually produced ballots (genuine or not) from 90 percent of its registered voters.

Hague contended that his success came about "because the people understand what I have done for them . . . and want me to continue doing as I have done in the past." Election superintendent John

Ferguson, a Hoboken industrialist, saw it differently at one point: "We know it is futile to arrest anyone belonging to the Democrat organization in Hudson County on election day. The accuser usually finds himself in jail as the arrested party by the time he gets to the station house. I reaffirm . . . the only way to have an honest election in Hudson County . . . is with a militia, and if the present conditions are to continue, it is futile and ridiculous for us to attempt to hold further elections."

"Duh Mare" continued to wield "a big stick," as Teddy Roosevelt had advised, against any friends who crossed him. In the spring of 1927, it was the turn of John Saul to feel Hague's blows. Saul, a longtime city employee who served as Commissioner of Parks and Public Property, took the liberty of dismissing a number of municipal employees during one of Hague's extended vacations. His budget-cutting move was infuriating to Hague. Saul was stripped of most of his duties and personnel, and was threatened with recall on the allegation that he had refused to take advice. Rather than wait until he was removed from his post, Saul resigned.

Such unsophisticated tactics brought new attention from the *Journal,* which printed a series of amusing, satirical letters by a local dentist (signing his columns "FLG") that criticized the Hague machinations. Pressure from City Hall was increased—with one charge being that *Journal* delivery boys were in violation of child labor laws—and the paper eased up a bit. It eased up still more when Hague ordered that the parcel of property surrounding the paper's headquarters be renamed "Veterans' Square." He himself had bestowed its earlier name, "Journal Square," after city and state funds had been used to create the uptown plaza and business district.

The *Journal* editors, however, could not refrain from printing the news of the "One-Day Republicans" scandal that rocked Jersey City in 1928, and of the two-year investigation into Hague's regime that followed.

Problems for "duh Mare" began when Jersey City's Republican faction hit upon a unique scheme to put one of their own in the governor's office in Trenton. Harry Moore's three-year term was up, and Hague would have to come up with a new nominee that would gain Hudson County's favor, as usual—but what if the Republicans themselves nominated a Jersey City "boy" as their choice? They had a ready, willing candidate, too. Robert Carey, a former judge, had known and opposed the Hague machine for years. He agreed to run.

But Hague knew that Carey first had to win the Republican primary in order to threaten him in the gubernatorial contest. He studied the slate of nominees opposed to the knowledgeable Carey in the primary and pointed a finger at Morgan F. Larson, a little-known Republican senator from Middlesex County. If Hague befriended him, the Mayor decided, Larson would win the primary, but be relatively easy to beat with a solid Democratic candidate in the gubernatorial race—easier, certainly, than the hard-fighting Carey.

And if, by some miracle, Larson won the gubernatorial contest—well, then Frank Hague would have a friend in Trenton, anyway.

On Republican primary day, the polls in Hudson County were swamped by thousands of voters who declared they previously had been independents, but who had now decided that they were Republicans—Republicans who wanted to vote for Morgan F. Larson. In addition, more than a thousand Democrats signed Republican nominating petitions to get on the Larson bandwagon.

An angry Bob Carey promptly charged that he had been "swindled out of the Republican gubernatorial nomination by the Hague forces." And a cry went up in Trenton for an official inquiry into Hague's ability to produce some 30,000 Democrats who became One-Day Republicans.

As the Mackay committee had done in earlier years, a new group of legislators headed by State Senator Clarence Case began looking into the affairs of Hague and his tightly controlled Democratic machine. The "Case Committee," as the probers were known, started with a query into the possibility of fraud in the Republican primary, but the investigation quickly mushroomed into a penetrating perusal of everything and anything touched by Frank Hague. Because the probe continued for many months in 1928 and 1929, it might be appropriate here to leave its findings for a future chapter and move ahead—while the investigators subpoena witnesses and ask their questions—to the municipal commission election of 1929.

It was a particularly bitter contest—one in which Hague not only had to fend off the charges of the Case Committee, which were filling daily columns in the *Journal,* but one in which he had a formidable opponent for the first time in years. The challenger's name was James "Jeff" Burkitt, a former riveter who stood well over six feet and who had no fear of "duh Mare" whatsoever. J. Owen Grundy, the venerable city historian of Jersey City for four decades (and a man given to wearing a long, old-fashioned preacher's coat, string tie, and broad-brimmed fedora in any weather), is one of the few men around today lucky enough to have witnessed the Hague-Burkitt battle. "I remember visiting Burkitt one day at his home and seeing him stripped to the waist, working out with barbells," Grundy recalls. "He had rippling chest muscles and huge biceps."

In addition to physical strength, Burkitt had a commanding voice. Delivering speeches in his native Alabama drawl, he dared to stand on the steps of the almost sacrosanct City Hall. There he would bellow for attention and shout, "I have a cannon loaded with facts!" Then he would unleash a barrage of facts and statistics, comparing costs of government, number of schools and parks, size of police force, and the like between Jersey City and its neighbors of equal size.

Seldom was he halfway through a speech before the missiles began flying. Tomatoes, rotten eggs, and worse would be flung at "Jeff" by loyal supporters of the Democratic party and Frank Hague. The inevitable finale: Burkitt's forceful removal from the scene by a squad of "Zepps" who would charge him with disturbing the peace.

An uncle of mine, Frank Kelly, a poorly paid lettercarrier on the economic scale but a man with the unconquerable soul of a great fighter, understood Burkitt's words and joined him in the anti-Hague crusade. Uncle Frank was a powerful speaker himself, given to quoting in loud tones from W. E. Henley's "Invictus": "I am the master of my fate; I am the captain of my soul." Standing on the flatbed of a truck, looking out over the small crowd gathered around him, he would plead for someone to join him in the battle against Hague. Quickly, people would walk away—before they were spotted by Hague's followers—and occasionally one would turn to give my uncle a "Bronx cheer."

"You cowards!" Frank Kelly would yell. "You Hague monkies! Come back here and fight like men." He was a fighter, ready to slug it out with anyone at any time, but Frank Hague understood that if you knocked a man down with a fist, he might get up and come back at you. He had other ways of taking care of people like my uncle. A Hague ward leader was given the job of postmaster; the postmaster saw to it that Frank Kelly lost his job—and, in turn, his home. He landed eventually in a coldwater flat, broke financially, but never broken in spirit.

Consider for a moment, if a Burkitt supporter received that kind of treatment from the forces of the Mayor, what Burkitt's fate was to be.

In 1929 a fusion ticket was running its own slate of commission candidates against Hague and his four choices. Burkitt served as the chief spokesman for the fusion five, although he declined to be a candidate himself. Instead, the maverick campaigner attempted night after night, day after day to make his voice heard throughout Jersey City. Soon, as might be expected, Burkitt was restricted by Hague's police in when and where he could speak. Burkitt's refusal to comply with "the law" brought arrests, beatings and more. Even during a trip to State House to encourage the removal of a Hague election official, Burkitt engaged Hague men in physical combat. It was inevitable that Burkitt would show up at a municipal meeting to confront the Mayor. Hague, presiding over the commission, was clearly amused at the sight of his opponent. Burkitt limped and had several bandages on his head and face.

"Some of your thugs beat me up," was Burkitt's reply when Hague asked—in all innocence—what had happened. Chuckling, Hague explained, "I'm not laughing at you—but your face looks so funny." Burkitt was ready to raise his fists when the Mayor suggested they settle any questions about his speaking permit "like gentlemen." Burkitt glared at him, raised an eyebrow, and said, "Oh? I didn't know you were one."

Burkitt's impertinence insured harsh retribution. He was not allowed to speak or hold an outdoor meeting within six blocks of one of

Hague's indoor meetings (and it was impossible to know where an "indoor" Hague meeting was being held). Burkitt and his handful of followers were also warned that if they posted notices announcing meetings on streetlamps, walls of city buildings, and property belonging to private citizens, they would be subject to arrest.

Burkitt swore open defiance of the ban on his posters. He announced that he intended to put a large sign on the corner of Academy Street and Bergen Avenue, and damn the consequences. Promptly at 8:00 p.m., a large truck drove up to the corner bearing a sign promising a Burkitt speech in a half-hour. In minutes the police were there to haul Burkitt and the truckdriver off to the precinct house.

Because the *Jersey Journal* provided needed support (in spite of owner Dear's appointment to the bench by Hague's friend, Governor Moore, three years earlier), "Jeff" frequently sought to make his speeches in Journal Square. (Hague might have ordered new signs posted, reading Veterans' Square, but the residents of Jersey City were slow to recognize the change in their everyday language.) In the midst of one speech, according to the paper's report, "Six thugs beat up 'Jeff' at Journal Square. He fell twice before the cops arrived." Burkitt's reward that time for speaking out against the administration was "a badly lacerated ear and various bruises and abrasions."

Against any one man, the crusading and fearless Southerner could give more than blow for blow. In a rowdy demonstration at the State House in Trenton, Burkitt bodily lifted a huge rival and threw him across the room, putting his opponent flat on his back and out of the fight. The kind of physical violence that Burkitt could deal out made police captain Harry W. Walsh reluctant to take him on single-handed. Each time Burkitt was arrested, Walsh made sure that there were plenty of policemen to help to do the job. Time and again, as Burkitt was dragged away, he would bellow in his unmistakeable Southern drawl that "Harry Wowsh is a phoney, a coward! He's tough 'cause he's got a gun on his hip an' a badge on his chest! An' he's got Frank Hague behind him! Anytime Wowsh wants to take Jeff Burkitt on man to man, just tell me the place an' time." Not surprisingly, Capt. Walsh postponed the battle to a future date.

Voters, particularly among the upwardly mobile families who had moved to the ''Hill'' wards, began to sympathize with the underdog Burkitt. Then, in the midst of one street battle between a group of Hague's opponents and supporters, an eight-year-old child, Catherine McGee, accidentally was struck on the head by a whirling baseball bat. The child died, and the *Journal* devoted a front-page sketch to the event, running a caption that said the drawing depicted the ''killing of Catherine McGee by four of Hague's Election Day thugs.''

In addition to its daily tales of the violence that Hague's forces—both uniformed and otherwise—committed in the name of free elections and order in the public streets, the *Journal* began to lay out for the voters details about the kind of government that held power over their city and their lives. The administration, said one editorial, ''has convicted itself of being unworthy of further public trust. The evidence consists of neglected schools, neglected streets, neglected parks, outrageous taxes, industries driven from the city, vacant stores, unemployment, graft, shakedowns, favoritism, and what not. These are no idle charges made in the heat of a political campaign. They are grave accusations that can be supported by public records and testimony given under oath.''

Evidently, Jeff Burkitt's repeated cries—''Jersey City is the highest taxed city in the nation, and it's not me sayin' that; the United States Department of Commerce said it!''—were starting to be heard by more and more people. Perhaps for the first time in his career, Frank Hague was worried.

The Mayor intensified his efforts, passing the word down to the lowest ward worker that no defection would be tolerated, no criticism would be heard without punishment. He repeatedly accused the *Journal* of ''yellow journalism,'' irresponsibility, and actions that may have stemmed from unknown political motives of the owners and editors.

On the eve of the election, Hague ventured into the heart of the Horseshoe, to speak extemporaneously and at considerable length (he typically outlasted even the longest-winded of his supporters) at his favorite school hall, P. S. 37. On the stage was a crude casket bedecked with funeral wreaths. Beneath it was a sign that read: "The End of Burkitt." And the loyal, the fearful, the undecided crowded in to hear Hague and a half-dozen other speakers verbally lambaste the rival who had devoted a full year to crusade against the administration, using his lion's heart and oratorical fervor to speak out against Hague on almost every street corner in the city.

Calling Hague "the immovable object" and Burkitt "the irresistible force," historian J. Owen Grundy says, "They were two street fighters who asked no quarter and gave none. Down deep, I believe Burkitt was the only opponent Hague really admired. He had the guts that only Hague could understand and respect."

Hague may have understood his opponent, and respected him—perhaps—but he had no intention of letting him claim victory. When the votes were counted, fairly or unfairly, Hague and his four choices for the commission had vote totals that ranged from 66,668 for the least popular man to 68,522 for the most popular. The best the five fusion party candidates could muster was a vote of 43,681 for one man and considerably less for the others.

And Jeff Burkitt trailed far behind in his one-man fight.

He left Jersey City shortly after the ballots were counted.

6

If the reader is not to be burdened with page upon page of testimony recounting the misdeeds—and some worthwhile achievements—of Frank Hague over the first decade of his reign, it is necessary to condense into manageable form the discoveries of the Case Committee that were made over some 18 months of hearings. One way, perhaps, might be to choose a single day—one, say, in late October, 1928—and imagine what it was like for the investigators, the suspected, and the spectators. What follows, then, is an impression of what such a day might have revealed, with the names and questions and answers taken from official records and newspaper accounts, but with the action compressed into a finite span of time. The technique, it could be argued, is similar to that used in time-lapse photography. . . .

On the ceiling of the large second-floor assembly room of the State Senate building in Trenton, a score of flies buzzed good-naturedly, clinging inverted only a few feet above the sextet of long-bladed fans that spun slowly in a tired attempt to move the stale air of the room about. The grey windows, jammed tight in their sills to keep out the autumn chill, let in barely enough light for the two custodians who entered to locate a wall switch and snap on the yellow ceiling bulbs.

"D'ja hear about the fight in Jersey City last week, Eddie?" asked one as he blinked up at the dim illumination. The other, a black who already was waving a cloth over the polished surface of a table that resembled a judicial bench, grunted a negative reply.

"No? You should a' been there. Allie Santora took on two guys, one after t'other. Knocked 'em both cold! On the same night! Nobody ever saw nothin' like it. If that don't get him a shot at Barney Ross an' the title, nothin' will."

Now the black was working on the heavy chairs. "I don't follow the fights much no more, not since Willard whupped Johnson befo' the war."

"You should. Hey, they got great battlers in Jersey City—'Irish' Bobby Brady," Lenny 'Young' Zazzarino, the 'Marion Bullet,' Standley Poreda, the Mack brothers. They're gettin' plenty of attention now that Frankie Burns and Joe Shugrue have retired."

Now the chairs were being straightened in neat rows. "You catch the exhibition ballgame Saturday?"

Nodding, the white man grabbed a wide dustmop and shoved it halfheartedly across the floor in front of the long table. "Nope, but I heard about it. Heard that your 'countryman,' the black guy, Dick Shade—"

"It's Seay, pronounced *shay*," retorted the black with a wide grin to show he was not criticizing anyone.

"Shade, Shay, what's the difference? Anyway, he played for $15 bucks just to say he was in a game with Babe Ruth and Lou Gehrig."

"Who got fifteen hundred apiece! Man, that's a shame. Satchel Page said that Seay—he's from Jersey City—would have been in the Hall of Fame if he'd been white."

The other slid the broom through the doorway and into the hall. "Ah, for that kind of thrill, I bet he would have played for nothin'. I know I would." He took a final look at the meeting room. It was still humid, full of heavy dust-laden air, noisy with the buzzing of flies and the whirring of the fans overhead. But the chairs were neatly aligned.

"Let's go," said the white man. "In a coupla hours this place will look like a subway station at rush hour anyway. It's clean enough." He walked into the hall, patiently waiting for his co-worker to follow him. "I'll tell you one thing," he said, shrugging his broad shoulders. "If I could fight or play ball—not even half as good as them twins, Maury and Joe Shannon—I wouldn't have to worry about my future. You know well as I do any athlete good enough to get his name in the papers ain't gonna be out of a job anytime. They all get on the payroll 'specially in Jersey City." He closed the door of the room tightly, checking to make sure it was not locked. As the two men walked down the corridor, he added a final statement: "Jersey City ain't a place to forget its heroes, Eddie."

* * *

Promptly at 10:00 that morning, roughly an hour after the two cleaning men had made the room ready, Senator Clarence Case of Somerset County slammed his gavel down on the wooden block atop the long table. As silence fell, he aimed his gaze out on a sizable crowd that filled every available chair and much of the aisle at the rear. With a nod to the male stenographer at the side of the room, he snapped, "Here we go again, Phil. You put in the heading—day, date, time, all that stuff." The secretary smiled, then jotted a few shorthand notes. "Gentlemen," Case said, making the single word into a question that demanded readiness from the fellow senators on either side of him. And, when there was no dissent, "Mr. Watson, call your first witness."

A stocky, red-faced man rose from his chair at the right end of the table. "Glad to, Senator," said Russell E. Watson, chief counsel for the committee's inquiry, "although I'm beginning to think that hearing any more testimony similar to what we've heard for the past few weeks is a waste of everybody's time."

There was a ripple of laughter from the spectators jammed into the room. "That's all right," called a rough voice from the rear. "It's cheaper comin' here than goin' to the movies."

Case slammed the gavel sharply, twice, three times to still the crowd. "I understand your frustration, Mr. Watson," he said, forcing a good-natured smile, "but call your witness. In this kind of situation, the sheer weight of the evidence can be important."

Wearily, Watson turned and barked out a name. A shuffling in the front row of people produced a standing figure, a jovial-appearing, muscular man in a suit that was obviously his Sunday best, albeit a bit frayed at the cuffs. The man, whose name was

Alfred H. Mansfield, stared first at the row of politicians in front of him, then turned to survey the audience behind him. Finally, with a "thumbs up" gesture that brought a laugh from the crowd, he strode forward and took the chair that stood raised on a small platform.

"Could we have your full name, please?" Watson said flatly.

Mansfield looked at him. "Uh, don't I get sweared in or somethin' first?" he asked.

"For the twentieth time," said Watson, struggling not to shout, "this is an inquiry, not a trial. We expect you to answer some questions, as truthfully as you can, but no one is accusing you of anything. Is that clear?" He fixed Mansfield with a baleful glare and got a noncomittal nod in return. "Just your name."

Alfred H. Mansfield, a crowd-pleaser, grinned and gave his name and, when asked, said that he had worked for the last 25 years as a health inspector for the Hudson County Board of Health. "It's the same as I told you last time, when I was here in July. Nothin's changed—not the name, not the job."

Watson nodded. "I understand that, Mr. Mansfield. I'm sure the Senator and everyone else here remembers your testimony then. We just wanted to go over some of it again, to see if we can understand exactly what you do for the salary you are paid."

"I don't mind," Mansfield said, settling his large frame against the hard chair. He got his laugh from the crowd. "But could we make it sort o' quick? This questionin' is tough on my behind."

Case raised the gavel, and the crowd quieted at the mere threat. "Could I save us time by going over some of the ground?" he demanded. "In your earlier testimony, Mr. Mansfield, you told us that as a health inspector for the county, you have no office, keep no records, and report to no one. Is that correct?"

"Yeh," Mansfield replied quickly. "I have a roving commission."

Watson nodded. "I remember, I remember. And it was at that point that we decided to take a recess. Now that you're back—and I understand that you still are on the Hudson County payroll—perhaps we could get specific about your duties." He paused, observed Mansfield nod condescendingly, and said softly, "Exactly what do you look for when you conduct your duties as a health inspector?"

"I—er—sort of go out and look for whatever I can find."

Over the laughter of the crowd, Watson demanded, "Exactly *where* do you look for whatever you can find?"

The witness rubbed a thick finger along the side of his nose. "Just 'bout anywhere, I guess."

Watson sighed deeply. "Can we get specific? Last week, for instance. Where were you looking last week?"

It took a moment of thought for Mansfield to remember that he had "dropped in on a couple of places in North Bergen, but I can't tell you just where, I mean, I don't know the street names in my head anymore."

For the crowd, it was better than Chaplin and Keaton together. For Watson, it was obviously a battle of desperation. "At these places that you can't quite remember, Inspector, what exactly did you do?"

"I was up there to check on horses and cows."

Under his breath, Watson doubted that the man could tell the difference but he asked aloud, "What were you checking for?"

"Foot and mouth disease." The answers were flicking out faster now, keeping up with the questions in table-tennis tempo.

"Can you describe this disease?"

"I—'m not sure."

Watson slammed his hand down hard on the table-top. *If I can't get answers,* the crowd could almost hear him thinking, *I'm damn sure going to get attention.* "Well," he roared, "how do you know when an animal has a foot disease or merely a corn?"

"I'm a health officer," Mansfield answered calmly, "not a vet."

In the roar that erupted from the crowd, a roar of laughter peppered with applause, Watson waved a hand almost drunkenly and stepped aside to let the grinning Mansfield move back to his seat. Turning to the tableful of investigators, he whispered an almost incoherent recapitulation of the witness's testimony:

"Twenty-five years on the payroll, gentlemen . . . never found a single violation of any city or state ordinance . . . president of a political club that collects no dues, but pays a small fortune in rent . . . seen going into Frank Hague's office for a conference before coming in here to testify, claims he was only using the toilet . . . ran a tavern during Prohibition and says he didn't know about the Volstead Act . . . and god-knows-what-else, and ask him what he does and he tells us he goes 'round looking for what he can see!''

Two of the senators on either side of Case reached out anxious hands, as if they expected the red-faced Watson to collapse. Case, however, nodded in a knowing fashion. "Mr. Watson," he said, "things are muddled enough without a show of histrionics on your part. The point is well made, but we must hear more. Please continue."

Watson shrugged and turned to call Mrs. Mabel Youngblood, a thin, nervous woman who rose slowly from a rear row and made her way carefully along the narrow aisle. In a trembling, soft voice, while her eyes remained fixed on the floor, she gave her address—49 Sussex Street—and admitted that she knew the name of (in Watson's words) "a member of the Democratic party named William McGovern."

"I guess you mean young Bill. He's a real nice one, he is. He is so good to us, me and my husband, I mean."

"How do you mean? Good to you in what way?"

The witness raised her eyes, opening them wide in surprise. "Why, on Christmas he brought us—me and Mr. Youngblood—a basket with chicken in it. And all the trimmin's. And he got one for Mrs. Ryan next door for New Year's 'cause I told him she didn't get one for Christmas. And he wrote to Washington for us, 'cause my husband—well, he ain't been workin' an' Mr. McGovern said he could get him veterans' benefits. And he did."

"Mr. McGovern is the Democratic committeeman in your—"

"Yep, and that's why I'm a Democrat, and the mister is, too."

Watson pounced on the opening. "But you voted Republican in the recent election, didn't you?"

The witness bobbed her head nervously atop her frail figure. "I didn't know it was wrong," she said, her voice quavering. "I was standin' in line at the pollin' place—it was in the front of the undertaker's store on Morris Street—and I wasn't feelin' good. I got this stomach tumor. It was actin' up and young Bill heard me complainin' and moved me up to the head of the line."

"And he suggested that you vote for the Republican candidate."

Now the head shook from side to side. "No, he didn't suggest nothin'. He just said when he was helping me through the little curtain that he was votin' Republican this time 'round."

Watson rolled his eyes to the ceiling and spread his hands in a helpless gesture toward the tableful of investigators. "Mrs. Youngblood, I wish I believed that you were as innocent as you appear."

A whisper of booing ran through the hearing room. In the rear, a newsman from the *Journal* nudged an associate. "They don't like him pickin' on a poor old woman," he said, leaning his head toward the crowd of spectators. At the table in front, Watson had dismissed the woman and begun reading into the record the names of 1,127 registered Democrats who had voted illegally—most as "One-Day Republicans"—in a primary election. "This is goin' to take awhile," said the *Journal* reporter. "Let's go outside and see if we can find Hague. Maybe he'll have somethin' to say."

"Duh Mare" was nowhere to be found, but the two reporters discovered his boyhood friend, John Malone, leaning against the marble-surfaced wall in the corridor. He nodded perfunctorily as the two men approached him, then raised a cautionary hand.

"I can't answer any questions, boys. Don't waste your time."

The reporter with the notepad slipped it into his pocket. "No questions, then, Needle-Nose. Not for the record, anyway."

Malone grunted. "Wise guy, I told you to cut out the 'Needle-Nose' crap. One more time and I won't answer nothin' 'less you call me Mister Deputy Mayor."

"All right, John," the older newsman said. "I was kiddin' around. Come on, off the record, how d'ya think it's goin'? They got anything solid on Hague, you think?"

"If crap's solid, they got somethin'," the slender politician snorted. "Go ahead, put that in your paper." He stared at the two reporters, then shook his head as a group of the senatorial investigators came from the assembly room and headed toward the toilets and the downstairs snack counter. "Look at that," he said. "This thing's been goin' on so long, them guys are gettin' as bored as the rest of the world."

"Hey, John, you think the *world's* concerned with what Frank Hague does?"

"Like hell it ain't! Listen, you lunkheads"—he scratched a match across the marble behind him and applied it to a thick cigar, puffing fiercely until the end glowed brightly—"you got any idea how far out Frank's word reaches? No, you guys think you know so much. Nothin'—that's what you know. Nothin' ! ''

With a wink at his partner, the young reporter urged, "Okay, Mr. Deputy Mayor, we know nothin'. So tell us: How's Hague do it? How's he keep everything runnin' so smooth?"

Perhaps Malone had had a drink too many that morning. Perhaps he was merely tired of hanging around the assembly building, gathering data to carry back to Hague. "But that's *my* job," he said. "I report to Frank, to the Mayor. Just me, nobody else. And what he wants done—*that* comes down through me. I tell the ward leaders; they're the generals for their sections of the city. They go to the committeemen, you know that; and them, the guys near the bottom, they keep the people in line."

The reporters were nodding eagerly, pretending to be students at the feet of the instructor. "But what if the committeeman can't keep 'em in line?"

A snort from Malone. "Then he's out and somebody else is in. If we need more committeemen, we get 'em, that's all. And if a guy does a good job, he moves up." He leaned back, tipping his head backwards to squint at the two men as if aligning them atop the length of gunbarrel that was his nose. "We work that way in the city, an' that way in Hudson County. An' we'll work like that in the state and maybe this whole damn country pretty soon." A cackle of laughter burst from the thin mouth beneath the nose. "And you dumb yokels don't think the *world* keeps an eye on Frank Hague!"

One of the reporters decided to sidestep the insults. "I think the world better keep a watch on 'duh Mare,' Malone, before he puts it in his pocket to use as a marble. Looks like he's gettin' ready to swipe it along with everything else."

"Yeh," the other jumped in. "Wait until he testifies this afternoon and tries to explain how he can buy estates, apartments, and all his other stuff on a salary of $8,000 a year."

Malone grinned, then ground his cigar out on the terrazzo floor. "He don't have to explain nothin'," he snapped. "He's the Mayor, and you guys better not get too tough with him. You *start* to, an' we just might leak the little story that a guy on your paper has also been a regular employee of the city for a long time."

"What 're you talkin' about, Malone? A *Journal* reporter on Hague's payroll?"

Again, the beady eyes squinted above the equine nose. "I ain't sayin' there is one, and I ain't sayin' there ain't, but I think it would be pretty interestin' if there *was* one, don't you? And there might even be a guy over at the *Observer* who sometimes gets a check from the Recreation Department. So if you birds think your underwear's clean, well, you got another think comin'."

Malone spun on his heel and walked along the corridor, dismissing the two reporters without a backward glance. Behind him, he knew, their faces had blanched and they were eyeing each other suspiciously. It was true; Malone searched his mind for the names of the newsmen and suddenly had them: George Farrant at the *Journal*, Herman Donsky at the *Observer*.

"Reporters!" he muttered under his breath. "They gotta eat, just like anybody else."

In the meeting room, Watson was going through an unending roster of fresh witnesses, calling them one after another and desperately trying to keep their testimony in focus for the senators. It was not a simple task, because the witnesses were prone to lapses of memory when asked about their jobs, their salaries, their voting records.

"Mr. Joyce," he said to a youthful employee of the city's transportation bureau, "it's a simple question: While you are a full-time salaried worker for Jersey City, how do you find time to appear as an actor in a play—called *The Shannons of Broadway,* I believe—in New York City?"

"Oh," the young man replied, "I know. It only ran a week. I took a vacation."

"And you took other vacations," asked an angry Senator Case from the table, "whenever you got a chance to appear on the stage?" He waved a gesture of dismissal before the actor could reply.

"While we're on the subject of theater," Watson said as he turned to the investigatory panel, "let's hear from Charles Suozza, gentlemen. He ran the Majestic Theater in Jersey City a few years ago. It was located right across the street from City Hall." It took only a few questions to elicit from the sallow-faced theatrical manager that while he operated a burlesque show for several years right under the nose of the Mayor and other officials, he paid $100 weekly "to keep from being bothered." His checks went to a member of the Board of Education—a revelation that caused a spectator in a front row to wonder aloud what kind of education the city's schoolchildren were getting.

"And I sent $500 to the Democratic fund," Suozza said.

"It's meaningless testimony," a newsman whispered to a rival reporter. "When Hague decided to prove what a god-fearing man he is and closed the movies and burlycue shows, he wiped out any harm this kind of payoff can do him. He'll say the guy's mad at bein' closed down, that he's making up his story."

The reference to the member of the Board of Education had sidetracked Watson's try at digging deeper into the matter of City Hall bribery. A clerk had been asked to reread some data previously uncovered by the Case Committee. In a matter-of-fact voice, he intoned that 27 percent of Jersey City's public school students attended class on split schedules because schools were overcrowded. Bayonne, Camden, Passic, Paterson, Trenton, and other cities had only one to seven percent of their students in a similar situation.

"I—uh, I don't understand," said one of the state officials seated at Case's side. "Figures have been presented here, I believe, that show the city can readily borrow $20 million for school construction."

Suddenly, the tall figure of Jeff Burkitt rose from the crowd at the rear of the room. "You want an explanation!" His booming voice echoed under the high ceiling, overcoming the rumble of the whirring fans with ease. "Frank Hague neglects the public schools so's not to make the Catholic school system weaker, that's what. An' he gets the Catholic vote for it!"

Case had to gavel the room into silence. "Mr. Burkitt," he called in a stern voice, "I must again ask you to refrain from making comments. Time and again you've thrown these hearings into an uproar—''

"I offer my 'pologies, Senator," drawled "Alabama Jim" in his softest Southern tones. "But it hurts me, truly it does, to sit out here and listen to you all tryin' to make sense out of anything Hague does when anybody can tell you the real reason he does it. An' that's to line his own pock—''

Slam, went the gavel. *Slam! Slam!* "Mr. Burkitt! You can be removed!''

The tall man waved a hand, nodding. "I know that, sir. My 'pologies again." He sat down, seemingly withdrawing from the fray, then rose up again with with a rush. "But, Mr. Case, Your Honor, sir, me and Judge Warren got proof that Hudson County's getting over five million a year in payoffs from gamblers! And every cent is headed Frank Hague's way!''

The room erupted. Several reporters battled their way through the doors to relay the charge to their papers. Applause welled up around Burkitt, and laughter surrounded the furious Case as he wielded his gavel. Watson shook his head, a mixture of amusement and chagrin on his face. Finally, as the room quieted, Case asked wearily, "Is there anything else you'd like to say, Mr. Burkitt, since you obviously have the floor? If so, please say it and let us get on with things.''

The tall Southerner reached up as if to tip an invisible hat on his head. "Jes one thing, sir. That is, if I kin?''

All eyes went to Case, who nodded in acquiescence. "Just be brief, that's all I ask.''

"Well, then I'd like to tell everybody that I am going to hold a silent prayer meeting—maybe just for three minutes— at the corner of Charles Street and Central Avenue. I'm goin' to pray that Jersey City is delivered up from the hands of Frank Hague and all those people robbin' its good citizens. And''—he noticed Case raise the gavel and he himself raised a cautioning hand—''I just want to invite all the good citizens to join me, that's all. Thank you, sir.'' He stood silent for a moment, and then marched up the aisle and out of the room, tall in his dignity.

"Call your next witness, Mr. Watson," Case said in the sudden stillness that had fallen on the room.

Atwood Wolf, a young lawyer who had been tarred with the "One-Day Republican" brush, took the designated chair. Watson led off with some routine questions, then asked about a charge made by Burkitt that Wolf had intimidated some building contractors. "I understand that you've been reported to have told them that if things did not go the way the Democrats want, Theodore Brandle—the leader of the Ironworkers—will pull their workers out on strike. Mr. Burkitt's exact words, I believe, compare Brandle's control of the workers with the control the Czar formerly had in Russia. Have you any comments on the charge?"

"Any comments?" snorted the angry young man. "Burkitt is full of brainstorms! He goes around maligning people, deliberately calling them filthy names, bad names, and getting arrested for using foul language. He's been tried on a number of occasions for it."

When the lawyer's testimony produced no conclusive evidence of wrongdoing, Watson returned to his unending parade of employees on the padded Jersey City payrolls. "Sheriff," he said to a stocky man who seated himself gingerly in the chair, as if afraid his weight would break it, "your nickname in the Fourth Ward, which you serve as leader, I understand, is 'Honest John'?"

A nod of John Coppinger's balding head was the response. Watson turned to the panel of state officials. "Senator Case," he said, "perhaps you'd like to ask a few questions yourself."

Case spoke in a clear voice. "Have you ever done anything since you were made sheriff except to sign checks?"

Honest John's reply was immediate. "No."

It took only a few questions more to elicit the fact that the sheriff had no idea of what his duties were supposed to be, no knowledge of what the staff he paid were supposed to do for their salaries, or even what their salaries were.

"I see," said Case as he studied a list, "that you have someone on your payroll with the title of Execution Clerk. Do you know his duties?"

Perspiring, Coppinger furrowed his brow in thought. "Uh—I—er, think he has something to do with keeping records of who gets 'lectrocuted."

Frank Hague (left) beside Franklin Delano Roosevelt on the latter's campaign for the presidency in 1932.

In 1938 Babe Ruth became a coach for the Brooklyn Dodgers. Here's Frank Hague reaching across the dug-out to shake hands with his friend the "Bambino."

Hague flanking President Harry S. Truman at a
Democratic rally at Lincoln High School in
Jersey City.

(Facing page) *The Mayors of Jersey City, 1838-1911*
Top row: John B. Romar, Samuel Westcott, Robert Gilchrist, Phineas
C. Dummer, Henry J. Taylor, David S. Manners, Cornelius Van Vorst,
Orestes Cleveland. Center row: William Clark, James Gopsill, Thomas A.
Alexander, Peter MacMartin, Peter Bentley, Charles H. O'Neil, Henry Trap-
hagen. Bottom row: Charles Siedler, Isaac W. Taussig, Peter F. Wanser,
Mark M. Fagan, H. Otto Wittpenn, Edward Hoos, Gilbert Collins and
Henry J. Hopper.

Two of the most powerful men in the history of New Jersey politics: the only 3-term Governor of New Jersey, A. Harry Moore, at the time Jersey City Commissioner of Parks, with Frank Hague during "Boys' Week" in 1924. The ceremony took place in the assembly chambers of the City Hall.

Hague leaving the Grand Jury room. Despite all allegations, Hague was never indicted or convicted of any wrongdoing.

Hague with Deputy Mayor John "Needlenose" Malone on the occasion of Hague's retirement in 1947 after 30 years as Mayor and 34 years on the city commission.

Frank Hague Eggers, the Mayor's nephew, receiving the gavel of office from his uncle. Eggers, who was turned out of office by the Kenny landslide in 1949, staged a successful comeback to the commission 4 years later only to die in office shortly after his return.

The 1949 victory by John V. Kenny defeated the Hague machine. Here a symbolic coffin is carried into City Hall as a city goes wild.

The night "the Little Guy," John V. Kenny, made history by sweeping Hague's vaunted machine out of office.

Hague's wife of more than 50 years, the former Jennny Warner, grieves at her husband's funeral. To her left is their son, Frank Hague, Jr., and their adopted daughter, Peggy Ann Hague.

Freedom from Bossism triumphs: The Kenny victory.

President John F. Kennedy in a symbolic linking
of hands with Boss John V. Kenny and then New
Jersey Governor Robert Meyner.

Case waited for the crowd's laughter to subside. "While you've been on the Jersey City payroll as sheriff, you've also been running a plumbing business, haven't you?"

"Yes, sir, and my people do excellent work, sir. If there's anything you need done, we—"

"I don't need plumbing, Mr. Coppinger. I need an explanation of how you can handle both jobs at once."

Again, the heavy brow wrinkled in concentration. The pause seemed to last forever, and then the answer came: "Well, Senator Case, sir, this sheriff's job only lasts for three years, and, you see, Mr. Case, that is, well, I thought maybe I shouldn't give up my plumbing business—just in case, er—Mr. Case, sir."

Fighting to control his temper, the investigator banged the gavel furiously and roared. "You mean you like the job's $11,000 salary!" When he got an affirmative reply, he asked a final question: "Sheriff Coppinger, do you know where the sheriff's office is?"

The sheriff-plumber nodded slowly. "I think so," he said, anticipating the gesture of dismissal and lumbering from the chair.

"Mr. Watson, I believe that some lunch might give us the strength to hear some more of this kind of thing," the senator said. "I suggest we adjourn until this afternoon. At that time, perhaps we can get some answers from the one person who might be able to cast the most light on the political system of Jersey City."

"I am assured, Senator, that Mayor Hague will be present," said Watson as he stuffed his briefcase with papers."

At the rear of the large room, a newsman whispered to an associate: "If an assurance from Frank Hague means anything." Rising along with the crowd of spectators, he pressed forward to approach Watson.

He did not have to hold out an identifying *Journal* press card. "You've got my sympathy, Russ. It's like slogging through the mud at Chateau Thierry, ain't it?"

Watson laughed. "We'll get him, Dan. You just wait and see. Case is really determined to get him this time. And we've got Burkitt to keep the pot bubbling, and a couple of longtime Hague enemies —oldtimer Mark Fagan and Monahan, the ex-police chief— they're all willing to help out."

The reporter played devil's advocate. He did not see how anything criminal could be proved, how Hague—who never put anything in writing in any form whatsoever—could be directly linked to payoffs or bribes or unlawful use of public funds.

Perhaps not, Watson agreed. "But the evidence of widespread corruption is piling up day by day, one bit after another, until we've got a huge pile, a gigantic wall, and on top of it sits Hague like a fat Humpty-Dumpty. All we have to do is put a crack in that wall and it collapses, and he comes down with it."

"Maybe so, maybe no. If you ask me, Burkitt's not good for much more than laughs when it comes to helping out. Take last month when he showed up in that 'speak' the night the feds pulled the raid. Sure, he proved that Hague lets bars operate illegally in Jersey City, but he was the one who ended up tradin' punches with a customer and got hauled off to jail."

Watson had an answer on the tip of his tongue when a murmur of shouts echoed down the hall outside the chamber. The reporter spun about, automatically reaching for his pad and pencil. "See you later, Russ," he called over his shoulder. "Sounds like somethin's going on!"

In a mob at the end of the corridor, a tall, stern-visaged figure stood silent, narrow eyes glinting as flashbulbs popped only inches away. Frank Hague's clothes were expensive, perfectly tailored, soberly cut to add to the impression of height. A tight collar encircled his thickening neck, with a narrow gold clasp tucked precisely beneath the narrow knot of the thin tie. Heavy jowls were beginning to show on the face, and circular bags were bulging beneath the eyes. A few rivulets of perspiration caught the flashbulbs' glare atop the rapidly balding pate.

Malone, holding off the crowd of reporters, raised his voice, demanding quiet "if you fellas want any kind of statement." The reporters obediently fell silent. Frank Hague, they knew, did not answer questions. He made statements.

"I have volunteered to come here to help out Senator Case," the Mayor said carefully. "This whole damn committee certainly needs help 'cause it doesn't know what the hell it's doing. It's made a lot of charges, and it's listened to a lot of charges. But none of the people here have any idea of what's really going on in Jersey City and Hudson County, and they're all making damn fools of themselves. I intend to tell them that if they took a look at Altantic City cr Camden County, by God, *we'd* be wearing a halo.''

One of the reporters waved a hand. ''Mr. Mayor—'' he began, but Hague ignored him and went on speaking. ''I also intend to ask the committee why it isn't concentrating its attention on important matters. Like those forty-dollar-a-day vouchers turned in by Judge Joseph Dear. Just because he owns the *Journal,* which has seen fit to trumpet the fact that it's the cause of this whole affair, well, I don't see why the public shouldn't get a look at his padded payroll.''

A buzz of excited whispers filled the corridor. And suddenly Malone was pushing through the crowd, aided by a half-dozen burly men whose manner immediately characterized them as members of the ''Zepps.'' As suddenly as he had come, Hague was gone, the door of an antechamber snapping shut behind him.

The parade of early witnesses after the lunch break were clearly acting the role of curtain-raisers for the day's star attraction. The investigators, including Case and Watson, dutifully asked their questions and listened to the answers, but everyone in the room knew that the big event was going to take place momentarily.

''As Superintendent of County Mechanics, Mr. Doody,'' Watson said wearily halfway through the afternoon,'' could you explain your duties for us.''

Perched on the edge of the chair atop the platform, James Doody eagerly answered. ''I do the best I can to keep my men busy.''

Watson flipped through a sheaf of papers. ''According to the records I have here, you have some 70 men on the payroll. They have assorted titles, haven't they? Such titles as 'cuspidor cleaner,' 'supervisor of sinks,' and 'foreman of vacuum cleaners.' '' He waited for the laughter to subside. ''And the records—which I must point out are rather skimpy since they make no mention of any work being requisitioned or being done—seem to show that employees hired for seasonal work remain on the payrolls of Hudson County all year 'round.''

The witness shrugged, and was promptly replaced by one of his employees—a rugged young man who gave his name as Chris

Niehaus and his address as 25 Condict Street. He testified that he worked for the county from 8 a.m. to 4 p.m. daily, and worked infrequently for the U. S. Trucking Corporation from 4 p.m. to midnight.

"How do you manage to hold down two jobs?" asked an incredulous Case. "When do you eat and sleep?"

"Oh, I can do it, sir. I sometimes just leave a little early."

Asked to describe his duties as a Hudson County employee, Niehaus mumbled something about "keepin' the roads in good shape and cleanin' up stuff that falls off trucks, just kind o' keepin' the roads clear, you can say."

Resting his chin on a cupped hand, a tired Case suggested that the witness "probably doesn't kill himself working." Niehaus nodded his head quickly, displaying a wide smile. Watson waved him out of the chair.

Case conferred with a group of legislators during a momentary break. The witness's testimony, he reminded the others, fit in nicely with that of a previous "inspector," one of a dozen employed by the city. The man's statements had shown that none of the inspectors actually checked the daily fare totals of buses hired to provide transportation. Consequently, the bus firms regularly underreported their gross receipts—a situation that not only permitted them to hang onto a large portion of the fares, but which enabled them to pay lower taxes to both Jersey City and Hudson County.

Because money was being saved, the bus companies were not loath to contribute to the Democratic organization's fund-raising activities. Such contributions, of course, were in addition to the "donations" made by all employees of the city and county—donations amounting to 3 percent of the worker's annual salary. So prevalent were the payments that the employees had come up with a couple of distinctive names for them. Some referred to the forced contributions as "Peter's pence," evoking memories of the familiar idea of robbing Peter to pay Paul. Others (including my father) glumly looked ahead to pay-day as "Rice puddin' time," indicating that a visit to the loan company might be required if our dessert for dinner that evening would be even something as prosaic as dry, barely sweetened rice pudding.

Testimony by a number of hardy souls before the Case Committee amounted to veritable oaths that such payments had to be made regularly in order to hold onto a job. Others had testified that when they failed to make payments, they were fired. Noting that the combined city and county payrolls totalled some $13 million, the investigators easily calculated that 3 percent in forced contributions gave the Democrats a healthy sum for whatever political and personal activities they might want to undertake. (It was not studied, by the way, how much money was funneled by "Uncle Frank" to certain members of the Republican-dominated legislature who on numerous occasions showed their own peculiarities in voting habits.)

"Excuse me, Mr. Watson," Case called to the probing investigator. "We were looking over some figures here, and didn't quite catch what Mr. O'Neill said. Could you go over that once again?"

Watson nodded, feeling his exasperation grow. He took a deep breath. He could not move too fast, he knew. He could not make it look as if he could not wait to get Frank Hague into the chair. He spoke slowly and carefully.

"Mr. O'Neill, as a supervisor with—er, rather vague —responsibilities, you more or less refused to answer our questions in a previous visit here, correct?"

"That's right." The words fairly exploded from the thin-faced Irishman's lips. Then, with contriteness: "But I got to thinkin' that me ma—she's goin' on seventy now—would die if she read in the paper that I done somethin' wrong."

"Then you're ready to recall what you can about these various reports on the work you supervised?"

O'Neill nodded briskly and sat up straight. "What I can," he said.

With a flourish, Watson pulled a sheaf of pages from a legal folder on the table. "I have here a report ostensibly written by the Hudson County Grand Jury on the excellence of various institutions within the county. It's an excellent piece of work, wouldn't you say?"

Smiling, the witness agreed.

"It certainly can find no fault with any county operation, can it?"

"No, I don't think so. It's a good report."

"And the members of the grand jury who wrote it and submitted it did a good job?"

O'Neill's face grew a shade redder. "Uh, yeh, I guess so."

The sheaf of papers was tossed into his lap roughly. "Except," snapped Watson, "the grand jury didn't write the report, did it? Every word of this report was written by you, wasn't it, Mr. O'Neill? Every word!"

The supervisor glanced at the papers, then shoved them to the floor. His color deepened, his voice roared in the stillness. "I'm not Hague! I'm John O'Neill. I haven't done anything wrong!"

A mutter—shock? surprise?—was heard in the rear of the chamber. A door swung open quickly as a loyal observer raced out to report to Malone, who would pass it on to Hague, that O'Neill had practically accused him of wrongdoing.

In the chair, the supervisor realized his blunder. He knew that he would have to take the offensive or his days in a cushy job were numbered.

The opportunity presented itself. "Nothing wrong?" sneered Watson. "You okayed the payment of a weekly salary to dozens of county employees who do nothing? You don't call that wrong?"

"Oh," responded O'Neill, matching him sneer for sneer, "you think it's a clean thing to have 40 employees in the senate and 72 in the assembly who get their paychecks the first day of the year and never show up after that?"

The crowd roared in amusement. Case, seeing the flustered look on the faces of his colleagues, smashed his gavel repeatedly onto the echoing wooden block, calling out at the same time something about filing contempt charges against the witness. In the hubbub, he gestured for a brief adjournment, and Watson felt his temperature rise in anticipation of the next person called to the chair. Approaching Case, he asked if the members of the investigatory panel had time to go over some previous testimony before Frank Hague took his place at the front of the room.

"I think we'd better," the senator said. "We might need a refresher course so that the Mayor's answers make sense." Gathering up his stack of memo pads, he led the way to a small meeting room as the group of spectators left behind laughed and joked, anxious as blood-thirsty Romans awaiting the start of the gladiatorial contests.

In the crowded meeting room, the senators leaned forward in heavy wooden chairs and tried to make something out of the depositions, records of testimony, and assorted financial documents spread on the table before them. There were hundreds—no, thousands—of pages.

"Where the hell do we start?" one of the men said, waving his cigar so animatedly in a hopeless gesture that an inch of white ash splashed across the papers.

"We know that he's been on the city commission since '13, and mayor since '17, and that his best salary has been $8,000 a year."

"And that he's made it plain that he devotes himself full-time to the job," another voice proclaimed. "He's got no other occupation."

Watson flipped through a pad. "Okay, in 1918—it could have been '19—John Milton wrote a check for $12,000 to buy the Jersey City lot where Hague built the apartment house he lives in. He paid Milton cash to reimburse him."

One of the senators cleared his throat. "We know, we know. The building's called Duncan Hall. Milton bought the rest of the land a couple years after the first deal—what'd he pay? $51,000?—with another check. And Hague gave him cash again."

A page of the pad was turned. "Then," Watson pointed out, "the mayor swapped the land for $65,000 worth of stock in the building company. Not to mention that he lives rent-free in an apartment worth $7,000 a year in rent."

A squat, balding member of the group stood up and announced that nature was calling him. "Besides," he said as he moved to the door, "we've heard so much about Milton buyin' this and Milton buyin' that and Hague passin' out cash like he was printin' it—well, I wouldn't be surprised to find out that 'duh Mare' owns this Goddamn buildin' we're sittin' in!"

The group laughed, and there was an occasional chuckle as individual members turned pages and saw the various "dummy" names that had been used by Hague and his loyal deputies to acquire property for him. There was John Milton, of course; and John J. McMahon, the register of Hudson County; and Thomas McNulty, and Patrick Casey, and Thomas Davis, and others who had signed checks to acquire real estate, stock, and other assets—and who then frequently were given a check signed by someone other than Frank Hague to resell the property. Hague himself always settled his debts by paying cash.

"Do we have time, gentlemen, to go through the Kerbaugh records?" Case asked. A half-hearted mumble of acquiescence set him turning pages and reading aloud. Fragments and notes from the pages of testimony were enough to make some of the listeners' eyes open in surprise and indignation:

H. S. Kerbaugh Realty, friendly with John Milton's law firm . . . bought a half-dozen pieces of property, most of which were promptly involved in condemnation proceedings for city and county municipal projects with the fortunate company profiting by—how much?—$628,145 in less than five years."

"Jesus H. Christ!" muttered a panel member who represented a downstate county. "If I could find that kind of deal in my area!"

A ripple of laughter ran around the table. Case hurried on: "Let's look at the work in Journal Square, the Boulevard Bridge construction."

"That's the one where the head of the Board of Education owned the construction company doin' the work?" a senator asked. "Ferris? Right?"

Watson nodded agreement now. Smiling, he found what he was searching for among the stacks of papers. It was a small, worn, leatherette-bound notebook. "And here," he said, withdrawing a slip of paper from the book, "we have our famous memo headed 'Boulevard Bridge' and listing the figure of 200,000 behind the words 'Hague and Freeholders.' "

It was Case's turn to grin. "You forgot the figures for Hague's lawyers, Russell."

A shake of the head. "Give me time, senator. I was getting to it: Ten thousand to O'Marra; fifty thousand to Mitchell."

There was a silence in the room. The light seemed to dim as the blue smoke of cigars and cigarettes filled the air.

"If only Ferris were alive to explain this," Watson said through clenched teeth. "Damn! Some people die at the wrong time."

"Those handwriting experts we hired," the downstate senator inquired. "They said the notes are in Ferris's handwriting, right? We've got that much to go on."

Case raised a hand. "Except that Hague's handwriting expert says the book's a forgery, and it's all part of a scheme of this committee—and yours truly, in particular—to hurt him politically. We can't get Ferris's former treasurer—"

"Bill Delehanty," Watson added, noting the senator's hesitation.

"Yes, Delehanty—to leave his comfortable home in New York and come in here to swear it's Ferris's book."

Several of the members shook their heads in unison. Then, a thin, grey-haired man, who looked to be the oldest on the panel, stroked the wisp of mustache on his upper lip and asked, "Should we try to pin him down on the sewer deal, Clarence? I know it was back in '18, but—"

Case spread his hands, then clapped them together in a gesture of hopelessness. "It's not going to be easy. Bank records destroyed, company records vanished, the out-of-town construction companies unwilling to cooperate, not enough solid witnesses—"

"But we've got enough on the Boonton Dam plant for anybody who's even half-honest. Jesus! The city engineers estimate the job ought to cost less than a million, and when it's built, the bill comes to more than $3 million! And the head of the contracting company swears under oath that he paid the city corporation counsel's intermediary $15,000 for his help on the job!"

Case shook his head wearily. "But the man's checkbooks vanished. His records vanished. So it's his word against whatsisname—"

"Milton," offered Watson. "John Milton."

Again, the silence fell heavily. Faintly, the ticking of a half-dozen watches could be heard, each tucked away into a vest pocket and secured by a length of gold or silver chain draped across a stout chest. Case moved his hand upward, sliding his thumb and two fingers into his pocket to draw his watch out. He glanced at it, then said as he wound the gold crown vigorously. "Gentlemen, our time is getting short." He looked into Watson's eyes.

"Russ," the senator said. "He's all yours—but give us a chance to get a question in edgewise, at least."

Laughing, the group filed back into the assembly hall. Like the members of the Supreme Court entering to take their places, they caused—by their mere presence—the crowded room to fall silent, with even a noted rowdy or two pressing his lips together in awed anticipation.

Watson gave a signal to a clerk, said a few words in a loud, clear voice, and stood waiting as Frank Hague strode into the room.

If Hague were nervous in the slightest, there was no sign of it. He smiled broadly at several friends and constituents in the spectators' seats as he walked easily along the center aisle, then casually reached to wave a hand of greeting at some of the politicians seated behind the table. He restrained himself from actually shaking hands with a few—after all, they were primarily members of the opposition party, and it might be embarrassing to them for their constituents to see how friendly they were with Frank Hague.

He did not wait for Watson to gesture toward the waiting chair, but moved quickly to it. Carefully, as if to avoid putting an unnecessary crease in his immaculately pressed trousers, he seated himself, then gave a nod to the investigator as if to say, "Go."

It took only a few questions for Watson and the panel, as well as the assembled crowd, to realize Hague's position. He would be glad to defend himself against any public charges made against him, but he had no intention of allowing anyone to look into his personal finances.

"Up to 1921," Watson asked after the preliminary routine of identification was out of the way, "you had no other gainful occupation than the offices you outlined . . ."

"Only my brain and the ability to see things," was the prompt answer.

"Did Mr. Milton purchase for your account the remainder of the land on which Duncan Hall stands and pay for it $51,000?"

Not bothering to glance at the table where his legal counsel sat, Hague answered, "I decline to answer."

"Did you reimburse him in cash for the $51,000?"

"I decline to answer."

"If you reimbursed him to the extent of $51,000 in cash, why did you handle the business that way?"

"I decline to answer." The response was coming quickly now, sometimes almost before the final rising inflection that marked the end of each of Watson's questions.

"I decline to answer" to whether or not he had bought property at Deal, N.J.

"I decline to answer" to whether he took title in the name of John J. McMahon as dummy.

"I decline to answer" to why his debts were not paid by check . . . to why he sometimes used a dummy buyer on transactions . . to why—well, to some sixty questions posed in rapid-fire order by the investigating counsel.

And then, looking as if the ordeal had irritated him as much as it would bother him to brush a fly from the sleeve of his pin-striped suit, Frank Hague had strode purposefully from the room. And was gone.

There would be an aftermath to the matter, of course. But it was to come more than a half-year later, some time after Senator Clarence Case had stepped out of the leadership of the probe—on his way to a supreme court judgeship—and had been succeeded by Senator Albert McAllister of Cumberland County.

The aftermath centered on several concurrent resolutions offered in the senate. They pointed out that Frank Hague had been subpoenaed to appear before a Joint Committee of the Senate and General Assembly of the State of New Jersey, and that he had duly appeared. He had, however, refused to answer a question put to him—"Now, during the years 1922 and 1923, did you have a bank account in the National City Bank of the City of New York?"—that had been deemed proper and pertinent. Such refusal to answer "is a contempt of the Senate and the General Assembly," and therefore "be it resolved . . . that Marine De Witt, Sergeant-at-Arms . . . is commanded to take and convey the said Frank Hague to the common jail of the county of Mercer, there to be confined until such time as he shall make known . . . that he is willing to answer the said question . . . ."

7

Frank Hague, recently reelected Mayor of Jersey City, was comfortably ensconced in his spacious Duncan Hall apartment when the sergeant at arms arrived with a warrant for his arrest. There was a delay, of course, before the doorbell was answered—time enough to permit the Mayor to make a few phone calls. While the arresting officer explained his purpose, a few minutes more passed—time enough to permit the arrival of Police Chief Walsh (or *Wowsh,* as Jeff Burkitt referred to him) and another large, burly officer or two.

Within moments, John Fallon, a state judicial official who bore the title of vice-chancellor and who had formerly been Hudson County counsel, was on the scene to swear out a writ of habeas corpus and free Hague, who technically had been placed under arrest—although he continued to sit comfortably in his own living room. And off to jail went the sergeant at arms, charged by Captain Walsh with disturbing the peace.

Soon, it would be found that the Court of Errors and Appeals upheld Fallon's contention that violations of the criminal law by public officials were strictly judicial in nature, and that under the New Jersey constitution the legislature had no power to conduct an investigation into such matters. Hague, Fallon argued, was under no obligation to testify.

"I am very much pleased and satisfied by the decision," Hague was quoted as telling newsmen. "It is exactly what I expected."

Having the Case-McAllister probe behind him allowed "duh Mare" to collect his breath and begin to lay plans for the decade of the 1930s that was fast approaching. Undoubtedly, he was glad that 1929 was almost behind him. Certainly, the election that year had been a close one. His refusal to testify about his finances not only made headlines in the feisty *Journal,* but in papers all over the nation. Local lawyer Robert Carey—whose bid for the Republican gubernatorial nomination had been upset by the masses of Democrats who had turned into "One-Day Republicans"—put it bluntly: "Frank Hague showed the yellow streak he has down his back."

Morgan Larson, the successful Republican contender for the governor's chair, publicly pledged to send Hague to prison if he won the election—a vow that made headlines and helped change the voters' impression that Larson had been boosted to the nomination by Hague's maneuvering. William L. Dill, the Democratic nominee, faced a dilemma: If he repudiated Hague, he would lose the sizable Hudson County vote; if he backed Hague, he would seem to be supporting a man caught in the bright glare of suspicion. He did his best to say little, but it was apparent that Hague's tarnished image was rubbing off on any number of Democratic candidates. Edward I. Edwards, under fire as he strove to hold on to his U.S. Senate seat, was one such individual. Al Smith, governor of New York and a close personal friend of Hague, was another. Smith, challenging Herbert Hoover for the presidency, had to struggle to avoid commenting on Hague's problems.

Silence proved of no benefit. When the New Jersey votes were tabulated, Hoover had crushed Smith by nearly 300,000, Larson had beaten Dill by some 156,000, and Hamilton F. Kean bested Edwards by almost 170,000. Hague's ticket in Hudson County grimly held onto power, with less than half the plurality it had in the previous election.

For Frank Hague, the near-defeat might have signaled the beginning of a serious slide into oblivion—but suddenly the citizens of Jersey City, of Hudson County, of the state of New Jersey, and of the United States had more to worry about than the doings of one politician and a steamroller political machine. Stock prices, which had soared for three years to double the investments of several million people, began to slide. Down, down, down they went—until on October 29, 1929, more than 16 million shares were thrown on the market by sellers anxious to get any price they could for their paper representations of confidence in the future of American industry. Order in the market was not restored until mid-November and by then some $30 *billion* in values had vanished into thin air.

The Great Depression loomed on a grey horizon.

The euphoria of the World War victory receded quickly. The dance craze, the abandonment of restraints that had produced an era of intellectual renaissance, the excitement over the widespread popularity of the automobile, the newfound power of the advertising industry to sell almost anything—these and the other facets of American life that had made the Twenties roar were replaced almost overnight by the single overwhelming concern of citizens to earn a living. There was no time for anything else.

Stepping into the White House after Calvin Coolidge, who knew little of finance and thought the boom times of the late 1920s constituted a phenomenon to be encouraged, Herbert Hoover found his campaign slogan, "Four more years of prosperity," turning to ashes on his lips. The eradication of so much monetary value in such a short time resulted in an immediate downturn in sales of any kind of consumer and industrial goods; the decline in corporate income forced employers to cut salaries and lay off workers; this produced further reductions in sales, which led to more layoffs and more firings, and so on until it seemed the cycle could only end in absolute collapse.

Breadlines and shantytowns—dubbed "Hoovervilles" by the cynics—became commonplace sights throughout the country. When veterans of the war marched on Washington, demanding bonuses they had been promised, they were driven away by armed federal troops. Violence flared time and again as hungry, underpaid workers pleaded for—then demanded—better pay and working conditions from their employers, and, often failing to get it, went on strike.

The unrest was plainly visible in Jersey City, where Hague's forces long had a familiarity with violence. One of the milder incidents took place when a crowd of 250 angry citizens stormed a budget hearing in 1930 to protest a tax increase. James F. Murray, Sr., a lawyer and longtime Hague opponent, led the charge of dissidents booing and shouting as Hague angrily banged his gavel like a trip-hammer.

The Italian-American community also was uneasy. Demonstrating the kind of progressive thinking that would be unfamiliar to Jersey City until several decades later, Italian-American leaders posed a challenge to Mike Scatuorchio. The Fifth Ward leader, growing fat on the lucrative garbage collection contracts awarded him each year, had lost contact with the ordinary laborers. Various Italian-American clubs throughout the city were tied closely to the regular ward clubs of the Democratic party, and a number of social and charitable clubs were strictly under the local control of strong-willed citizens who resented the implication that they answered to Scatuorchio. All at once, some 200 representatives from all wards were clamoring for patronage and recognition from the Hague regime.

Scatuorchio managed to prevent the formation of a citywide federation of Italian clubs by establishing an advisory council of civic and political leaders. He also secured from Hague a promise of more jobs, including an additional assembly seat for someone of Italian-American heritage. But one of the leaders of the anti-Scatuorchio movement—a Ninth Ward Italian who owned a bottling plant—was handled in typical Hague fashion: His bottling plant was harassed by the city's health authorities repeatedly.

Such activities did not escape the notice of the *Journal's* newsmen. Several vigilant reporters kept a close eye on the comings and goings of city officials, often with embarrassing results. One noticed, for example, that Roger Boyle, a fire chief who had been unable to testify before the Case-McAllister committee because of a mysterious stomach ailment, was now back at his high-salaried position. The ailment, it seems, had been cured as mysteriously as it had appeared. The newspaper made much of the travels of "Wandering Roger."

Brushing aside the paper's demands that Boyle and others in his administration should come clean about the corruption charges regularly levelled at them, Hague claimed that the worthwhile deeds of his reign were being overlooked. He insisted that attention should be paid to his support of a movement to consolidate all Hudson County municipalities into a single large city, and he even said that he would resign to show his sincerity if that would help bring about consolidation. He also continually advocated improved transit systems that would provide better access to Hudson County, urging an extension of the subway system from the Kill Van Kull on the south to the Bergen County line on the north.

But the citizens and the newspapers found it difficult to get excited over such mundane matters. Times were much too difficult—and how difficult they were can only be detailed when it is made clear that in 1929, the year before the Crash, things for the great majority of the country's population had not been all that good. According to studies by the conservative and cautious Brookings Institution, only 2.3 percent of American families had incomes of more than $10,000 a year. Only 8 percent had incomes of over $5,000. Some 71 percent had total annual incomes of less than $2,500. And 60 percent had incomes under $2,000, 42 percent under $1,500, and more than 21 percent under $1,000 per year. Admittedly, prices were inflated in 1929, but the Brookings economists calculated that an income of $2,000 was enough to supply only basic necessities—which meant that in 1929, more than three-fifths of the entire population lived at poverty levels.

It was small wonder that a year later, when poverty had truly become a national phenomenon, Frank Hague's interest in a subway extension was not uppermost in the minds of many citizens. They increasingly were becoming concerned, however, with how much money was being siphoned from their skimpier paychecks and emptier pockets by the chicanery of their political leaders. And they paid attention when a long-simmering feud between Hague and a former supporter flared up to focus newspaper headlines and the gaze of federal authorities on the Mayor's activities.

Edward I. Edwards, the wealthy Jersey City banker who had pledged his political influence and wealth to Hague—who had in turn used it to defeat the valiant H. Otto Wittpenn—was in 1930 simmering over Hague's refusal to repay the favor. True, Hague had supported Edwards first in his successful bid for the gubernatorial seat in New Jersey, and then had backed him in his ascendancy to the U.S. Senate. Now, however, when Edwards wanted to return to the senate, Hague had pledged to stand behind State Senator Alexander Simpson.

It must be said that Hague could explain his reasons. Edwards showed increasing signs of mental strain, going so far as to have publicly predicted that a civil war would break out if Prohibition were not repealed. When Edwards got the news that Simpson was Hague's choice, he turned violently against his former champion. In a statement to the press, he condemned ''self-proclaimed leaders who might—instead of sojourning in Europe or basking on the warm sands of Florida—make some decent effort to lighten the burden of government and reduce the oppressive taxes that now have our people dismayed and discouraged.''

From his residence in Palm Beach, where he was basking along with numerous multimillionaires who were struggling to hold onto their estates in the wake of the Crash, Hague responded: ''Poor Teddy, somebody ought to call a doctor. It looks to me as if he has had a bad night. I am sorry, but he had his chance and kicked it away, so why blame me? I think that if he keeps applying the icebag he'll realize what a fool he's made of himself.''

Perhaps teetering on the brink of insanity, Edwards was infuriated. ''Icebag! Icebag?!'' Seething, he began to sputter about ''Three percent bags! Christmas kiddie bags!'' He claimed that Hague had extracted hundreds of thousands of dollars from the Al Smith presidential campaign kitty, and had made millions by forcing the police, firemen, sanitation workers, and other city employees to fill his bags with their hard-earned cash. Hague, said the angry Edwards, was ''a political Messiah and creator of political peonage.''

The charges and follow-up investigations brought headlines, if little else. On March 1, 1930, the *Journal* used its largest type to report that Hague's tax bill amounted to $1,000,865. In smaller type, it noted that he had paid a fine of $865 and still owed the million. ''I don't know where they got their figures from,'' scoffed Hague. ''They are ridiculous and nonsensical and they flatter me.''

His attitude—*so what?*—probably was much the same a few
months later when, in 1931, Edward I. Edwards committed suicide
by firing a .38 calibre bullet into his right temple.

At the time, "duh Mare" had other things on his mind. A group
of independent bus owners, led by Frank E. Schoenfeld, a Hudson
Democratic assemblyman, urged that the city government should be
changed to a city manager plan. Previously, the bus owners association had supported Hague, but they had grown weary of his
awarding choice bus routes to his old favorite, the Public Service
Corporation. Now they sought advice from George L. Record, the
aged but still-brilliant political thinker who 30 years previously had
been the "high priest" of Mayor Mark M. Fagan's "New Idea"
party. The Schoenfeld-Record alliance first considered urging the
recall of Hague, but then decided that the chance of success would
be greater if it worked toward the city manager plan.

The movement withered almost before it had time to take root.
Hague's city clerk ruled immediately that many of the names on the
petitions promoting the city manager plan were fraudulent, and the
judges in Hague-controlled courts upheld the ruling. For the once-
powerful George L. Record, it was a last gasp in the political arena.
Within two years he would be near the end of his life. He often
could be seen walking alone along Bergen Avenue, with only a
faithful dog to keep him company. On one such evening, two young
men approached him. One was John R. Longo, a youthful labor politician who long would be a Hague opponent; the other was J. Owen
Grundy, who would go on to become Jersey City's official
historian.

As they watched Record approach, the pair noticed that despite
his out-of-fashion clothes, he walked tall, with his white hair ruffled
by the evening breeze. They called to him. "Mr. Record," asked
Longo, his voice filled with awe at the opportunity to question a
man he had admired for years, "could you answer a question? You
once were celebrated as the nation's premier reformer. You associated with presidents and advised them. You once were one of the
state's most outstanding political figures. Now, you're alone
—without a legal practice to speak of, without the press hanging
onto your words. With—well, with only a loyal dog at your side."

Longo's question almost could not leave his lips. ''Why?'' he finally asked. ''Why?''

Record smiled, recognizing the sincerity behind the indiscreet question. ''Boys,'' he said, ''someday when you get older you'll learn that when you are right, you'll always be alone. When you're absolutely right, you'll be absolutely alone.'' And with that— followed by a courteous ''Good evening''—George L. Record strode into the night. (Years later, as he recalled that event and that evening, Longo said, ''As I watched that tragic, beautiful figure disappearing into the darkness, I thought of Jesus Christ.'')

With the Schoenfeld-Record opposition sidetracked, Hague in 1931 also acted to eliminate another growing source of trouble. Union leader Theodore M. Brandle, who once had said that ''men of Hague's type should be elected for life and not have to be annoyed every four years,'' had prospered under his close alliance with the Jersey City mayor. He had established a bank and a bonding company, started his own construction company, and had been named director of the state Iron League. Not surprisingly, he also opposed any employment of non-union labor—and threw up a picket line to keep non-union workers off the job when the Pulaski Skyway was being built. Fighting broke out and one man died as a result. When Hague ordered the police to arrest Brandle's pickets, the union leader established a field hospital for his men and used his own funds to pay strike benefits.

The mayor vowed to bring Brandle to his knees. Calling his former friend a ''labor racketeer,'' Hague saw to it that Brandle's local was put into receivership and the ironworkers promptly deposed their leader. Soon, his bank collapsed and his prosperous bonding company failed after it received no more Hudson County contracts. In time, Brandle was indicted on racketeering charges.

Brandle tried to discredit the Mayor in return. He claimed to have loaned Hague $60,000 to settle an IRS demand against the Mayor. But an eyewitness to the proceedings says no monetary exchange took place: ''Hague had tons of money, but he was not in a position to show it.'' Hague gave Brandle a note, ostensibly in exchange for the $60,000, and then used his own funds to settle the IRS claim. Brandle was supposed to destroy the note, but never did—and that might have been the last time Hague trusted anyone with something on paper.

Hague's success in dealing with Brandle would shortly help him gain control over many more labor unions in the city and county. And his display of power continued to garner votes for him in each election. In the general election of 1931, his support of A. Harry Moore saw that politician returned as governor in a record victory that carried in a Democratic assembly. Moore promptly reappointed Joseph A. Dear to the Court of Errors and Appeals, and—surprise!—the *Jersey Journal,* of which Dear was a co-owner, began to lose its anti-Hague flavor.

The country's inability to shake off the Great Depression made it obvious that a Democratic victory lay in store in the looming 1932 election. The only question was which of several strong Democratic candidates would get the nod from the party to oppose the fading Hoover. At the convention, Hague served as floor manager for his old tenement house pal, Al Smith, and stated publicly that Franklin Roosevelt would be incapable of carrying any state east of the Mississippi. But when FDR won the nomination, Hague immediately promised him that he could produce one of the largest rallies ever held in America.

That August, Roosevelt agreed to see what the Jersey City mayor could do. He accepted an invitation to visit Governor Moore's "little White House" at Sea Girt, N.J., and travelled in a motorcade through the Holland Tunnel. A first stop in Hague's birthplace, the Horseshoe, brought on a carnival atmosphere and an official welcome from John V. Kenny, the powerful leader of the Second Ward. On went the motorcade to Hague's ornate mansion in Deal, where the future president and the reigning mayor shook hands as flashbulbs exploded to record the meeting for posterity.

The scene at Sea Girt exceeded FDR's optimistic expectations. Thousands of automobiles and hundreds of buses had brought countless cheering citizens to the scene. As the limousines inched their way toward Governor Moore's residence, the roar of the crowd drowned out the roar of the sea nearby and parachutes carrying miniatures of Old Glory fluttered down on the assemblage. And the band, playing "Happy Days are Here Again," did its best to compete with the sounds of fireworks overhead.

Roosevelt's words had to make even the usually serious face of Frank Hague break into a broad smile: "Never in my life have I seen or heard of a bigger or more enthusiastic representation of citizens than we have here today. And may I remark that there is no person who could have organized such a day as perfectly as Mayor Hague of Jersey City, the State Democratic leader. It is just wonderful."

A few moments later, after a speech by Moore, as the three political leaders met the press, Roosevelt spoke expansively: "Mayor Hague is an old friend of mine. We have campaigned together in the common cause before, and I'm happy that we are working together in this cause."

The overwhelming plurality of Roosevelt—and of Governor Moore in the election the previous year—strengthened Hague's hold on the city, county, and state. His machine appeared invincible. By the time the commission election of 1933 neared, the anti-Hague forces were but a shadow of what they had been four years earlier. Roosevelt was pushing his "New Deal" vigorously, putting people and money to work through a mass of social programs—but Hague was pointing out to his Jersey City constituency that he long had been responsible for free medical care at the Medical Center, for free baskets of food distributed to the needy, for job upon job upon job for the party faithful, and so on. "What 'New Deal'?" he might have asked. "It's the same deal we've always had in Jersey City."

Supported now by the *Journal* and its rivals, Hague brushed aside minor opposition from a fusion party ticket headed by his old foe, James F. Murray, Sr., an alumnus of both Saint Peter's College and Fordham University. Spattered frequently with eggs tossed by Hague supporters when he tried to speak, Murray took to surrounding himself with bodyguards—only to find that he promptly was accused of associating with criminal elements. (Two of the men named in a *Hudson Dispatch* report of the day later became known to me. One, Tony Cupo, is not only a fine gentleman, but is loved and respected in the Village section of Jersey City. The other, George Geirer, was a distributor for the respected *Newark News* and a longtime Democratic committeeman. In no sense was either a racketeer or criminal—which might lead one to wonder about the biased reporting of the newspapers of the day.)

Playing on the possible underworld connections of his rivals, Hague plastered the city with ads and signs proclaiming ''No Vice, No Crime, No Racketeering'' and stepped up his attack on ''racketeering labor unions.'' In a newspaper interview, he explained that ''Jersey City police don't wait to see a crime committed. They don't wait for a complaint. When a gangster or racketeer shows up, we lock him up under the disorderly persons act. There's no bail. He gets 90 days. When he gets out and persists in hanging around, we give him another jail dose. We keep that up until he departs.''

Despite brilliant speeches by such men as J. Owen Grundy and Raymond Chasan, a courageous and principled champion of civil rights, Murray's ticket continued to lose ground as the election neared. In a final blow, Hague's commissioner of finance stated that Murray had become a candidate only after he had been denied a city contract to furnish shoes for the poor. The city, said the commissioner, had determined that Murray's shoes were of inferior quality, with soles virtually made of paper. Labelled in the newpapers as ''Paper Shoes Murray,'' the opponent and his supporters went down to a three-to-one defeat at the hands of the voters of Jersey City.

The celebration of victory brought thousands to City Hall, where they were allowed to shake hands with Mayor Hague and Governor Moore, who was, of course, always a ''Jersey City boy.'' Hague used the occasion to announce that a $3 million addition would be added to the Medical Center. Adjacent to the Margaret Hague Maternity Hospital would go a new facility for tuberculosis patients.

The applause rang out, loud and long. *Depression*? Maybe elsewhere, but not in Jersey City as 1933 dawned. Frank Hague, Mayor, had plenty of plans to make the years ahead better.

8

His personal fortune growing with each passing day, his powerful arms stretching now all the way from Jersey City into the White House, "duh Mare" was free to turn his attention during the next four years to several things that he enjoyed—sports and his beloved Medical Center—and to several things that he despised: Communism and the labor union movement.

On the sporting scene, Hague was quick to point with pride to any Jersey City citizen who achieved celebrity status. One such opportunity occurred in the Rose Bowl game of 1934 when a graduate of Dickinson High School, Al Barabas, scored a touchdown that gave Columbia a 7-0 upset victory over Stanford. Hague immediately fired off a congratulatory telegram promising a "big celebration" upon the youngster's return. (During his long reign, Hague had time to acclaim the prowess of other Dickinson athletes—Guido "Galloping" Baratelli, Ed Franco, and Al Blozis, among them. Blozis, an All-American at Georgetown who later starred for the New York Giants professional team, died in World War II; in 1980, the then-Mayor of Jersey City, Thomas F. X. Smith, honored his achievements and his memory by affixing his name to a senior citizens' project at the Medical Center.)

But Hague did more than merely acknowledge his town's heroes. Early in 1937 he officiated at the opening of what was said to be the finest stadium in the country built expressly for minor-league baseball. Built with federal funds provided by FDR, the stadium was naturally named Roosevelt Stadium. It was designed with 25,000 seats, but on opening day, a crowd of 31,234 men, women, and children squeezed through the gates. Hague saw to it that the largest crowd ever to witness a minor-league game would be on hand. Local merchants were asked—*ordered* is perhaps a more fitting word—to buy tickets and distribute them free to needy youngsters.

Reportedly, some 60,000 tickets were sold—and no one ever questioned where the money went that represented the difference between the tickets sold and the number of spectators at the game. It wasn't a time for casting aspersions on anyone, and certainly not on the political machine that had given the citizenry a chance to take their minds off the Depression by providing a splendid sporting event. The band was there, playing the kind of music that Hague loved—"Let Me Call You Sweetheart," "Wearin' of the Green," and "Take Me Out to the Ballgame." Dressed in a wrinkled tuxedo dangling over baggy baseball pants and with a crushed top hat on his head, a famed comedian—Al Schacht, "the clown prince of baseball"—was there to draw laughs from spectators who saw how remarkably his attire contrasted with that of the dignified Hague. A. Harry Moore was there, too, in his role as a U.S. Senator whose name was being bandied about as a potential presidential candidate at some future time.

And, squeezed into a bleacher seat in the lower right field section, an excited youngster named Thomas F. X. Smith stared in awe at the players, the musicians, the dignitaries. And even when our beloved "Joiseys" lost in a hard-fought 12-inning four-to-three battle, the magical quality of the day could never be erased.

Let the Red Wings take their victory back to Rochester—that was the thought in the minds of thousands of people. *Jersey City has the stadium, the excitement, and the champion: Mayor Hague.*

Not everyone, to be sure, applauded Hague's methods, which were so entrenched by now that they were accepted as routine by most citizens. When a Jersey City saloonkeeper died after an altercation with some of the local police force, the dead man's daughter charged police brutality. A prosecutor who investigated the situation found no cause for action. Instead, Hague ruled that the saloonkeeper's widow could tend bar in her late husband's stead—despite a Jersey City law that said no females could drink at a bar. Hague did not change the ordinance; he merely made the widow immune from it.

In retrospect, it seems amazing that Hague noticed no parallels between his methods or those of the people under his immediate jurisdiction and the ones employed by the dictatorial-minded rulers in countries he visited abroad. Now fancying himself as a world traveler, the mayor frequently embarked on a great luxury liner to make his way to Italy, Russia, South America, or Africa. At home, Acting Mayor Arthur Potterton was given the task of issuing an occasional pronouncement to keep Hague's name fresh in the newspapers and in the minds of Jersey City residents.

One such pronouncement was made when Hague acted to restrict the rights of union laborers to demonstrate and picket in order to gain redress against their grievances. After the nation's highest court overturned an attempt by the Jersey City mayor to restrict union demonstrations to a handful of isolated places within the city, a spokesman for a union of furniture workers compared the plight of members in Jersey City with those of workers in Nazi Germany. Responded Potterton, after some prodding by Hague over ship's wireless: "Mayor Hague has always been a friend of organized labor and will always be."

A friend, yes—so long as the unions were on his side. To keep them on his side, the Mayor seized upon the threat of Communism—the evils of which he had witnessed in his travels—and vowed to help the unions resist any infiltration by the Red Menace.

"I saw a prison filled with 100,000 persons," he told a cheering crowd after a trip to Russia. "All political prisoners, because they dared to criticize their government. That's what they do to them there. If those communists who agitate here should stand up in Moscow's Red Square and speak as they do here, they would only live long enough for the nearest soldier to shoot them."

For a public that received meager news of the world only through local newspapers purchased at the price of a few precious cents, or through brief radio broadcasts, the dangers of the communist menace could be made to seem very close at hand. Democracy had to be preserved at all costs, and Hague took numerous opportunities to tie his name with that of Franklin Delano Roosevelt, the champion of the Democratic party. Roosevelt, said the Mayor, had saved Jersey City from bankruptcy with a massive infusion of federal funds. Still, huge cuts had to be made in the salaries of city and county workers and some 50,000 people went on the welfare rolls.

But under the government's Works Progress Administration and the National Recovery Act, as well as a host of other relief organizations, people went to work even as the federal deficit climbed higher. Jersey City was the recipient of Roosevelt's largesse in the form of $1.5 million for the baseball stadium, $5 million for the Medical Center, and hundreds of thousands of dollars for street repair, among other things. So grateful was Hague for his friend's contributions that he publicly turned his back on another old friend, Al "The Happy Warrior" Smith. At a Democratic rally, Hague responded to a Smith plea for an anti-Roosevelt faction within the party. "I charge them with buying up Communistic candidates and with being responsible for spreading false Communistic propaganda against President Roosevelt of which that man spoke," said the man who had served only a few years earlier as floor manager for Smith's unsuccessful bid for the nomination.

If things were bad in the rest of the country, they seemed less so in Jersey City. My sister Regina, an "A" student at Fordham who had to leave school at the end of her freshman year because money was in short supply, obtained an NRA job. My sister Florence similarly got work, because the unemployed in Jersey City found governmental jobs in plentiful supply. And although his predecessor, Mark Fagan, had started free medical service for indigents in the city, Frank Hague expanded the concept to include anyone who had an "in" with the party. The song "Pennies from Heaven" reflected the attitude of numerous Hudson County citizens when they looked upon the benefits of having Hague at the reins.

Many breathed easier, too, because it was readily apparent that crime was not visible on city streets. Hague believed in attacking the problem of youthful offenders at its source, rather than wait until young boys gone astray had turned into hardened criminals.

Always ready to admit that "I myself was what you might call an incorrigible boy," Hague established a Bureau of Special Services that dealt with juvenile delinquency in a variety of ways. Psychology and psychiatry were used, but so was good old-fashioned "shellacking" in the event that more modern methods did not produce immediate results. Dr. Thomas Hopkins, an assistant superintendent of schools, was made head of the bureau and told to see that youthful offenders were kept out of the courts and the jails.

"Penal institutions," explained Hague, "are nothing but schools of crime. I will not allow a boy in a patrol wagon, in a cell, or in a court."

It was an incident stemming from the Mayor's firm belief that he knew best how to turn a youngster from the path of crime that later would plague him. Once, addressing a gathering at Emory Methodist Church on the corner of Belmont and Bergen Avenues, he told the story of two 12-year-old boys who had been deemed incorrigible and were destined to be committed to a correctional institution. In a heart-to-heart discussion with the youngsters, Hague determined that their antisocial behavior grew out of their dislike for school. He learned that the two would prefer jail to school, and suggested that they might go to work—instead of to school—and help support their mothers. The boys agreed readily, but school authorities protested that under law, children under the age of sixteen had to attend school. Exempting the youngsters—as he previously had exempted the saloonkeeper's widow—from the regulations, Hague said, "In this case, I am the law."

Shorn of its explanatory clause and the background of the story, "I am the law" became synonymous with Frank Hague in newspaper stories and on the lips of political opponents who would challenge him over the years.

Writing as one of some 3,000 youngsters whom Hague's Special Bureau was said to have saved from prison during the six years of its existence, I can state that I have no doubt as to its efficiency. As a parent, it is possible for me to look back and realize that one aspect that made the Bureau work was its ability to remove a mischievous youngster from the traditional judicial and penal punishment meted out to "big shot" criminals. The Hague approach gave the youthful braggarts nothing to swagger about—and few wanted to talk about the severe beating they received (and their fathers, too, if *they* complained).

By the time the municipal election of 1937 rolled around, Hague's 100 percent-American stance—on crime, Communism, good old hard-work values, and all the rest—left little room for critics to maneuver. Attack the Mayor and his values, and you were a communist. Support him, and there was a job, food, medical care to be had. When the votes were counted, the Hague ticket controlled nearly 95 percent of the 117,000 total. "Duh Mare" received his seventh term as a member of the commission, his sixth as mayor. With only a few thousand votes to their names, the opposition—which had called itself "Democracy Against Dictatorship"—sent a terse message to City Hall: "We concede the election."

His hand gripping the sceptre of Jersey City power ever more tightly, Hague was ready to do battle with a new rival. Reverend Lester Clee, a clergyman from Essex County, had begun riding a statewide "clean government" movement in the early 1930s and now had begun mounting a campaign for the gubernatorial seat held by his fellow Republican, Governor Harold G. Hoffman. Where Hoffman and Hague had coexisted peacefully, "duh Mare" recognized a formidable enemy in Clee, whom he scornfully referred to as a "Black Protestant."

Acknowledging that none of his close circle of Democratic friends had the stature to upset Clee, Hague turned to an old friend. A. Harry Moore, who had gone onto the U. S. Senate after his two terms as governor, agreed to try again for his old job. In a fiery speech, the senator responded to familiar charges of "Moore and Hagueism" with these words: "How that issue has fallen! And why not? No man can point a finger of blame at what Frank Hague of Jersey City has done. This is the cleanest city in the United States, thanks to a great humane mayor."

On election night, Republican headquarters throughout the state went wild as returns poured in to show the crusading Clee leading by more than 85,000 votes.

And then the Hudson County tally appeared.

Moore had swept the county with a 130,000 vote majority, enough to send him to Trenton as governor by some 45,000 votes.

"Fraud!" shouted Clee.

"Count 'em again," said a confident Hague.

Clee did, and when his recount showed only a gain of some 820 votes, he instigated an investigation by the legislature into the possibility of voting irregularities. Concentrating on Republican districts that had voted overwhelmingly for Moore, Assemblyman Henry Young, Jr., demanded that the Republican Commissioner of Registrations, Charles F. Stoebling, furnish all records relating to the election. Stoebling was reported seriously ill and unable to leave his luxury apartment on Glenwood Avenue.

Stoebling's chief assistant, Alice Seglie, was ordered to produce the sought-after books. She agreed to do so only if her boss gave authorization to unlock the vault. But Stoebling was too ill even to discuss the matter on the telephone. Furious, the assembly met in Trenton and ordered the sergeant at arms of the legislature to bring the books from Hudson County. Now, Hague's Hudson County police blocked the way, and when it was suggested that the state police might have to be called into action, it was realized that only the governor had the authority to order such a move. And the governor, of course, was A. Harry Moore—a man who certainly saw no reason why he should aid anyone in perhaps upsetting his own recent election.

"I have no authority to order the safe opened," said Moore. "Go to court."

Unable to obtain the voting records, Young's committee followed the path laid down years before by the Case-McAllister investigators and began calling an endless parade of witnesses to prove fraud.

One witness, a rabbi who had moved from the Third Ward to Providence, R. I., in 1934, claimed that he was nowhere near Jersey City when someone voted in his name on election day.

Two men confined to the county mental hospital said that anyone who contended that they had voted in the election had to be crazy.

Mrs. Rose Velardi, a Republican assigned to keep an eye on voting procedures, said she had been given $5 by a Democratic committeeman to look away at one point. Retorted the Democrat: "She's sore at me because I didn't give her no Christmas basket last year."

Other witnesses cited impropriety after impropriety—ranging from bungled attempts to intoxicate voters or seduce them with amorous caresses to promising them future jobs in return for the right vote—but the star witness of the probe was one Theodore Zelinski, who on election day bore the title of "deputy superintendent of elections." Zelinski—who, as an uncle-in-law of this writer, has long familiarly been known as "Teddy"—testified that he attempted to stop two people from collaborating inside a polling booth in a district where Moore chalked up a 433-to-1 victory over Clee. His effort, he said, was met with physical resistance from several men: William McGovern, the Democratic First Ward leader; Phil McGovern, the commissioner's brother and judge of the election board; and John Chunka and Floyd Chuck, described as "hoodlums."

After a flurry of fists, Zelinski summoned a policeman, but the officer began to cart the complainant away when instructed to do so by McGovern. Then, "Teddy" told the Young investigatory committee, McGovern evidently had a change of heart and offered him $100 to forget the entire matter.

"I regret not taking the money to this day," Zelinski said. "I should have given it to charity."

Although Phil McGovern and others subpoenaed to appear before the committee refused to testify on charges raised by my uncle, the testimony he gave was supported by at least one other deputy. All of the massive weight of the sworn statements, however, proved feather-light when vice-chancellor Henry T. Kays ruled that the legislation creating the Young committee was unconstitutional. Within hours, the election officers who had been placed under arrest were free—and the ailing Stoebling recovered from his illness.

All questions about Moore's election as governor were forgotten, and the only question seemed to be who might succeed him as U. S. Senator. Who else, speculated newspapers and the public, other than Frank Hague? Floods of congratulatory telegrams poured into City Hall early in January, 1938, when Governor Moore stopped by to visit the Mayor who had just reached age 63. Would Moore offer the senate seat as a birthday present?

"No one in New Jersey is better fitted for this high post," declared Moore as he rested a firm hand on the Mayor's shoulder for the benefit of the assembled photographers. He went on to praise his friend "as a citizen and as a leader," and then stood silent, waiting along with the crowd for Frank Hague to speak.

Choosing his words carefully, Hague thanked Moore for the tribute—and said he was forced to decline the offer. Making it clear that he would avoid giving any indication that he was running away from a fight, the Mayor declared that the importance of mounting "an anti-Red war" against the threat of Communism required him to stand by his guns in Jersey City. Not for him a senate seat, not while there was work to be done to protect the welfare of his constituents!

There was work to be done, certainly. Hague and the city faced a threat.

How much of the threat stemmed from Communism, however, was uncertain. During his last four-year term, Hague's efforts to retain strict control of labor organizations had caused a number of major companies to desert Jersey City and Hudson County, and in their place had come smaller firms of the "sweatshop" variety. The newcomers paid less in taxes than the larger departing companies, and their non-union workers drew less in salaries (which meant they also paid less to support vital city services). Hague tried to lure new industry with signs proclaiming "Jersey City—Everything for Industry" at highway entrances to the city, but he attracted only the attention of a young labor organization, the Committee for Industrial Organization. The CIO, having grown in two years to a membership of four million, set out to bring Jersey City workers into its ranks. To Hague, who had reorganized the American Federation of Labor organization in Hudson County and defeated Teddy Brandle's ironworkers, the CIO had to be "cut off at the pass." Any group that managed to get control of the minds and purses of thousands of workers—and voters—could mean trouble for the Hague regime.

The battle began with a CIO attempt to stage a demonstration—one that was shattered by an onslaught of Jersey City police. Calling the quick attack "the most illegal and terroristic greeting the CIO has received in any part of the country," the labor organization managed to open a small office on Academy Street. Recognizing that the courageous leader of the United Mine Workers, John L. Lewis, was a powerful force in the CIO, and knowing that Lewis was no stranger to the use of violence, Hague probably realized early on that he was in for a lengthy fight.

In retrospect, the objectives of the CIO were simple: to distribute leaflets urging the unskilled and largely uneducated laborers of Jersey City to join the industrial union. And Hague's objective was even simpler: to stop them.

In an early fracas, the force exerted by the police seemed enough. Clusters of CIO pamphleteers were carted off to jail, charged with unlawful assembly, and given sentences of from five to 30 days by judges all too willing to keep "duh Mare" happy. Undaunted, the CIO leaders decided to try to bring the workers to them, instead of taking their leaflets to the workers at their jobs. They tried without success to rent a meeting hall in Hudson County. No owner was going to make his place available to an organization despised by Hague; that kind of action could cause plenty of trouble later with fire inspectors, health inspectors, and all the rest. When the CIO next asked for a permit to hold an outdoor meeting, the request was turned down on the ground that anti-CIO feeling within the city might result in violence.

The Mayor fanned the flames of anti-CIO feeling at every opportunity. He did it by proclaiming that the labor organization was part of a gigantic communist conspiracy that was out to destroy the very foundations of America. By latching onto the "Red Menace," Hague found a theme that diverted public attention from the worsening economic situation in Jersey City. There was no time for intellectual debate, no discussion of the possible merits of a communistic system vs. a capitalistic one. Communism was the enemy—things were that simple. And the term "Communism" was applied not only to the CIO, but to the American Civil Liberties Union, the Socialist Party, and any other organizations or individuals who drew Hague's wrath.

With Police Chief Walsh proclaiming that "Jersey City is not Moscow," and the Mayor warning that if an ACLU free-speech lawyer appeared in Jersey City, "his friends will not see him for a long time," the stage was set for a confrontation that would end with the humbling of Frank Hague. But it would be a long time coming.

It is possible that the Mayor welcomed the influx of lawyers, civil libertarians, and others who sought to aid the CIO in its effort. As Dayton David McKean pointed out in his study of the Hague machine in action, *The Boss,* the citizens of Jersey City were starting to become aware of what today would be called "a negative cash flow." They were paying the highest taxes in any American city, and yet Jersey City had the highest debt rate—$181 per capita—of any city of its size. Delinquent taxes climbed from $1.9 million in 1934 to $4.4 million in 1938. More than 15,000 homes were turned over to the city in 1935, and the city narrowly avoided bankruptcy by threatening to stop interest payments and forcing bond holders to accept new bonds. But certainly the populace could not lay the blame at the feet of Frank Hague; after all, time and again, he had been voted into office and cheered at each appearance, each pronouncement. If anyone had begun to have doubts, if anyone had started to think about criticizing "duh Mare" and his tactics—well, suddenly, there was a scapegoat:

Communism.

Citing a 1924 law against the dissemination of "fake advertising," Hague prohibited the CIO workers from distributing their leaflets. To do so, the organizers had to show up at industrial sites early in the morning and beat a hasty departure before police could arrive. But a case that was working its way through the courts—and on up to the U. S. Supreme Court—was decided at an inappropriate time for the Mayor. With Chief Justice Hughes declaring "the liberty of the press is not confined to newspapers and periodicals," the court struck down a Georgia law almost identical to the one in anti-distribution Jersey City.

Immediately, distribution was begun of a leaflet announcing that a pro-CIO speech would be delivered in Jersey City by Norman Thomas, the widely-known socialist. When the police seized some of the circulars, the CIO said it would file suit in Federal District Court—and Hague backed down. But, he made clear, his attitude toward the invasion of business or industry by "outside groups" was unchanged.

That attitude became evident when Thomas arrived for his speaking engagement. The political leader had spoken in Jersey City on many previous occasions, but this time was denied a permit as "a dangerous communist agent." When he showed up in front of a waiting crowd of 5,000, he was taken by Hague's police forcefully to the waterfront and placed aboard a ferry to New York City. He immediately returned by subway, was again arrested, and sent back on a Manhattan-bound train.

Hague defended his police officers' actions by stating that Thomas, a former presidential candidate, had been escorted out of the city for his own safety. Two U. S. congressmen—Jerry O'Connell and John Bernard—were among the many Americans dismayed by the situation. They announced that they would speak in Jersey City before a large labor meeting. But when they arrived at Journal Square, they found it roped off by police—and behind the ropes were some 20,000 unruly pro-Hague citizens who had been urged to attend by newspaper ads calling for a demonstration of "Americanism." The congressmen cancelled their speeches as fighting broke out between pro-CIO groups and World War veterans, many of whom were in uniform.

To Frank Hague, the victories seemed momentous. But he was not dealing any longer with local politicians, labor groups, saloonkeepers, and the like. He was dealing with names that had access to national publicity outlets. *The New York Times, Life* magazine, the *Washington Post, Baltimore Sun,* and other publications carried the story of repression in Jersey City. J. Edgar Hoover's FBI was asked to invoke the Lindbergh kidnapping law against Hague after the Norman Thomas seizure, and President Roosevelt was asked his view of the situation at a press conference. Although the embarrassed Roosevelt tried to pass off the matter as "a local police problem,'' he is said to have later told the U. S. Postmaster General to warn Hague about going too far.

It was natural, in the atmosphere of name-calling and flying fists, for an old antagonist of Hague to return to the scene. And suddenly "Jeff" Burkitt was back in town, taking up quarters in the Hotel Plaza, and loudly proclaiming in his Southern drawl that he would speak when and where he pleased, with or without a permit. He decided that his initial soapbox would be the corner of Sip and Bergen Avenues.

When he stepped up into the rumble seat of his car and raised his voice, Police Chief Harry Walsh was ready for him. Burkitt had time only for a few of his choicest epithets—"yella-bellied coward," "tough guy with a gun on his hip," and such—before Walsh and a flying squad pulled him from the car and into the street. But a strange thing happened as the cops pummeled the aging "Alabama Jim." Voices from the crowd of 1,000 people protested loudly—*daring to speak against Hague's tactics*—and compared the police to Hitler's storm troopers. "Let him speak! Leave him alone!"

It did no good. In his cell the next morning the weary battler read the papers and realized that his day had passed. The *Journal,* which in its anti-Hague days had gleefully reported the colorful exploits of "Jeff," now simply referred to "Burkitt" and wasted little space on the story of his arrest. And the courts would have none of his explanation that he was merely exercising his right as an American to speak freely: Charged with using indecent and profane language, he was sentenced to six months at hard labor—and served every day of it.

The treatment might have broken the spirit of a less-impassioned warrior, but not that of Burkitt, according to an eyewitness—John R. Longo, who served alongside "Alabama Jim" during part of his term. And what put Longo, another Hague opponent, in prison? A charge of being a communist, of being involved with a fake petition, and—well, perhaps Longo himself should relate the tale:

"Tommie," he told me during an interview in the late 1970s, "in the 1937 primary, Lester Clee, a reform Republican, was on a crusade to end Hague's days in the state. He declared for governor.

James Murray, the anti-Hague spokesman in the county here, was negotiating to run a Democratic slate against the Hague ticket. His idea was to keep the Democrats so busy in their own primary that they would not have the time or spare votes to interfere with the Republican contest. But when Murray failed to come up with a ticket, we saw an opportunity for real political responsibility against Hague.

"We were young men, Tommie, barely 21 years of age, first-time voters mostly. We assembled a primary ticket of assemblymen and freeholders. Each candidate was to concentrate on competing with the ward leader's strength in each of three wards. It was just a test, really, because Hague's freeholders had no fear of being beaten—but they were worried that for the first time the voters in their own neighborhoods would have an opportunity to say how they felt about the men."

At least one of the ward leaders had reason to worry, it was later revealed. According to Longo, Teddy Fleming, of the Sixth Ward, and the father of an author who wrote a number of anti-Hague pieces, was not well liked by his constituency; and, of course, none of the men wanted Hague to see any sign of weakness at the grass-roots level.

"Duh Mare" was further riled by the name selected for Longo's group: Young Democrats Marching with Roosevelt.

"When I went to file the ticket," Longo continued, "the county clerk refused to accept it. He declared that it was not according to legal form. Before the day ended, I returned with a new petition filled with new names. This time, the clerk threw it outside his window and said that it was illegal, that it contained phony names and insufficient names, and included other violations. He did not even examine it. I left the petition on the window sill in front of him and walked out."

Although two newspaper reporters witnessed the confrontation, their presence had no effect on the clerk. The petition was not accepted and was never filed. There was no opposition in the Democratic primary. It was the following year—1938—when Longo's document found its way onto the news pages.

Speaking at a meeting of the Holy Name Society at his church, the youthful political thinker proposed a resolution stating that it was possible to be both a good Catholic and a member of the CIO labor movement. In the Hague-fostered hysteria of the time, in which the CIO and Communism were synonymous, Longo fought strongly for the resolution—and the group finally voiced approval.

"Overnight, my action became part of the national spotlight. An appearance on a radio program in New York was convincing enough for writers to declare that Hague had not bamboozled *everyone,* that some people in the city were repulsed by his charges. There was pandemonium in political circles. The machine and Hague himself—I was told by newspaper editors—had become infuriated by my action."

Others were upset, too. The Catholic Church ousted Longo, but reinstated him after a national outcry produced support from such distinguished clerics as The Right Reverend Monsignor John J. Ryan of Catholic University. Still, it was Hague's wrath that Longo felt most severely.

"From out of nowhere came an indictment charging that a year earlier I had filed fraudulent nominating petitions. Wherever I went for help, I found that I was a pariah. No one would dare help me. I ended up at City Hall in New York and asked Mayor LaGuardia for his assistance. I had campaigned for him and he got hold of Vito Marcantonio, a Harlem lawyer and president of the Fiorello H. LaGuardia Association there.

" 'Marc,' La Guardia said, 'go across the river and represent this fellow.See that they give him a pat on the ass and end the case.' "

The young attorney was to discover that Hague's prosecutors and courts were out to teach a lesson to any foe of the Mayor. Despite the testimony of the two reporters who had seen the clerk refuse to accept Longo's petitions, a jury found the defendant guilty of gaining signatures on the petitions "improperly." As the judge prepared to pronounce sentence, Marcantonio pointed out that ten of the 12 jurors in the box were either themselves on the city or county payrolls or had as many as a half-dozen family members drawing a salary that was paid, albeit indirectly, by Frank Hague.

It was to no avail. Longo received nine months at hard labor in the county jail—where, at least, he had a first-hand opportunity to watch the volatile antics of his boyhood hero, Jeff Burkitt.

"Jeff was fearless," Longo related, his eyes moist and shining with the memory. "I was in what they called the upper cell block, Jeff in the lower one. But every morning, like a war chant, he'd yell, 'Hagueism must be destroyed! ' And he'd send his tin cup rip-racking across the prison bars, making a shrill echo all through those hollow chambers.

"We couldn't talk during our long hours on the rock pile—the prison authorities changed the rules of conduct on my arrival—but that didn't stop Jeff Burkitt. I can still see him, placing his 14-pound sledge hammer down and waving wildly to me, shouting, 'Stay in there, John! Keep your chin up, Longo! Hagueism must be destroyed!' I was frightened stiff. They'd haul Jeff away and throw him in solitary, and I imagined they'd come after me in the dead of the night and throw me into a river nearby."

Longo served his time peaceably, preferring to wait until another day to fight. The incorrigible Burkitt, on the other hand, was often beaten by guards, poked with the lighted ends of cigar butts, and otherwise mistreated. But it evidently meant little to a man who had so often been bloodied by Hague's detectives and Walsh's officers.

Marcantonio, who was to go on to defend numerous communist sympathizers and himself was branded as a communist during his term in congress, "never charged me a dime," Longo recalls. In an effort to have his term reduced, Longo's uncle, Nick Florio, a famous trainer of fighters, arranged a meeting between Longo and Jack Dempsey, the heavyweight boxing champion. Then Dempsey phoned Hague, whose admiration for famed athletes was well known, to plead that the sentence be reduced.

"Hague said he could help if it was a murderer," Dempsey told Florio, "but Longo—that's something else."

While Burkitt and Longo languished in their cells—where they were regularly visited by J. Owen Grundy who brought word of what was going on in Jersey City—Hague carried on his anti-Red, anti-CIO battle like a mad general. A rabbi who had testified for Longo as a character witness during his trial was informed that his congregation would have to vacate the Jewish Community Center. In a second attempt to speak in a public park, Congressman Jerry O'Connell was confronted by a mob, then seized by the police. Returning to Washington, he stated wryly, "I'm glad to be back in America." He also presented a letter to President Roosevelt that called for Hague's dismissal from the Democratic National Committee.

The president, noting that the signatures of 32 members of the House were on the letter, was compelled to take action. He discussed the matter with Attorney General Homer Cummings, who ordered an investigation of the free-speech complaints in Jersey City. As if that were not embarrassing enough to Frank Hague (who showed no signs of public embarrassment, it must be noted), "duh Mare" found himself praised on official Nazi radio as "a man fighting for the cause in the United States."

Words—whether printed on letters or broadcast on the air— were not about to change Hague's mind or approach. That, the CIO realized, would have to be done by court order. The organization filed a suit asking injunctive relief to restrain Jersey City authorities from interfering with its drive to organize the area's workers.

With the case set for Federal District Court in Newark, both sides turned to some of the finest legal minds available. Spaulding Frazer, dean of the Newark Law School, and Morris Ernst were chosen to represent the CIO. Hague called on John A. Matthews, a leading Catholic layman, to present his views to Judge William Clark, a maverick Republican.

Having devoted much of his time over the years during which he held power to avoiding court appearances, Hague surprised everyone by seeming to relish a chance to speak out on the communist menace.

He was to spend six days on the witness stand.

In the beginning, he was cheered as he entered the courtroom. Tall, florid-faced, vigorous in appearance, and smartly dressed as always—dark suit, white handkerchief in the breast pocket, black tie fastened with a pearl stickpin—the Mayor doffed his gray fedora and took the stand.

Frazer and Ernst evidently had worked out their plan of attack carefully. The elderly Frazer, who at least was a New Jersey resident, would probe gently, merely trying to gain understanding. The fiery Ernst would bore in for the kill at every opportunity.

Hague reacted almost as if he had been programmed to do so: Wildly gesticulating, he publicly charged Ernst with being a "mastermind of a communist attempt to overthrow the government by first getting control of the CIO and the American Labor Party." Time and again, the Mayor rose from his seat to take a fighter's stance, while apprehensive guards would move a step or two forward as if to prevent him from attacking the judge, lawyer, or witness.

Contending that his actions were solely aimed at defeating the communist conspiracy, Hague denied that Jeff Burkitt had been jailed at one time for attempting to speak without a permit. "Oh, no," the Mayor indignantly told the judge, "he kicked a police officer in the chest. There's a vast difference in that. His language was something terrible." Then, after insisting that "Burkitt and his crowd" had been given 400 to 500 permits to hold meetings, he managed to pick out less than a dozen from an official police list.

When he was questioned about an incident in which Samuel Macri, an organizer for the CIO, was knocked unconscious at a speaking engagement in the company of Representative O'Connell, Hague found humor in the recollection. Macri, who had reportedly been out cold for 24 hours, complained that he was turned away when he went to the famed Medical Center for emergency aid. "If he was unconscious, how could he remember being turned away?" And, the Mayor pointed out, Macri had shown up at the Margaret Hague maternity facility, so it was not inconceivable that he would have been denied treatment. "He wasn't having a baby."

There was little laughter in the courtroom, however, during the bulk of His Honor's testimony. Treating Hague deferentially, Frazer asked for an explanation of the incidents where such notable citizens as Norman Thomas had been "deported."

Q.: Do you consider it an arrest when a police officer puts them in a car and takes them somewhere besides the police station?

A.: No, I think he is doing them a favor.

Q.: Do you think it is neighborly to dump into another city those you don't want in Jersey City?

A.: If they come from another city and they are dumped back, I think that is neighborly.

Asked who determines which citizens are "decent people who can circulate petitions," and what "constitutes material that is acceptable to the community," Hague responded with the statement that the Jersey City police had wide discretionary powers. Such powers, he noted, could be exercised in accordance with "circumstances."

Frazer honed in on the frequent use of the word "invasion" by the Mayor in reference to communists. He asked for an explanation of the term.

"When Harry Bridges, a noted communist, ordered 500 of his strong-arm men to invade Jersey City and destroy the shipping industry, that's an invasion," snapped Hague. "And when Carney, in a public declaration, says he is going to invade Jersey City, 3,000 strong, law or no law, that's an invasion!"

Q.: Did Mr. Carney invade Jersey City with 3,000 men?

A.: No! He was afraid to!"

At times, said the Mayor, people had to be arrested in Jersey City for their own good, "to protect them from harm." Mistreat a prisoner? Never! Burkitt's complaints? "Someone hit him with an egg or something." Then, "Maybe it was a case of eggs, I don't know."

If a novelist were to write of Hague's appearance on the stand, it might resemble a scene in *The Caine Mutiny* where Captain Queeg loses control of his faculties. Skillfully prodded by Frazer, cleverly enticed by Ernst, the Mayor soon was declaring that he did not believe in civil liberties for anyone who sought the overthrow of the United States government—even if the individuals only voiced such ideas—and he advocated that concentration camps should be established for "Reds," that alien radicals should be deported, and that all public officials should follow his lead. Asked if he really believed that those preaching the merits of communism should "go back" to Europe, Hague was vehement:

"They should not *go* back. They should be *driven* back if they came here to oppose this government, and if they were born here, they should be sent to a camp in Alaska."

As the Mayor grew more adamant, Ernst demanded to know if he would abide by the findings of the court; in other words, would he obey a federal order to stop interfering with the CIO's actions?

"No one will restrain me when there is danger of anyone losing his life and when circumstances demand that I ignore him," was the reply. Reminded that he had once said "the nightstick must prevail," he explained that the statement referred to the need to break up gangs of "thugs" that operated when labor racketeering was at its height. Yes, he admitted, he had ordered his troops in with nightsticks when "labor thugs" had threatened violence unless a trucking operator paid time-and-a-half to employees who had not worked overtime. The "thugs" had posted "outside pickets" to harm the trucker's business. "Outside pickets" were defined as: "All those foreign groups coming in from Brooklyn and New York to picket and create all sorts of scenes."

On Thursday, June 23, 1938, Hague concluded his testimony. His attorney, Matthews, as short and squat as Hague was tall and overpowering, helped him make a number of points in his final words as a witness:

The CIO and the American Civil Liberties Union, he said, were directed by communist leaders and therefore were not entitled to the protection of the constitutional guarantees of free speech and public assembly. "If they were high class citizens and they met in a peaceful, orderly manner, they have perfect rights; but if prior to that they were advocating the overthrow of the government, they were dissatisfied with everything that America gave them, and why, of course, I don't assume they have any rights."

Furthermore, Hague carefully pointed out, his administration had "cleaned out" the unsavory elements from Theodore Brandle's ironworkers (including Brandle himself) and from the local American Federation of Labor groups, while attracting "hundreds" of new industries to Jersey City "because it is free of labor difficulties."

It was a performance filled with bravado, and Hague's closest associates sensed that he was using the witness stand as a podium to reach a national—perhaps international—audience. A headline in *The New York Times* noted his "100 percent Americanism," and other publications seemed impressed by his "honest, forthright and sincere" replies and his refusal to sidestep questions posed by the CIO lawyers.

But the preponderance of publicity was anti-Hague. Roosevelt and various members of his "New Deal" organization—including Harold Ickes and Henry Morgenthau—affirmed the American ideal of every citizen's right to express an opinion. Some 50 newspapers ran editorials that referred to "megalomania" and "distortion of Catholic teaching," and individual critics called for everything from investigating Hague's physiology for a possible glandular disturbance to prosecuting him under an 1870 civil rights statute.

While the press and the public debated the case presented by both sides, Judge Clark deliberated conscientiously—and five months later issued a 15,000-word decision. He asserted that people had a constitutional right to travel freely in Jersey City, and that "deportation" as practiced by Hague's police was illegal. He invalidated the city's procedure for issuing permits said to be necessary if anyone wanted to speak to a gathering in a public park. And he declared that there could be no interference with distribution of leaflets, or with peaceful picketing.

For the moment, it appeared that Frank Hague—the man who had won victory after victory in his career—was beaten. The CIO and ACLU leaders hailed the Clark decision and proclaimed "an end to sweatshops in Jersey City, for now we can organize without interference from Hague."

But "duh Mare" was far from whipped. "There shall be no letup in the city's drive to keep out the radicals and Reds!" he declared.

And he promptly filed an appeal, vowing to carry the fight all the way to the Supreme Court, if necessary.

It would be necessary.

9

Possibly—only possibly—the decision handed down by Judge Clark surprised Frank Hague. Clark, however, was said to be one of only five judges in the entire state of New Jersey who did not owe allegiance to the Hague machine. As an example of how tightly the machine controlled the judicial system, let's look at the appointment by the newly-elected (for the third time!) Governor A. Harry Moore of a judge to the state's highest court, the Court of Errors and Appeals. Moore, with dozens of possible candidates to choose among for the open position, pointed his finger unerringly at Frank Hague, Jr., the 34-year-old son of "duh Mare."

Nepotism? Of course not. After all, young Frank *had* attended Princeton. Well, to be sure, he did not graduate from there, leaving after being required to repeat a number of courses during a summer semester. He transferred to the University of Virginia. There, he passed 11 of the 20 courses he took in law school—a record that caused him to drop out and enroll at Washington and Lee. Without earning a law degree, he passed the New Jersey Bar examination on his first try.

Even though one may consider Moore one of the great governors of New Jersey (as I do), one has to raise a querulous eyebrow at his reply when he was asked why he had nominated the younger Hague for the important post: "I knew the appointment would make his dad happy." *The New Jersey Law Journal* editorialized against the appointment, but to no avail. When the time came for confirmation in the state senate, the seven Democratic senators quickly gave approval, and they were joined by seven of the 14 Republicans, whose votes were necessary if young Hague was to become a judge in New Jersey's highest court. The word was that former Republican Governor Hoffman had given a nod out of deference to his old "friendly enemy," Mayor Hague.

"Now," said a newsman of the event, "When Dad says, 'I am the law,' Sonny can say, 'You're right, Pop!' "

In return for his aid, Moore assured Hoffman that several of his favorites who had been appointed to jobs in the previous administration would stay in their posts. "In patronage matters," the governor had once said, "I am strictly organization. All there is to say about patronage is that we are entitled to our fair share of jobs."

Perhaps—and, again, only *perhaps*—the public might have been dismayed by such blatant statements if the entire world had not been trembling on the brink of World War II, if just across the Hudson River the glories of the New York World's Fair of 1939 were not on display, and if the last vestiges of the Great Depression were not being shucked off as the nation stepped up its defense production.

In such a time, the antics of Frank Hague and his powerful police force could easily be thought to be minor distractions, sometimes amusing, sometimes less than amusing—but generally of little significance. When, for example, three of Police Chief Walsh's toughest cops—whose names, Fletcher, Okonski, and Menge, have always made me envision a sign on the door of a Madison Avenue advertising agency—"legally kidnapped" socialist leader Norman Thomas and deported him via a ferry, the man-on-the-street tended to laugh. After all, no one was hurt. (Recalling the amusing fracas recently, an aging Jimmy Menge finds it hard to criticize Hague: "Sure," he says, "he had the 3 percent thing going, but those of us who paid it looked on it as 'union dues.' " And, he remembers, when his partner, Frank Okonski, was found to have a brain tumor, the Mayor took care of all his medical expenses, "It didn't cost Frank a dime.")

Hague used other means to retain control of the police force. The officers were paid 40 percent to 50 percent better than men who held the same jobs in other cities (so a 3 percent kickback did not strike anyone as being out of line). And the Mayor made sure that the men had one of the finest gymnasiums in the country to work out in—to enable them to stay physically fit for their own well-being, but also because Hague insisted on his "army" looking good. A six-day work week kept many officers from becoming overweight and also provided the city with additional patrol hours. To keep their jobs, the men were required to observe the moral code laid down by the puritanical Roman Catholic mayor, who delighted in proclaiming that "Jersey City is the most moralist town in America."

While the big names of organized crime—Al Capone, Frank Costello, and others of that ilk—spread their tentacles into plenty of states and cities, Hague made sure that he controlled who operated on his turf. Gangsters who attempted to infiltrate Hudson County met immediate opposition from the Jersey City Police Department, and the department was said to be regarded with more fear than the FBI.

Prostitution, particularly loathsome to the mayor, was non-existent—at least so far as anyone could tell. It was difficult, of course, to verify many of the crime statistics reported by the Jersey City police, and the FBI refused to publish them after 1935 because they were considered to be so unreliable. Everybody knew that gambling existed, however: Playing "the numbers" and illegal betting on horse racing was tolerated, so long as the people running the operations were on Hague's "approved" list. That meant no rough stuff would be tolerated. The kind of gamblers Hague liked was represented by the man who, more or less, was given the franchise to operate a numbers racket in Hudson County. This was Joseph Moriarity, a tall, quiet, timid-looking individual who might well have been taken for an accountant. Having started out as a young money-maker by selling newspapers, Moriarity carried the nickname of "Newsboy" throughout his career—which proved so profitable that when $2 million was once found in an abandoned garage on a desolate side street, he denied ownership. "It's not mine. I dunno how it got there," he said as the money was confiscated by detectives. He knew there was plenty more where it had come from.

"Newsboy," "Rusty" McAvoy, "Spike" Connolly, "Lefty" Marchitto, and "The Iron Horse" Maschucci—these were some of the names of the policy makers and others who had their fingers on criminal activity in a Jersey City that was free of racketeering, vice, and crime, according to Frank Hague. Before Moriarity took the title of gambling king in Hudson County, one Charles Goode bore it—and served at the same time as Hague's Democratic leader in the Second Ward. Crime had other close ties to City Hall: Daniel Casey, Jersey City's director of public safety, once assigned a special squad of police to investigate the numbers ring and find out who was running it. When the report uncovered the name of Pat Casey, the director's brother, the investigation was promptly called off.

With such close ties between his administration and the lawless on the one hand, and his administration and the courts on the other, Frank Hague was a picture of confidence at all times. The anti-Hague, pro-CIO ruling of Judge Clark was appealed to the Third Circuit Court of Appeals in Philadelphia. Hague shrugged off a defeat there, and shrugged again when President Roosevelt showed his approval of the Clark decision by giving the justice a higher judicial post. The Mayor sent his assistant corporation counsel, Charles Hershenstein, to the Supreme Court with another appeal, but by the time that august body upheld the Clark decision once again—in mid-1939—the nearness of war and the excitement of the World's Fair occupied people's minds. It was simple for Frank Hague to issue a proclamation that said to the CIO: "The doors of City Hall are always open to you. We want you to come and discuss labor problems."

Although New Jersey CIO leader William Carney viewed the court decision as "the opening gun to rid this state of Hagueism," he realized the fight was over and the immediate thing to do was organize the labor force in Jersey City. Two officials of a union local met with Deputy Mayor John Malone and the Mayor's personal representative and nephew, Frank Hague Eggers, to discuss a walkout at a local manufacturing plant. Workers had been ordered off the job after the manufacturer announced a series of salary cuts. Following the meeting, the cuts were rescinded and the employees went back to work.

If the populace of Jersey City took little notice of Hague's defeat, and if the Mayor himself tried to make light of the entire affair, there was one man—much higher up—who was well aware that the time had come to pull away from a politician who seemed about to embark on a long slide down. That man was President Roosevelt, and he seized an immediate opportunity to tighten the screws on Hague. Governor A. Harry Moore, despite an appeal by the Mayor to seek the governorship for an unprecedented fourth term, declared that he had no intention to run.

"I'm tired of public office," Moore said. "I want a good long rest. I want to be free of job-hunters, of the worries and cares that rest on the shoulders of an officeholder. I want to get away from those whom I, in honest effort, displeased. I'm tired of taking the abuse of folks who demand this and that when I can't grant them their requests."

With Moore out of the picture, Roosevelt called in his secretary of the navy, Charles Edison, the son of inventor Thomas Edison, who was a Jersey native. Ray Chasan, counsel for the independent City Affairs Committee of Jersey City, years later would describe the scene to me. Edison was quite hard of hearing, as his father had been, and Roosevelt had difficulty making it clear what his plan involved. Because the war situation called for a display of nonpartisanship on the part of the president, he wanted to add some Republicans to his overwhelmingly Democratic cabinet. "So, Charley," barked Roosevelt, "I want you to resign as secretary of the navy to run for the gubernatorial post in Jersey. Then I'll replace you with Frank Knox."

Edison, whom Frank Hague had once tried to seduce with a promise of support if the inventor's son ran for the U.S. Senate, saw a chance to battle Hague outright. "No!" he said incredulously.

The President, not accustomed to hearing a negative word from those around him, raised his voice, wondering if perhaps Edison had misunderstood him. "I said I want you to run for governor of New Jersey, and you said—what?" he asked.

Smiling now, Edison repeated his exclamation, "No!"

Roosevelt turned to an aide, muttering under his breath: "The son of a bitch is really deaf!"

Chasan laughed as he recalled how in future years, after Edison was elected to the state's highest political post, "whenever a backbreaker was making unreasonable demands on the governor, he would quietly reach into his upper left shirt pocket and turn off his hearing aid.''

By asking Edison to go for the gubernatorial spot, Roosevelt saw an opportunity to put a lid on Frank Hague, who had increasingly become a source of embarrassment. For some time, various advisers had warned the president that the ties between Hudson County and the White House should be severed, but Roosevelt had resisted. Once, when a close associate said, "We shouldn't bother with Hague; he's a son of a bitch," FDR had nodded in agreement. But then he shook his head: "Yes, but he's *our* son of a bitch," he replied.

The announcement that Edison would oppose Republican State Senator Robert C. Hendrickson in a bid for the gubernatorial slot riled Hague, but he could say little about his true feelings. Earlier, when Edison had chosen the post of secretary of the navy instead of opting to try for the governor's job, Hague had issued a flowery, flattering statement: "The name of Edison is honored in our state as in no other state in the country. The president has taken out of our party in New Jersey a wonderful candidate for governor.''

Yet, Hague knew, it was the same Edison who had turned down his promise of support in a senatorial race with the declaration: "We'd rather be respected than elected.''

Forced to support Edison—or oppose the wishes of the president who was struggling to keep the threat of Nazism from the nation's shores—"duh Mare" determined to give an example of the strength he felt sure he still possessed. He engendered a plurality of 153,000 votes in Hudson County for a $21 million relief bond issue, enough to let the question squeak through in the state by 50,000 votes. He also came out in favor of pari-mutel betting at Jersey racetracks. An old opponent, Reverend Clee, sought to use the betting issue to mount a campaign for the gubernatorial nomination and organized a number of church groups behind an anti-gambling platform.

The Roman Catholic Church, however, was in no hurry to oppose one of its leading members. Hague made much of the fact that the only ones who stood to suffer from the introduction of legal track betting would be the illegal bookies and policy makers—a move that linked Clee's groups with the denizens of the underworld. When the votes were counted, racetrack betting became part of the Jersey scene by a plurality of 156,815 votes—of which 133,501 were supplied by Hudson County.

Clee continued to battle by demanding that the state immediately had to begin using voting machines in elections to prevent, in his words, "the kind of trickery that the Hudson County Democrats were adept at accomplishing." Hague could not oppose the idea, but bridled at the fact that Clee's "Clean Government" group—based in Essex County—singled out Hudson as the site where the machines should first go into use. He charged Clee with trying to win the voting machine contract for a firm that had been involved in a 1937 corruption scandal. Shaking a weary head, Clee passed his anti-Hague mantle to a fellow Republican, State Senator Hendrickson. The candidate immediately began to level charges, noting that U.S. Attorney General Frank Murphy and the FBI were said to be looking "into political racketeering, crime, and corruption in Jersey City and elsewhere in Hudson County." Thinking that it would help him in the race against Edison, Hendrickson called for an investigation of the charges.

Murphy, however, was named by Roosevelt to the Supreme Court, and any investigation was sidetracked. Before he stepped out of his post as attorney general, he noted that "there was no evidence in the department to warrant prosecution" of Hague, so far as federal laws were concerned.

Despite a speech by Edison at a Sea Girt rally, in which he announced that if he were elected, "you will have elected a governor who has made no promises of preferment to any man or group," Edison knew that Hague would have to back him. Election day came—and went, and Edison annihilated Hendrickson by nearly 64,000 votes statewide, with Hudson County turning in a plurality of 109,000 to overcome a Republican advantage everywhere else in Jersey.

When the new governor was sworn in a few weeks later, Frank Hague was not on the scene. Asked about the mysterious absence of the Mayor, Edison tersely replied, "Well, I guess it's a long trip from Florida."

To reporters on the scene, it was obvious that Hague's lust for the political wars was waning, and that he preferred more and more to warm his huge frame in the Florida sunshine. He had been noticeably shaken when a longtime and fiercely loyal companion, Michael I. Fagen, died—an incident which seemed to set "duh Mare" musing about past glories. It was Fagen who had urged that federal funds contributed by President Roosevelt should be used for needed sewer construction rather than for a Jersey City baseball stadium.

"Lemme ask, Mike," said Hague, "which will the people see—the sewers or the stadium?" Fagen's reply was obvious. "You got your answer," Hague had snapped. And the stadium had been built.

Edison wasted no time letting Hague—and the newly re-elected Roosevelt—know the new situation in New Jersey. He ripped out a direct phone line to City Hall that had been as much a part of the governor's office as the huge desk and overstuffed chairs. And he began to put up his own candidates for openings in the courts, the highway commission, and the Hudson County tax board. One such appointment—that of Frederic R. Colie to the State Supreme Court—drew a blistering series of threats from Hague. Colie had taken part a few months earlier in an unsuccessful Republican attempt to block the appointment by Governor Moore of Frank Hague, Jr., to the Court of Errors and Appeals.

Still, there was little that Hague could do to show his ire—unless he could defeat Edison on a highly visible public issue. He mulled various ideas over in his mind while he dined sumptuously at his home in Deal, the sprawling apartment in New York, or the sun-drenched Florida retreat. With war looming ever nearer he knew the issue of Communism was a relic of the past. (He himself had chosen not to attend a baseball game one afternoon while cheering crowds awaited elsewhere his appearance at an Americanization Day Rally, complete with signs proclaiming: "Stand Shoulder to Shoulder With Mayor Hague to Keep Communists Out.") No, Hague realized, he needed a different kind of issue—something that would mean real profit or loss to his constituency.

He found an opening when Governor Edison instituted a new Hudson County tax board. The board, taking note of the fact that two railroads operating in the area had recently gone bankrupt and that two others were in severe financial difficulty, reduced assessments on the lines. Having long squeezed the railroads for all that he could get from them, Hague saw red. He contended that the railroads owed Jersey City and Hudson County millions of dollars in back taxes—somewhere between $23 million and $46 million—and said that he wanted them to pay up promptly.

Suddenly, the battle lines were drawn. Charging that the various power companies and others bearing the name of Edison profited from the railroad-connected business contracts they held to the tune of more than $10 million, Hague claimed the governor was giving his customers favored treatment at the expense of the citizens of New Jersey. He pointed out that eight years of litigation, culminating in a decision of the U.S. Supreme Court, required the railroads to pay in full—and that the only concession Jersey City might give would be to let the railroads pay what they owed in installments over a period of time. A furious Edison admitted that his companies did some $3 million worth of business a year with the railroads, but insisted that his tax board's action in reducing the assessments was necessary to help save a struggling industry.

The matter found its way to a session at the State House in Trenton, where a bill to provide tax relief was to be voted upon by the assembly. Hague dispatched Peter P. Artaserse, a trusted lawyer, to carry the battle for his delegation, while Edison's primary support was furnished by Alfred E. Driscoll, a Republican senator from Camden County, who himself was to later serve as governor of the state.

While opponents wrangled within the ornate building, Hague and Edison threw verbal darts at one another from their offices. The governor stated publicly that Hague's opposition to his tax bill was not caused by the Mayor's concern for the citizens of New Jersey, but because Hague was still smarting over the appointment of Frederic Colie to the State Supreme Court. "Mayor Hague," announced Edison, "is trying to pay me off with calculated abuse."

The abuse, calculated or otherwise, was evident in Hague's numerous pronouncements. Edison, he claimed, was a "betrayer" of the people of Jersey City, Hudson County and the state. Driscoll jumped in to charge that Hague had called the governor "the chief thief" and members of the legislature who supported his plan "petty thieves." Hague countered by blasting Driscoll's "unwarranted attack," and said the verbal brickbats "will not stop me in exposing this outrageous deal by the railroad lobby." He promised that there would be a series of explosions in the legislature before he was through, and conjectured that Driscoll's rebuttals were the result of "a guilty conscience."

Edison was the first to lose his cool, and began issuing statements of questionable veracity. He contended that he had received only nominal support in his election success from Hague, when everyone knew that Hudson County's 100,000-vote majority had put the governor into office. Without the vote from Hudson, "the Gibraltar of Democracy," the wealthy heir of one of America's greatest geniuses would not have won. In contending that Hague was "a self-chosen boss of the Democratic party in New Jersey . . . who no longer is free to carry on his attempts to exert control over the high courts of the state," Edison rightfully recognized Hague's unhappiness over the Colie appointment, but he was far off the mark about the Jersey City hero being "a self-chosen boss." Every Democratic governor from Edward I. Edwards in 1919 to Edison himself, some 21 years later, owed his election to Hudson County and the peerless county boss—and had been all too willing to help that individual stay in control. Every Democratic leader in New Jersey recognized Hague's right to his 25-year reign as the state leader.

As Hague continued his opposition, Edison's anger increased. He finally told newsmen that he had discussed his intention to appoint Colie with Hague in a telephone conversation that the mayor had instituted from his Florida vacation home. Hague, he said, "promptly turned loose on me a torrent of imprecations and threats that he was going to ruin me if it were the last thing he did." Other researchers have quoted some of the phrases within the "torrent of invective": "Damned ingrate" and "Benedict Arnold" are among the milder, printable ones.

Without denying the substance of the telephone conversation, Hague responded by stating that he had not placed the call; the governor had called *him*. Edison's motivation, he said, was to try to flatter the Mayor by clearing Colie's appointment with him—but, at the same time, the occupant of the state's highest elected office was telling the public that he was independent of any bosses. "Hypocritical" was the term Hague applied to such actions. He insisted that his own report of the phone call would be verified if Edison made available the telephone bills from his home in Lewellyn Park; they would show that the governor had called Hague's secretary at his private home number to request the number of the mayor's Florida residence. Edison, of course, had no intention of complying with the Mayor's demand, and both men took a moment to catch their breath as the date neared for the tax bill vote.

An all-night session of the assembly in late July produced a final, irreconcilable break between the Mayor and the governor. The Edison-endorsed bill passed in the assembly by two votes, in the senate by one. The favorable outcome was partly the result of a series of meetings between the governor and individual assemblymen and senators—meetings in which, Hague promptly charged, Edison had promised political favors in return for a favorable vote.

"In the early hours of the morning," Hague shrilled in a press release, "the most disgraceful betrayal of the people that has occurred in the history of New Jersey was perpetrated in the State House at Trenton when the Governor of the State of New Jersey, in order to culminate his efforts to put over the $121 million tax deal, bartered a Common Pleas Judgeship for the necessary deciding vote in the House of the Assembly."

Edison's reply—as might be expected—was that while he had met with various people, as Hague stated, no coercion was used to obtain favorable votes. And any persons appointed to any offices were well qualified for the posts.

The tax relief bill was to prove financially unrewarding to Jersey City and other Hudson County municipalities, and it was a natural consequence that Hague's failure to fend it off would be seen by his longtime supporters as a sign of eroding power. Still chafing from his defeat at the hands of the CIO and the courts, Hague this time was not about to concede victory to his opponents so easily. He vowed a continuing battle against the railroads—and pledged to spend millions if necessary to force them to pay the other millions that he said were due Hudson County—and he grew more determined than ever that Edison would regret having raised a challenge to his regime.

He decided to make a political move that would let him regain stature if it worked, and would make Edison look small if it failed. He sent his old friend, former Governor Moore, to confront Edison. At the meeting, Edison later recalled, "Moore said that Hague really liked me, and that as vice-chairman of the Democratic National Committee, Hague thought I would be a splendid candidate on the national ticket—and that the White House itself was within my grasp. I was told that I was the only man in the East logically suited for the presidency, and that it was foolhardy for me to wreck the party that would elect me president."

If Edison had accepted the bait, it appears in retrospect, Hague would have eliminated his enemy and would have assured himself of a friend in the White House when Roosevelt stepped down. But an adamant Edison chose to make demands in return for any concessions: Hague would have to resign both as mayor and as vice-chairman of the Democratic organization, and his hand-picked congressional supporter, Mary Norton, also would have to step down. Hague was prepared for the rejection.

"I don't know what pipe the governor is smoking," he told newsmen, "but it is evident that he should change his brand. The best I can do is make him president of a Democratic ward club. Maybe that is the presidency he was offered. At least, that is the only price his peace terms would be worth."

The audacity of the tall Irish battler from the coldwater flats of the Horseshoe won him some applause, and let his supporters know that he would not rest until Edison choked on his own words. With Moore, Artaserse, and O'Mara, Hague told a cheering mob of some 20,000 people at Lincoln High School that he would fight to the finish against Edison and the legislators who allowed "the choo-choo tax steal." He also denounced the legislature for creating four new judicial district courts to supersede local police courts. "What ever happened to Home Rule?" thundered the Mayor. Because the bill creating the new courts did not abolish the municipal courts, Hague ordered local police and sheriffs to ignore them and continue to bring miscreants to the traditional courts they had long used. His idea was to starve the new courts out of existence, to leave the judges appointed by the legislature sitting high on their benches with nothing to do.

The newly appointed judges, however, soon had their hands full dealing with cases brought forward by Hague enemies. Vincent Ferro, an independent political leader, lodged false-arrest charges against Daniel Casey, Hague's public safety commissioner. A group of policemen, said Ferro, arrived at his home around sunrise one morning and carted him off for questioning, contending that he and his family had allowed the notorious "Jeff" Burkitt to use the Ferro address as his own when he registered to vote. Ferro alleged that he was literally kidnapped and held incommunicado. The case went in and out of courts for several years until Ferro—who by then was a soldier stationed on a South Seas island during World War II—signed papers presented by a representative from the Army's Judge Advocate Department which dropped the charges against Casey.

Another case that kept the new courts occupied involved charges of criminal libel brought against several Hague officials by an author, Marcos Spinelli. It grew out of the mayor's ever-present willingness to taint any opponent with the smear of Communism, a smear that Hague once admitted depended on his own definition of a communist. "A communist," he said to an inquiry, "is a man who is subject to Russia, a radical opposed to the American principles and American institutions, whose sole purpose is to overthrow our government, whose sole purpose is against all types of religion, all types of government, except the Soviet government in Russia." Asked if a communist would have to have all these factors present in his makeup, Hague responded quickly: "Well, I wouldn't say that. I would have to just see what his contacts is, and who his associates are, and how he performs. I will judge him as I find him."

"Duh Mare" was quick to judge Marcos Spinelli, but he had a specific purpose in charging the man as an enemy of the United States. It was not the author himself, but his wife who posed a threat to the Hague regime. Grace Billotti Spinelli, a longtime Jersey City resident, agreed to run on an anti-Hague ticket in the commission election of 1941. By doing so, she secured herself a place in the political history of "the Mecca of politics" by becoming the first and only woman ever to run for the mayoral post against Hague.

Her candidacy stemmed from the desire of Republican William E. Sewell, county leader and superintendent of elections, to show his own strength against the Hague machine. He had done well in the hard-fought 1940 campaign, helping Republican incumbent W. Warren Barbour win another term in the U.S. Senate by defeating Democratic nominee James H. R. Cromwell. The victory was a sizable one, in view of the fact that Cromwell was the husband of Doris Duke, the country's richest heiress, and he had been named by President Roosevelt as our ambassador to Canada. (During a pre-election party at Duke Farms, the estate of the heiress's late father just outside Somerville, Frank Hague looked over the magnificent grounds and said to his friend, John Malone: "What a helluva place this would make for a clambake.")

Anxious to put together a strong slate on a fusion ticket, Sewell first chose David A. Nimmo, a Republican lawyer who had served as an associate counsel in the Case probe of Hague's finances and who was active in the American Legion. His next selection was Jacob Raab, a professional engineer and a Republican from Hudson County. Then he added Joseph White, a young attorney in Sewell's law office, and Thomas Herlihy, an employee in the Superintendent of Elections office. Both were Catholics and nominal Democrats. The list totalled four candiates for the five commission slots, and Sewell discussed the fifth opening with a longtime Hague opponent, John R. Longo. Could Longo come up with another possibility, someone who could get votes?

Turning to Longo was a natural move. He was a regular among the group of dissidents and political planners who gathered nightly at Bickford's Cafeteria on Journal Squre to express dismay at Hague's every move. From the 1920s onward, the "cafeteria statesmen," as they were dubbed, huddled over their cups of coffee and discussed ways to wrest the reins of power from those richer, warmer, fatter souls inside City Hall just a few blocks away.

Open around the clock, Bickford's was divided into two areas. There was the cafeteria part, with formica-topped tables and a line of people shuffling their trays along the stainless-steel rails while they strove to stretch their meager handful of change to cover as many dishes as possible. And there was the "Spanish Room" at the rear, where white cloths covered the tables and a waitress took the orders of more extravagant diners.

Where a person sat, of course, indicated his social and financial standing. At the bare tables, lingering over a cup of coffee and a Danish, might be a bookie who had been cleaned out by a long-shot winner, a budding athlete, or a young entertainer still waiting for the break to make him famous. One such performer, who showed up almost nightly in the late 1930s and early 1940s, was a skinny kid from Hoboken, Frank Sinatra. He was befriended by John V. Kenny, a faithful Hague lieutenant and boss of the Second Ward, whose father—Ned Kenny—was the saloonkeeper who had given Frank Hague his start early in the century by asking the young Irishman to run for Constable. Kenny had taken to dropping into the cafeteria to grumble that Hague seemed to be passing over loyal supporters in favor of moving his nephew, Frank Hague Eggers, up the political ladder. Now he began putting his political clout behind the youthful crooner, helping Sinatra obtain night club engagements. It would pay off in later years when Sinatra's mother, Dolly, would show up at vote-raising rallies to boost Kenny's efforts.

During his heyday, "Jeff" Burkitt was a Bickford's regular. Others included Owen McCabe, a policeman and sometimes prizefighter—he fought as "Young Rector, the Fighting Cop" —and police lieutenant Joe Murray. Frank "Elmer" Russello, a handsome and smooth-talking East Coast counterpart of movie star George Raft, and shifty-eyed Joe Sesta, along with Lou Messano (who reminded people of comedian Ed "The Firechief" Wynn) and Joe Soriero, made up the Italian faction, mulling over ways to dethrone Frank Hague. They were joined by a Polish contingent, whose members boasted such names as John Romanowski, Charles S. Witkowski, and the Zelinski brothers—Benny, Teddy, and Charlie—from Gammontown.

And John Longo was there, smarting over the Hague charges that had led to his imprisonment, making himself available to the newspaper reporters who knew they could always get a quote against Hague from somebody at Bickford's. From the *Journal,* George Clark, Eli Ives Collins, and Steve Haff competed with a group from the *Observer*—John Burke, Len Ford, and Howard Lamb—and Leo Hershdorfer of the *Dispatch.*

Longo's willingness to speak out drew the attention of Sewell, and it took only a few moments for the quick-thinking John to propose a candidate for the commission slate. He introduced Sewell to Mrs. Spinelli, who was employed by the YWCA. Attractive and charming, yet with the heart and fire of a crusader, the diminutive lady agreed to be part of the ticket. The newspapers loved the idea. In sizable features in papers both in New Jersey and New York, Grace Spinelli was called "the little woman running for mayor against Hague."

At City Hall, Hague waited until the election neared, and then uncorked his bombshell. Marcos Spinelli, he charged, was a communist who had written a licentious, red-tinged novel, *From Jungle Roots*. The book was ordered taken off the shelves of the Jersey City Public Library (although it is doubtful that any citizen had ever checked it out to read it). The commissioner of public safety, Dan Casey, jumped into the fray to state that he had uncovered a connection between Spinelli and Vito Marcantonio, the New York congressman who had made a career defending communists. The fact that both Mr. and Mrs. Spinelli were friendly with John Longo was also brought out to prove the unworthiness of Hague's opponent.

The charges were enough to upset the ticket's momentum. David Nimmo, who had been Sewell's most attractive candidate, announced that his position as a Legionnaire required him to withdraw from the race until the situation was thoroughly investigated. He conferred with Colonel William H. McKinley, the Jersey City National Committeeman of the American Legion, and eventually decided that the charges were unfounded. He returned to the campaign trail, but the damage had been done. A libel suit filed by Mrs. Spinelli's husband against Hague and Casey (who had said Marcos Spinelli "is one of the leaders of the communist movement in the country") also could not cancel the "smear" in the public mind.

The fusion ticket went down to a humiliating defeat. Hague's slate almost duplicated its incredible success of 1937 by trouncing the opposition, 101,848 to 13,563.

As the familiar party names gathered in City Hall to pump Frank Hague's hand, a testimonial dinner was staged at the Fairmount Hotel to honor Grace Billotti Spinelli. It was organized by J. Owen Grundy, the former editor of the New York City *Villager* and a member of the "cafeteria statesmen," to show the esteem in which the community held the battling young woman. A number of prominent socialites were present—Mrs. Edward A. Jones, Mrs. J. Morgan Hollway, and Mrs. John E. Fairbanks, among them—as were Edith Welty, the independent mayor of Yonkers, N.Y., and New York City councilman Robert K. Straus (whose father headed Macy's Department Store and was Roosevelt's ambassador to France).

Nearly twenty years later, I was to meet Mrs. Spinelli personally. A small, quiet, and sedate lady, she approached me in my capacity as an official at Saint Peter's College with the request that I help her husband find congenial employment. As I searched my files and contacts, I found it difficult to believe that this demure and personable woman could be capable of listening to obscenities, much less use them. Yet Frank Hague had charged that his first female opponent had shouted obscenities and was trying to seize the government!

When it came to crushing an enemy, I realized, chivalry toward a member of the opposite sex was not a part of the character of Frank Hague—despite his public pronouncements about the elevated nature of women. An enemy was just that—an enemy.

And Hague's world recognized only enemies and friends. There were no others.

10

Lesser men—those without the physique of a fine athlete and the mental agility of a modern computer—would have been tired after some 40 years of political warfare. But Frank Hague, now in his mid-60s, let others see no signs of weariness. Oh, he spent more and more time away from City Hall, warming himself in Florida or California or Europe, but those close to him explained his absence as yet one more sign of how tightly he controlled city and state government. Perhaps the impression was calculated for its effect—to indicate his disdain both for Governor Edison's enmity and President Roosevelt's snobbery towards him—but, as I look back at Hague's actions, it is difficult to think other than that he was confident of his own political immortality, and saw no reason to believe that he would be less than triumphant in the long run.

As a youngster just entering the formative teenage years, I was becoming more and more aware of the importance of politics in Jersey City. In 1937, the father of one of my playmates was Joseph Ambrose, a poll watcher for the Hague machine during that year's general election. Ambrose, who had strong control over the fifth district, was challenged by an assemblyman, Sydney Goldberg, who had sponsored several election reform bills. The challenge was met by a typical answer from Ambrose: A single blow to Goldberg's face that sent the assemblyman crashing through the screen door into the gutter outside. Playing with my companion, on Henderson Street and Newark Avenue, I knew my pal's father had shown everyone who was the boss, and Goldberg, picking himself up from the street, knew it too. (Some four decades later, Joe Ambrose, aged but still a fighter, was to be one of my staunchest supporters in my mayoral campaign.)

If my early recollections of the political wars were overly colored by the prevalence of violence, it does not seem unusual. While my schoolmates talked of baseball and championship prizefights, they also told stories—some overheard from parents' conversations, others patched together from confusing newspaper reports—of brutal incidents that seemed part of each election. In the same 1937 voting turnout, for example, a group of some 30 longshoremen wielding baseball bats drove a half-dozen state troopers from a polling place. The police contended they were on hand to guard the safety of some youthful poll watchers whose self-appointed task was to insure an honest count. The workers claimed that the youths themselves were attempting some sort of ballot fraud. On the school playgrounds, groups of excited children took turns acting out the conflict that had taken place, just as we ritualized an attack that sent Republican John Grossi, who later served as a judge in the juvenile and domestic relations courts, to the hospital with a broken nose.

Still, with the formal declaration that the United States was at war in December, 1941, it became evident to young and old alike that the energy required for physical combat would have to be conserved to use against the nation's enemies. The idea of fists-and-ballbats was supplanted by one centered on M-1 rifles, tanks, and warplanes. Also, many of the young toughs who were formerly counted on by the Hague machine to battle any opposition marched off to serve their country in uniform, leaving behind a group of aging ward leaders who were less inclined to wave threatening fists at their rivals.

If Hague noticed that the men around him were growing old, it did not bother him. Why should it, when his wealth and power enabled him to consort amiably with such personalities as William Randolph Hearst, movie star Joan Blondell, athletes Babe Ruth and Jack Dempsey, and political figures Al Smith and Jimmy ''Beau James'' Walker. Deeply loyal to those who had earned his respect by their long labor in his vineyards, Hague felt certain that the men and the few women who worked under his direction were the best to be had anywhere, and that his own ship of state would plow on unchanged by time.

Legal challenges, he knew, would be ably met by John Milton, with an assist from the skilled talents of John J. Quinn and Charles Hershenstein, while Peter P. Artaserse, Edward J. O'Mara, and N. Louis Paladeau were capable enough to handle problems with the legislature. And, always, always ready to put the best face on things from a public relations standpoint was John H. Gavin, an able writer who had joined the City Hall team in 1926. A Jersey City native—a graduate of Saint Peter's Preparatory School and Saint Peter's College—Gavin had joined the flourishing *New York World* as a copy boy at a salary of four dollars a week. Working with some of the country's most talented writers, he had risen to the post of city editor, where he attracted Hague's notice and made the transition to the political arena. His highly literate press releases had much to do with the Mayor's continued eminence, even when Hague rivals were claiming victory.

As the country moved toward a wartime footing, the wily Jersey City ruler realized that it was no longer necessary to grind his rivals into the dust. He still had money and patronage at his disposal. One young challenger's brash approach caught his attention, and gave him an opportunity to demonstrate how securely he kept his opposition to a minimum. The youthful critic was T. James Tumulty, a young man newly licensed to practice law, who showed up at a budget meeting at City Hall. After listening to Hague and the other commissioners routinely assign funds for various projects, the young lawyer began to make derisive remarks and—making a wordplay on the popular Notre Dame backfield—called Hague's acquiescent four commissioners "The Four Horsemen of the Affirmative."

Amused by the interloper's audacity, Hague called out to him, "Young man, just what do you find wrong with my budget?" Tumulty, grinning, replied: "Just one thing, Your Honor. I'm not in it."

Hague laughed and said he would take the matter under advisement. A few months later, Tumulty "picked up the *Jersey Journal* and discovered he had been appointed an assistant corporation counsel.'' The appointment was a complete surprise, more so because a few weeks earlier John Malone, Hague's deputy, had denied Tumulty a job.

"You have to get acquainted," Malone said. "You should hang around a while, join a ward club, get to know people."

Tumulty, who already weighed over 250 pounds and was on his way to better the 300-pound mark, grew red in the face. "Get acquainted?" he shouted. "My family has been here for almost 200 years!" He stomped out of Malone's office, vowing to become a Republican and defeat Hague's machine.

It was not so easy for the Mayor to make peace with everyone who opposed him. In an apartment building known as Hampshire House, on Sip Avenue near Journal Square, a number of ousted politicians joined with some of Jersey City's leading intellectuals to form a new anti-Hague group. Including several members of the Bickford's Cafeteria regulars, the City Affairs Committee grew out of J. Owen Grundy's proposal that some sort of continuing organization be formed to battle the indomitable Hague. The site was the apartment of Judge Ashley B. Carrick, who—although he was legally exempt from the draft by virtue of his judicial position—had resigned his post to enlist in the army as a private. While Carrick packed his bag, Grundy and Dr. Irving Schuman suggested prominent citizens who could serve on the committee.

"I suggested James E. Pepe, a friend of Ashley's father, Judge Charles L. Carrick," Grundy recalls. "Then there was Reverend George G. Hollingshead, the superintendent of Goodwill Industries; Paul E. Doherty, a New York lawyer who lived on Arlington Avenue; my Park Street neighbor, James M. Keeffe; John R. Longo, of course; and Murray Greiman, Irving Eisenberg, Leo Rosenbloom, Emil Perkin, Elias Jacobowitz, and Ray Chasan. Each of us started out the next day to recruit, and in a week's time, we were organized. I brought in Doherty and Keeffe, Dr. Schuman brought in Greiman, Carrick got Pope, and so on." The young group was organized so meticulously that its charges against Hague's County Tax Board were instrumental in Governor Edison's decision to replace the board with one that might treat the railroad interests more favorably.

Spending his days at the track or on the golf links, and with so many bank accounts that his wife Jennie once had to respond to a newspaper ad calling attention to a $300 "dead account" inactive for some 21 years, Frank Hague could easily shrug off the opposition, no matter how effectively it was organized.

He was, it was soon realized, making a mistake.

As Richard J. Connors points out in his carefully researched work, *A Cycle of Power,* the Civic Affairs Committee's ability to survive without a sizable organization or grass-roots appeal posed a threat "not to Hague's hegemony directly, but to the absoluteness of his control." The group, notes Connors, tried to remove some of the atmosphere of fear of—and dependence upon—the Hague organization by local property owners and, by so doing, sought to weaken its hold on the city and county.

There were other threats confronting Hague, and they involved things over which he had little control. Long dependent on his success at turning out large numbers of voters when it counted, the Mayor found himself faced with the fact that Jersey City's population—which had crested at 316,715 in 1930—had declined by nearly 5 percent during the decade. The low birth rates of the Depression years, coupled with restrictive U.S. immigration policies and the flight of wealthier residents to the suburbs, were unsettling the population pattern Hague depended on for support. His traditional support groups, the Irish and the Germans, no longer comprised the largest foreign-stock categories of citizens in Jersey City; the Italians and Slavs had outgrown them, and larger numbers of blacks were moving in.

Longtime loyalties, however, caused the Mayor to continue to dole out positions of prestige (judgeships, U.S. Representative, and others) and patronage jobs to members of the same groups he had worked with over the years. He convinced himself that the Italians, Poles, and others who were passed over in favor of Irish Catholic or Germanic contenders themselves came from groups too factionalized to mount a sustained protest. Unschooled himself, he knew that the city's downtown wards were, as always, largely dominated by the poor, the ill-educated, and the unskilled. The uptown wards, Connors points out, at the beginning of the 1940s had been taken over by people who were only slightly higher, on the average, in social rank. Both groups had proved highly susceptible to the blandishments of machine politics through the past few decades, while Hague's natural enemies—the upper-middle-class white Anglo-Saxon Protestants—had moved outside the city's periphery to wealthier areas. But even with his basic opposition out of the picture, Hague was finding it difficult to placate his remaining constituency.

Under Roosevelt's New Deal, which was designed to pull the nation out of the Great Depression, the Jersey City faithful had prospered mightily. The Federal Emergency Relief Act had enabled the Mayor to dole out some $500,000 each month to hungry families, and by 1939 the Works Progress Administration had poured nearly $50 million into Jersey City and Hudson County. In *An Unsavory Alliance,* Professor Lyle W. Dorsett flatly states that "New Jersey was one of the worst states in the nation when it came to political abuses in FERA and WPA."

But suddenly, the nation was at war, and there were jobs aplenty for the unemployed. FDR, who had needed Hague's help to turn out a favorable vote, seemed solidly entrenched with the populace as the man who had pulled the country out of Hoover's Depression and who would lead the nation to victory over the Axis.

"If Hague wants to go on passing out jobs and Christmas baskets to the poor and needy in exchange for votes," was the word from Washington, "he's going to have to foot the bills himself."

The county payroll, which had grown from 1,981 in 1933 to 2,598 in 1939, levelled off sharply. State patronage was cut off, and the Depression-born programs of aid were curtailed or eliminated entirely. New federal agencies that were created to deal with wartime emergencies were not comparable to those of the 1930s which had provided extensive local patronage while allowing a large measure of local control.

Forced to depend on his city payroll to feed his machine, Hague found it necessary to ladle out jobs and salary increases slowly. The meager growth rate, along with the Mayor's natural inclination to continue to rely on his old guard, did not satisfy the ambitions of younger party members. Soon, Connors reports, several workers were bemoaning the passing of the parades and parties of yester-year, and were complaining that the only festive occasions they had to look forward to were funerals.

Dissension increased as young loyalists noted that (as the 1940s dawned) some precinct leaders had been in office for 20 years, 30 years, or longer. Few neophyte politicians were getting the training they would need to keep the machine functioning, and Hague himself could not move through all the various party circles to seek and select bright newcomers. Those who were brought into the organization were the highly visible individuals—such as T. James Tumulty—who made an impressive appearance at budget meetings or started local political clubs. Hague was always ready, of course, to provide work for relatives of older organization stalwarts. The war had scarcely been on a few months when he began finding jobs for veterans and "war heroes"—not from any sense of responsibility to the men and women who fought to preserve America, but because he realized that the veterans would soon comprise a category of voters, just as the Italians, Germans, and other ethnic groups had to be patronized in order to secure their vote as a bloc.

If anyone had a complaint—and more and more of the party faithful were growing restless—Hague was seldom on hand to listen to it. John Malone, the deputy mayor, sat in City Hall and passed problems to the Mayor by telephone. But Malone, depending on the ward leaders and a network of spies to keep him up to date on what was going on within the party ranks, got very little information about what was going on in the community at large. If the citizens were irate over the fact that no new public schools had been built since 1931; if they were furious over the deteriorating sewer system and the disintegrating, pot-holed streets; if they were frustrated by a series of strikes by garbage collectors, and if they were incensed at the poor service provided by the independent bus companies licensed by City Hall, Mayor Frank Hague was likely to hear little about it while he basked in the Florida sunshine. Perhaps Malone saw no reason to worry him with such matters. But Malone had spies telling him who within the party was jockeying for power and position, who wanted more money or a new title, and who had failed to drum up the right backing for which new proposal. *That* sort of information could be passed on to Hague.

"By the 1940s," John Milton told the inquiring Connors, "Hague felt that he had built up an inexhaustible reservoir of good will (because of past services and favors) that could be tapped at his pleasure. So he didn't work as hard anymore, and this meant that his organization didn't either."

The Mayor, however, was still a force to be reckoned with, even when he was ostensibly taking things easy.

Governor Edison found that out when he decided to follow up his tax board and Judge Colie victories with a sweeping rewrite of the New Jersey constitution. A commission was appointed to draft a model constitution that would break Hague's stranglehold on the state's judicial system, reorganize the executive department, restructure legislative apportionment districts, and provide additional relief for the railroads. Edison could well afford to be independent: Under the law restricting the governor to a single term, he did not have to be concerned about gaining or opposing Hague's 100,000-vote pluralities in the next election, and so thought that he could follow the best course for the citizens of the state.

The challenge was enough to bring Hague rushing from Florida, nostrils flaring and eyes flashing to do battle. He found allies in the state's rural communities, which managed to control the state senate despite the fact that they had only 15 percent of the state's total population. Reapportionment would cause them to lose control. And, warned the *Jersey Journal,* the constitutional commission was in danger of being controlled by two longtime Hague opponents—one was defeated gubernatorial candidate Robert Hendrickson; the other, Arthur Vanderbilt of Essex County, whose name itself signified wealth and power. Such men, said the influential newspaper, would use the commission "for the purpose of revising the constitution to suit themselves and the interests they represent: the railroads and other malefactors of great wealth."

Hague lined up enough support in the legislature to block the proposed referendum, winning his point when he suggested that the attention of the state and the nation should not be focussed on such a picayune matter as a new constitution while the world was at war.

Edison, smarting, wrote a letter to Local Government Commissioner Walter R. Darby in which he said that "Jersey City's finances were in such deplorable shape that a thorough-going reorganization might be the only solution." He next began a legislative campaign that would result in the assembly passing a bill to put the question of constitutional revision on the ballot in the 1943 general election.

The governor hit close to home, as well. James F. Murray, a staunch Hague foe in Hudson County, was appointed to the vacant office of county register and received assurances of Edison's support in an anti-Hague primary movement. He even sought a post for John Longo by naming as county clerk a lieutenant of Hoboken Mayor Bernard N. McFeeley, who supposedly had turned against Hague after years of supporting the Jersey City boss. By promising Edison support in his anti-Hague crusade, McFeeley was successful in getting the county clerk post for his city commissioner, William H. Gilfert.

Edison, thinking that he better have an ally on hand to keep an eye on the turncoat faction, insisted that Gilfert name Longo his deputy. Then, after a suitable period of time, Gilfert could be moved up to a judgeship and Longo would remain as county clerk. The plan proved too complex, and when it became evident to Gilfert that he was not going to be made a judge as quickly as he desired, he showed his anger by firing Longo. Hoboken Mayor McFeeley accused Edison of going back on his word, and with Gilfert at his side he posed with Hague for news photographers at a Jersey City Giants baseball game.

The photograph, inscribed by Hague to the effect that his supporters were "still with me, Charlie," made its way to a fuming Edison.

The governor looked about the state for other influential politicians who might help him break Hague's vise-like grip on the affairs of virtually every county. He found a group of mayors—Donovan of Bayonne, Stilz of West New York, and Thourot of Union City—who were smarting under the cutback of federal job programs. Hesitating and fearful, they promised their support.

And Frank Hague decided to show them once more who ran the show.

Evidently at the Mayor's orders, the Hudson County prosecutor swept through Bayonne with a series of vice raids. The culmination was the indictment of Mayor Donovan by a grand jury. Hague threw his backing to a rival candiate for the mayor's job, Dr. Bert Daly, in the next municipal election and Daly won easily. Not only did the victory infuriate Edison, but Stilz and Thourot saw how their permanency in office rested on allegiance to Frank Hague, and they promptly returned to the fold.

Leo Rosenbloom, the anti-Hague lawyer who had been named to head the Hudson County Board of Taxation (at the urging of the City Affairs Committee), suddenly found himself charged with being a "draft dodger." A subsequent indictment was dismissed, but in the furor Edison had to demand the dismissal of the entire draft board. Such incidents, amusing as they were to Hague and his cronies, proved devastating to Edison's plans to bring about great changes in Hudson County and the state. Normally mild in manner and calm in speech, he used the occasion of his final annual message to the people of New Jersey to attack what he called the undemocratic conditions that existed in Hudson County.

"There is no freedom of speech, religion, or press without fear in the county," Edison told a statewide radio audience. Noting that Hague had publicly advocated "concentration camps for citizens whose political opinions he did not like," the governor explained that he did not want "to destroy Hague and his henchmen as individuals, but the things they stand for, the tyrannies they promote, and the stifling of democracy they foster." In the days remaining to him in office, he stated, "I want to take their hands from the throats of our courts and judges, our prosecutors and our grand juries."

If Frank Hague heard the broadcast—and Frank Hague seldom bothered to listen to the mutterings of *outgoing* political figures—his response probably was a gutteral curse and a question: "What the hell does he think he's been tryin' to do these past years! Let him keep on tryin' for all the good it'll do him!"

Neither was Hague overly concerned when he learned that the Democratic Governor Edison was whispering in the ear of Walter E. Edge, a 75-year-old Republican who had previously served as governor nearly a quarter-century earlier. If Edge, who had almost beaten Calvin Coolidge for the vice-presidential slot in 1920, would promise to continue Edison's programs—said the son of the great inventor—he would get the support that would assure him another term as governor of New Jersey. Hague, who had appointed his nephew, Frank Hague Eggers, as his secretary to learn the City Hall routine and had made the young man a city commissioner in 1942, saw no reason why Governor Edison should not try to designate his own heir-apparent. And if Edison wanted to choose a man once called by U.S. Senator William H. Smathers ''a 75-year-old grouse-shooting, patriarchial, reactionary has-been''—well, that might just make it easier for the Hague machine to take the election.

Actually, as the Mayor was soon to learn, it would not be easy. It would, in fact, not be possible.

A major reason why an elderly Republican who had been away from the political scene for several decades once again moved into the State House was that the country's prosperous wartime economy created little voter dissatisfaction with New Jersey government. How could anyone be upset with the way things were at home, when overseas the tide of battle was just beginning to turn in the Allies' favor . . . when the almost-revered Roosevelt was freezing prices and wages to prevent inflation . . . and when, despite the wartime necessity to sacrifice, prosperity was spreading to larger numbers of Americans than ever before.

In *The Big Change,* Frederick Lewis Allen notes that by 1943, ''the last appreciable unemployment . . . had been soaked up.'' Citing signs of prosperity everywhere, he writes: ''It was hard to get a hotel room in any city. Restaurants in which it had always been easy to find a table for lunch were now crammed. Sales of fur coats and jewelry—many of them for cash across the counter—were jumping. Luxury goods for which there had long been a dwindling market were suddenly in demand; the proprietor of a music store reported that he was selling every grand piano, new or renovated, that he could lay his hands on . . . The government was doing what it could to reduce spending and thus slow down inflation—through price ceilings, rationing of scarce and essential goods, wage freezing, excess-profits taxes, and record high personal income taxes—and with some success. Yet the prosperity was there, paradoxically over-flowing . . . .''

If the money in their pockets was not enough to make people happy, the news from the battlefields seemed encouraging.

Roosevelt and Churchill met at Casablanca to agree on a goal of unconditional surrender by the Axis powers, and then a beaten, freezing Nazi 6th Army surrendered at Stalingrad. The war turned around virtually overnight, and it was only a few weeks later when the remnants of the German forces in Africa tossed in the towel to end the fighting there. In the summer, allied troops landed in Italy after sweeping through Sicily. As the end of the year neared, Churchill, Stalin, and FDR were preparing for a conference in Teheran to plan an invasion that would carry the allies to Berlin.

Without dissatisfaction to cause them to clamor "time for a change," the voters went to the polls and did what their leaders told them to do. Hague's constituency in Hudson County offered up a 100,000-vote Democratic plurality for the Mayor's choice for the governorship: Vincent J. Murphy, former mayor of Newark. Jersey City was carried by Murphy to the tune of 80,000 votes. But, statewide, the voters followed Edison's urging that they cast their ballots for Edge, and the Republican took his seat in Trenton with a 130,000-vote majority and a vow to continue to pursue the programs of his predecessor.

Hague, true to his nature, vowed just as swiftly that he would fight any Edison-inspired ideas to the end. It was a case of two former friends turning against each other, for Hague had been cooperative with Edge when the latter served as governor from 1917 to 1919 and during his term as U.S. Senator in the 1920s. Now, however, Hague realized that if Edge somehow managed to win a new constitution for the state, his power and career would come to a sudden end.

The reason: The proposed constitution would give the legislature power to probe the activities of municipal authorities—and it would be reasonable to assume, from his all-too-evident methods of handling budgets and revenues, that Hague would not be able to withstand an impartial investigation.

Aware that Hague would battle constitutional change with the same fervor he had used to turn aside a legislative probe in 1929, Edge began sniping at Hague's domain in other ways. The Republican-dominated Legislature had refused to go along with a number of appointments proposed by Governor Edison in his last year, looking forward to the time when a Republican could ladle out the jobs. Now Edge found himself with a number of judgeships and other posts to fill. He quickly appointed four new judges for Hudson County, and he secured legislation that authorized the governor to appoint new jury commissioners there.

Hague, who had been called "the Hudson County Hitler" by an enemy or two, must have felt much like the Nazi fuehrer himself as he saw the allied armies moving in from all sides, causing his own realm of power to shrink and dwindle in size. And Edge was not finished. The governor pushed through new legislation mandating the use of voting machines for all elections in Hudson. And he removed from the state tax board all members who seemed to be obstructing the work of the county tax board, which was largely made up of members approved by the Civic Affairs Committee.

Then, as if to prove that Hague's puritanical outlook and claims to morality were only a guise to fool the voters, Edge appointed a new attorney general for the state and instructed him to seek out and prosecute any evil that could be uncovered in Hudson County. Daniel T. O'Regan, the Hudson County prosecutor and a close friend of Frank Hague, was ordered to step aside while Walter D. Van Riper did his job.

What a job! Acting with the relentlessness and perseverance of Inspector Javier in Victor Hugo's *Les Miserables,* Van Riper swooped down in a series of almost daily raids. He claimed to have uncovered gambling in all its nefarious forms—horse parlors, crap games, card parties, and even Bingo games. Most of the Bingo games were fundraising efforts of the Catholic Church, but they were outlawed by Chief Justice Thomas J. Brogan of the state supreme court.

As often happens when the jailed become the jailers, the rights of the defeated were frequently disregarded with the same aplomb they had displayed when they held power. The new jury commissioners appointed by Governor Edge were naturally anti-Hague, and they made certain that citizens associated with the Hague organization were excluded from juries. Not surprisingly, most of their selections could be classified as opponents of the entrenched administration. Whenever the grand jury met, "shock waves" rippled through City Hall and the other seats of Hague's power, recalls John Longo.

Sheriff William J. McGovern, who previously had the authority to select grand jurors, was himself indicted and charged with failure to fingerprint three Jersey City tax office workers who had been indicted for minor infractions related to their public duties. The trio was subsequently exonerated, and the charges against McGovern were dismissed by the court after the powerful First Ward leader appealed his case. He charged that the jury commissioners had conspired to select grand jurors who were inimical to him and his political cause. An example of the type of jury commissioners named by Edge: Mary Doherty, the wife of Hague foe Paul Doherty, who presided over the Hudson County Tax Board.

Van Riper's raiders continued to enmesh Hague supporters in their thrown nets. Investigations in Union City, Hoboken, and Jersey City produced a number of indictments of police officials, including that of Jersey City Police Captain Edward "Monk" Gordon, a staunch Hague supporter. Gordon was subsequently exonerated of the charge that he had failed to close gambling and numbers-betting establishments.

The fact that Van Riper's victims often were cleared did not appease Hague. He set his own investigators to work, and suddenly the newspaper headlines trumpeted the news: "Van Riper Indicted!" A Federal Grand Jury called in the crusading Attorney General of the State of New Jersey and hit him with two indictments; one charging him on seven counts of dealing in a black market in gasoline through a service station that he owned in West Orange, N. J.; the other involving several checks that supposedly had been raised to higher figures before they were presented for payment. During the trial, Van Riper skillfully steered his testimony to blame Frank Hague "for my unhappy situation as a defendant," and he was personally acquitted of the black market charges, although his West Orange company was judged guilty. The official beat the check-kiting charges, too, but the indictments and subsequent publicity destroyed his zest, aggressiveness, and boldness.

Frank Hague smiled as he felt the heat from Van Riper's attacks fade, and he turned his attention to the larger challenge brought on by Governor Edge's call for constitutional change.

Press releases, realized the old campaigner, could not stem the tide. The people would have to see him in person, hear his ungrammatical but fiercely determined speeches, feel the fear that only an impassioned Frank Hague could instill in them. Up and down the state he stomped, shouting at crowds in Morristown. Garfield, Lodi, city after city.

"Home rule will be doomed," he cried. "Home rule will be doomed if the constitutional change referendum of the railroad lobbies is adopted!" he thundered. "These people who want to steal home rule from 531 municipalities are trying to put over this document—while six hundred thousand of our young men and women are out of the state fighting in the armed services!"

It was a tune that he knew would appeal to rich and poor alike: Loss of local control over the individual's destiny, coupled with a ringing call for patriotism and fair play. How could anyone vote to make any change while the nation's finest young people were occupied with more serious matters—such as merely staying alive.

When Governor Edge responded by ordering Van Riper to provide New Jersey residents in the armed forces with a booklet on the issue, so that they could cast absentee ballots, Hague charged that the booklet was slanted in favor of the proposal. Adoption of the measure, shouted the Mayor, would turn Van Riper into a "czar!" But, lest anyone think that he was against progress, Hague let it be known that he supported a constitutional convention where delegates "representing every shade of thought" could be elected by the people.

His strident cries for fair play and a democratic approach were echoed by the Catholic Church and other groups, and when a referendum on the proposal was held in November 1944, Hague was triumphant. The constitutional change commission was defeated by 150,000 votes—of which Hudson County provided 80,000, and Jersey City, 50,000. Chortling, clapping Malone and his other cronies on the back, Hague appreciatively read the "tributes" tossed his way by his defeated enemies:

"The final gasp of Boss Hague in an effort to perpetuate his corrupt Jersey City dynasty." That was from Governor Edge.

"A bully, a dictator, and a coward." From former Governor Edison.

"Opposition marshalled under the whip of Mayor Hague, whose personal interests in defeating revision must be obvious to all." From Arthur Vanderbilt, representing the railroad interests.

Not one to remain silent, a smiling Hague gleefully gave a statement to the reporters who thronged around him and asked him to reply to an Edison charge that "bosses, urban and rural, are happiest in the dark."

The former governor, said Hague, "vents his spleen by calling this large majority of citizens who supported my position 'a corrupt gang.' The corrupt ones meet with him in the halls of the State House—and are the railroad interests."

But he was not finished. "I doubt, however, that anyone is interested in Edison's views. He's the most thoroughly discredited politician in modern state history. As a leader, his following consists of his butler Milligan." Then, referring to a minor scandal that Hague's followers had exposed—in which it was learned that Edison had served gourmet foods, billed to the taxpayers, at the Little White House at Sea Girt—Hague added: "I hear that Edison is even suspicious of Milligan, who has become temperamental since he can no longer serve truffles, caviar, paté de fois gras, steel-headed salmon and assorted liquor at the state's expense, and billed to the taxpayers under such names as hams and oranges."

The smile of victory was still on his face when the Court of Errors and Appeals, New Jersey's highest court, gave Hague reason to broaden his grin. It decreed that the railroad compromise legislation adopted in 1941 and 1942 was unconstitutional. The railroads were to pay up more than $28.5 million in back taxes and nearly $21 million of the sum was to go to Jersey City!

"We won, Johnny! We won!" a jubilant Hague shouted to John Milton. Rushing to his office came his nephew, Eggers, the legal wizards Hershenstein and Artaserse and O'Mara, ward leader Kenny, and dozens of others, all crowding in for a manic display of congratulatory back-slapping. And over the din and laughter, Hague's stentorian voice could be heard, shouting again and again, "We won! We won!"

Edge, Edison, and the railroad interests, however, were to prove every bit as tenacious as the Mayor; as he did, they had the financial resources to carry on the battle. They let Hague know that they would be back—to propose new constitutional change legislation, and to carry the railroads' case further in the judicial system.

"Let 'em," Hague muttered. "Let 'em do what they want. What the hell do I care!" And he used the traditional New Year's Day celebration at City Hall to announce that he would run with his own slate of candidates in the May 8 Jersey City Commission Election. Congresswoman Mary T. Norton made her way through the baskets of flowers and embraced "duh Mare" while alert newsmen noticed that she had been given advance notice of Hague's intentions: On her bosom was a shiny new campaign button endorsing the Hague team.

And when the Mayor rose to announce that the men who had served with him during his seventh term as mayor and his eighth on the commission would be with him as he tried for an eighth and ninth respectively, applause and cheers rang out from all sides. Leading the enthusiastic endorsement was a delegation from the Congress of Industrial Organizations, the same CIO that had tangled bitterly with Hague just a few years previously.

The campaign would turn out to be one of the most difficult in the Mayor's long career—he would emerge victorious, of course—because the world around him was changing swiftly and drastically.

In increasing numbers, the veterans of World War II were returning home as the war entered its final phase. Roosevelt, Stalin and Churchill met early in the year to plan the defeat of Germany at their famed Yalta conference; later the bodies of Italian dictator Benito Mussolini and his mistress were displayed hanging upside down at Italy's Lake Como; and Hitler's suicide in a Berlin bunker was announced. To the young men who had been distracted from the influence of the political machine by the immediacy of the war, there were more important things to be done at home than plunge into the world of politics. There were jobs to be found, homes to be made, old friendships to be renewed.

There was something else, too. Says author Connors: "In their service-connected travels, many Jersey Cityites learned that boss rule was considered outdated and disreputable by their fellow Americans. The city and the regime which they had been taught to regard with pride were scorned and ridiculed, largely because of national publicity emanating from the CIO affair, in which the Mayor had shown his antagonism towards such basic liberties as freedom of speech and freedom of assembly. In the long run the advantages to the Hague regime of the CIO fight were dubious. When those in the armed services learned that 'civil liberty' was not an ugly phrase, that freedom of speech was not a cloak to hide communist subversion, they began to question the whole moral posture of Frank Hague.''

Writing in the *Jersey Journal,* a columnist said: ''. . . veterans of World War II who had been needled by their buddies about Hagueville and Haguetown . . . . Jersey City veterans . . . had seen their city held up to ridicule. 'Why are we fighting a war for freedom here,' they had asked themselves, 'when we live under a dictatorship in our home town?' ''

Realizing that the time was fast becoming ripe to unseat Hague, Governor Edge urged the legislature to pass a bill that would distribute the interest monies owed by the railroads to all the state's municipalities rather than to only those in which they owned property. Then he began to search for a group of commission candidates that might give the Hague machine a run for its money. He found the nucleus of the team through an editorial by J. Albert Dear, Jr., the editor and half-owner of the *Jersey Journal.* Paul Doherty, a staunch foe of Hague, would ''provide a refreshing change in the present City Commission lineup,'' said the newspaper.

Doherty, president of the anti-Hague Hudson County Tax Board, needed little other encouragement. He quickly organized a slate under the banner, ''The Liberty Ticket.'' His fellow candidates were Joseph J. Loori, a fellow member of the tax board; Michael Fiore, a schoolteacher; Joshua Ringle, known as ''Mr. Republican'' in Jersey City, and Arthur J. Wilson, a flamboyant chiropodist who could not help but create attention everywhere he went. Tall, lanky, and constantly wearing a grin on his face beneath a broad-brimmed Western hat that he donned to camouflage his partly bald pate, ''Doc'' Wilson looked as if he belonged on the vaudeville stage. A ladies' man, Wilson brought to the ticket an easy-going air of informality that, it was thought, would balance the seriousness of the other commission candidates.

Unfortunately, the doctor's flamboyance proved too much for Leo Rosenbloom, the campaign manager. Rosenbloom's basic approach was to conduct a high-level challenge, documenting the evils of the Hague regime and explaining with facts and figures how a new group of commissioners could set things right. In contrast, "Doc" Wilson showed up at meetings to hold aloft a huge horsewhip and demand that it be used on Hague and his fellow campaigners. "Horsewhip them!" he would shout. "Hague knows no other language." In a short time, the other four commission candidates had disavowed Wilson's tactics. There was no need to go so far as waving a horsewhip and calling for physical abuse, noted schoolteacher Fiore—not when it was so easy to point out to the voters the utter worthlessness of Frank Hague. And Fiore did just that in a speech reported in the *Jersey Journal*:

"You good people, who only read about Frank Hague in the newspapers, should know him better . . . I'll help you, by painting a word picture of Mr. Hague's activities all the year around. When I'm through, you'll wonder whether Frank Hague is mayor of Jersey City or ambassador *from* Jersey City . . .

"It's New Year's Day. Mr. Hague is at City Hall for his reception with the jobholders, sinecurists and other miscellaneous pad-boys, who each year are ordered down to the hall to pay their respects. That's not all they pay to the Hague machine . . . Incidentally, you'll notice that though this is a legal holiday, Hague is hard at work. That's the funny part about Hague: He works on a legal holiday, when everyone else is off, and he vacations the rest of the year when everybody else works.

"As soon as his New Year's reception ends, Hague grabs the first Pullman out of Jersey City and heads for Miami Beach. He dosen't mind garbage in Jersey City streets as long as he has the moon over Miami. He loves Miami Beach because that's where the temperatures are high and taxes are low. Of course, taxes in Jersey City don't worry our mayor, because he doesn't pay a single penny of taxes in Jersey City. He knows better. After all, isn't Jersey City the highest taxed city in the United States?

"About April 15, Hague comes back for a visit. Why April 15? Mr. Hague has to return to sell 60,000 tickets for the Jersey City baseball Giants, even though the ball park only seats 24,000. Every year our mayor parades across Roosevelt Stadium and then throws out the first ball. Of course, he doesn't pay for the ads telling people to come see him and support the team. No, sir, Jersey City pays the bill for that. Oh, well. The game's over and Hague leaves for his summer home in Deal.

"Hague enjoys the sunshine until about mid-September. Then he's off to Mount Clemens, Michigan, for the baths. He enjoys the waters for about six weeks and gets back to Jersey City just in time for the November election. You know, Hague is always around at election time to tell the people what a great guy he is and how he loves them and what he's going to do for them, and what he did for them, and how he loves the babies, and how nasty the railroad lobby is, and how lucky the people are that he's mayor of Jersey City. As soon as the November election is over, our millionaire mayor shoots back to Miami Beach and waits for the New Year and his next reception at City Hall."

With anger creeping into his voice now, Fiore continued: "Meanwhile, the poor people, the little people back in Jersey City are stuck with high taxes, smelly garbage, millions of rats, firetrap schools, broken streets, open and unsanitary sewers, no bus shelters, sinecurists, padded payrolls, insufficient parks and playgrounds, and ghost-town slums. These people pay taxes in Jersey City, so they can't afford Miami Beach. Hague gives them absentee government in return. Absentee government? That's Hague's system of keeping the boys in line by long distance telephone. It's just another reason why Hague's fame has become Jersey City's shame. This kind of absenteeism by Hague is sabotage, no different from the sabotage of a war worker who stays away from his war plant!"

Long used to shrugging off such attacks, Frank Hague yawned and occupied himself with a few speeches in which he contended that Doherty, Rosenbloom, and the others opposing him were mere tools of former Governor Edison. The commissioners on the Hudson County Tax Board, he said, had given the railroads some $30 million worth of reduced assessments and had forced him to eliminate a large tax cut planned for the people of Jersey City.

Several major world events were to play a part in his election victory. Less than a month before election day, President Roosevelt died, and the populace was too caught up in mourning and in the assumption of the presidency by Harry S. Truman to pay much heed to speeches of Doherty and his fellow campaigners. Joyous fervor began to grip the country as the allied armies closed in on Berlin. Only a week before the voters were to turn out, the German capital fell, and on May 7, the Nazis signed unconditional surrender terms at Rheims. As a result, election day coincided with Victory-in-Europe Day, and the voters woke to full-page ads in local papers (paid for, of course, by the taxpayers) showing a huge portrait of Frank Hague and his fellow commissioners. "We thank Thee, our Heavenly Father . . ." the headline on the ad said.

With such fortuitous timing, Hague and the others had no need to ponder ways to rig the voting machines that were used for the first time in every city district. Doherty's fusion slate managed to double the vote that the previous (1941) ticket had achieved, but Hague and his fellows swept to victory with a plurality of 50,000 votes.

On New Year's Day, a beaming Hague looked through the crowd of well-wishers to see a tall man in a broad-brimmed hat pushing forward to reach him. It was "Doc" Wilson and in his hand was a horsewhip.

"When people recognized me," said Wilson (who would become one of my biggest supporters in 1977), "they began to pull themselves away from being too close to me. It was like I had leprosy. But when they saw me present Hague with my horsewhip to use on Rosenbloom and his interests, and when they saw Hague thank me, they all started to cheer and shake my hand."

Laughing above the thundering laughter all around him, Frank Hague may have realized on that day in January 1946 that he had won his last election.

But I doubt it.

11

Good God! The man was nearly 70 years old! Would he never quit, never retire, never die?

The thoughts of Hague's enemies and rivals could almost be heard echoing through the corridors of the State House, in the restaurants and streetcorners outside City Hall, all over the wards of Jersey City, across the entire state.

"Retire? Quit? Die? Why the hell should I?" Frank Hague might have replied. "Things are just goin' fine for me."

Things were not going fine, however, for the opposition. Governor Edge, forced to retire from office because of the state's one-term limit for governors, met with former Governor Edison to settle on a possible successor to carry on the battle. Their choice was Alfred E. Driscoll, a Republican who promised to fight for tax relief for the railroads and a new constitution for New Jersey.

Everyone knew that the constitution was the key to ridding the state of Hague. Some of the mayor's bitterest enemies recalled that Postmaster General James Farley once had wanted to jail Hague on mail-tampering charges, but that he had been dissuaded from the idea by President Roosevelt. Now, the revered FDR was dead, and although Hague's support had been instrumental in helping Harry S. Truman attain the vice-presidency in 1945, the new President would not go out of his way to help the Jersey City boss. If a constitutional convention could open the way for a legislative look into Hague's finances, a jail term might solve the problem of getting him out of office for once and all.

But Driscoll would not continue his predecessor's attacks on Hague that called for vice and gambling raids and the appointment of hostile judges. It had to be obvious to "duh Mare," Driscoll reasoned, that constitutional change was going to come about eventually. He decided to give the aging warrior a chance to avoid ignominious defeat. "You've said, Frank, that you would be for a convention with delegates chosen by the people to represent every shade of thought," the Republican governor told the Democratic mayor. "Well, how about coming up with some names of people to consider as delegates."

While Hague stalled for time, refusing to pick up the olive branch, he had occasion to ponder that Jersey City residents in larger numbers were grumbling about the many problems they faced. He had promised—in a speech prepared for him to read shortly after the voters returned his commission slate to office—that things soon would be different:

"We are evolving an intelligent and well-balanced program for the postwar period that will eventually mean a newer, greater, and better Jersey City. . . . The forward-looking program, which will get underway as soon as hostilities terminate, provides for new schools and the reconstruction of others, the erection of a 14-story hospital school addition to the Medical Center, several new incinerators for garbage disposal and the elimination of unsightly garbage depositories, new parks and playgrounds, recreation centers . . . modernized and motorized street-cleaning apparatus [much of Michael Scatuorchio's garbage-handling system still depended on outmoded horse-drawn carts], modern sewer cleaning machines, miles of new streets. . . . "

It was not easy for Hague to make such promises, to outline such specific remedies for the city's ills. For decades, he had been able to stay in office by simply promising "good government" and by detailing the evils of Communism, the railroad barons, and other "un-American" influences. Now, he sensed a change in the air. It had been forcefully driven home to him when his own candidate for the gubernatorial position, Jersey City native Lewis G. Hansen, pulled only half of Hague's predicted 125,000 majority vote in Hudson County in the battle with Driscoll. In the contest, Driscoll racked up the second highest winning margin recorded in New Jersey until that time.

But the idea of spending millions of dollars to improve Jersey City—that was anathema to Hague! There was some money in the coffers, to be sure: The individual tax rate was being pushed higher by postwar salary increases and the need to maintain his beloved Medical Center at any cost. But at the same time, the new Hudson County and state tax boards were reducing assessments on corporate taxpayers.

Slowly, but inexorably, the Mayor began to feel a chill that the bright Florida sunshine could not erase from his bones. In early 1946, his long-time ally, Thomas Brogan, resigned as justice of the supreme court on the circuit in Hudson County. The circuit came under Chief Justice Clarence Case, who had led the investigations into Hague's affairs when he was a Republican state senator in 1928. The City Affairs Committee, less strident than before, continued to snipe at "duh Mare" in budget hearings. And Governor Driscoll's soft line toward his fiefdom actually weakened Hague's rule by removing his favorite appeal to Jersey City voters: Republicans in the State House were out to *destroy* Jersey City, and only he, Frank Hague, the savior of Hudson County, could stop them!

Not one to leave memoirs behind, or to explain his actions while he undertook them, the Mayor offered no explanation for his sudden and surprising announcement on June 4, 1947, that he intended to retire in mid-term.

"I'll step down on June 17," he said, "my thirty-fourth anniversary on the Jersey City Municipal Commission. And my vacated office will be assumed by my fellow commissioner, Frank Hague Eggers."

The simple announcement undoubtedly was preceded by a lengthy and stormy meeting between Hague, his nephew Eggers, John "Needle Nose" Malone, and various legal advisers led by corporation counsel Charles Rooney. Astute political observers turned up plenty of reasons for the changing of the guard. Foremost was the fact that the constitutional convention, scheduled to begin meeting in late

June, might prove successful in its deliberations—with a new constitution soon giving the legislature the power to probe into the financial deals of local officials. By taking himself out of the picture, Hague made it less likely that he would be questioned . . . indicted . . . *jailed*.

Despite his frequent absences from City Hall, Hague had seen what could happen to the boss who stayed on the scene a day too long. Mayor Bernard McFeeley of Hoboken had followed the Hague tradition, doling out patronage to his Irish compatriots and his relatives and employing political shakedowns to line his own pockets. When a group of angry policemen kicked off a drive in 1946 to put city employees under civil service, the groundwork was laid for a slate of candidates to dethrone McFeeley and his relatives. A string of indictments followed. Hague, who had lost control of the Civil Service Commission in Hudson County, saw the handwriting on the wall.

"Goddammit, Johnny," he is thought to have said to Deputy Mayor Malone, "don't you understand? *I'll* still be running things, but that nephew of mine will be out there taking the heat. If there's a problem, you phone me—catch me at the Hialeah track if you have to—and I'll make the calls that settle things. Why in hell should I hang around here until somebody wants to make headlines by demanding an investigation?"

Malone probably nodded. "But what if our new little mayor tries to run things on his own, Frank? What if he changes who *gets* what, who *does* what?"

A broad grin must have swept over Hague's face. "Johnny, Johnny, don't you think I thought of that? Look, suppose I named somebody else mayor in my place—maybe Johnny Kenny, over there in the Second Ward, or Bill McGovern in the First? Or anybody else. They're young guys, tough guys, still wet behind the ears, and they might want their *own* say-so on things, right? Ah, but little Frank Hague Eggers—he's my flesh and blood, and he knows he better do what Uncle Frank says and wants. Or Uncle Frank might just change his will."

Now Malone was the one to grin. "And that will's got plenty in it to pass out! Frank, you think of everything."

Hague leaned back in his large leather chair. "Right," he snapped. "Now let's think how we're gonna have a retirement party like this city ain't never seen!"

The setting for the spectacular farewell was Dickinson High School, perched at the edge of the Palisades to overlook downtown Jersey City and the Hudson River. In the auditorium where a fiery Hague had often spoken to throngs of cheering admirers, a capacity crowd saw him stand tall and erect at 72, surrounded by floral tributes, his fellow commissioners, and dignitaries from the local, state, and national political scene. One after another, a string of speakers trumpeted Hague's praises into the microphones. As an example of the kind of thing that was said about "duh Mare," this seems as good a place as any to reprint the words of Dr. Thomas White, a noted heart specialist who was recruited to work at the Medical Center and served there for a number of years both before and after Hague's death.

For Frank Hague *did* die. Before he had figured he would, of course—it is reported that his last words, spoken to John Malone and John Milton at his bedside in his posh New York City apartment, were: "I never thought you two bastards would outlive Frank Hague." His death, however, was nearly a decade away on that night at Dickinson High School when speaker after speaker recalled Hague's lengthy political history.

Let Dr. White's words—as they appeared in a medical publication—provide an idea of the kind of thing that was heard that evening by the party faithful:

> In 1913 he became a City Commissioner and in 1917, at the age of 41 years, he became Mayor . . . . In 1922, he decided to put into effect his long-dreamed plans concerning health care . . . . He began . . . to seek an outstanding hospital administrator. After two years of persuasion, in 1924 he induced Dr. George V. O'Hanlon to . . . head the yet-to-be Jersey City Medical Center . . . . Next to arrive was Miss Jesse Murdoch, R. N., Director of Nurses . . . .
>
> It is an indication of Frank Hague's vision and drive that he succeeded in having two such outstanding persons relinquish their

high positions in New York City on his promise to build a Medical Center in Jersey City which they could run with a free hand . . . . In their later years, they reaffirmed that Mayor Hague had fulfilled his promise to them.

The good doctor had some observations to make in regard to one of the criticisms that had been levelled at Hague during the later years of his career:

Under his direction, 50 years ago, youngsters were no longer booked at police stations for petty crimes. They were evaluated by physicians, psychiatrists, and educators at the Medical Center and their family background studied. Constructive decisions were made, and Mayor Hague sometimes sat in on these evaluations. In one instance where an overgrown boy, in a low grade for his age, had become a chronic truant, he suggested that the youngster be taken from school and given a job. He was told that the law required that the lad remain at school until the age 16 years. Hague indicated his disagreement with this legal technicality. Out of a reference to his remarks during that episode came the widely published, distorted and wholly out-of-context statement, ''I am the law.''

Tribute? Could there be words more apt to provoke applause and cheers and roaring ovation than such as these:

Frank Hague was a professional politician of times now past. Entirely through his own resources, he was a state and national leader in the Democratic Party for many years . . He used these same qualities to build a unique institution and he anticipated the present-day concept of governmental concern for people's health by fifty years or more. . . . He was a one-man organization both in politics and in his supervision of the Jersey City Medical Center. He was a loner, the boss, the top man. There was no second in command. There is no one . . . on a Federal, state, or local level with the stature of Frank Hague.

Imagine—just imagine—that if such fulsome praise were lavished on Frank Hague by a fellow human being some 15 years after his death, what were the words heard on that farewell appearance in the heart of Jersey City that hot June night?

A newsman got what he thought were Hague's final words insofar as his political career was affected. In answer to a question, Hague explained what his immediate plans were: "Get plenty of rest. Go to bed early nights and duck newspapermen."

He had, of course, no such intentions. Deputy Mayor John Malone and Corporation Counsel Charles Rooney, along with the rest of the City Hall central staff, stayed in place to guide—or control—new Mayor Eggers. Hague, as usual, made the required phone calls from Florida or his New York City apartment, and would show up in Jersey City whenever he felt like it. One occasion, for example, was at the swearing-in ceremony of new police and firemen a few months after he had passed the symbolic gavel of power to his shorter, heavy-set nephew. Hague used the appearance to make a fatherly speech to the young officers, lecturing them on their duties and responsibilities to the citizenry. A few short months later, Hague hit the headlines with a vitriolic blast at Paul Doherty and Leo Rosenbloom, blaming the tax board members for reducing the city's assessed valuations on railroad property, with a resultant pressure on the "little guy" to pay heavier taxes.

Rosenbloom said that Hague "must have obtained most of his facts and figures from the *Daily Racing Form*," and had the satisfaction of seeing his statement run in the papers next to a wirephoto of Hague, tanned and immaculately dressed as always, in a box at a Florida racetrack.

While he placed his bets at the windows of distant racetracks, "duh Mare"—he would retain the appellation throughout his life—began to hear rumors of troubles within his political family back home. To fill the vacant commission spot that resulted when he moved Eggers into the mayor's office, he had appointed Ninth Ward leader and former city clerk Phil McGovern as a commissioner. And to the vacant city clerk slot went Francis X. Burke, a WWII veteran and winner of the Congressional Medal of Honor. The appointment of the army veteran showed the growing numbers of returning servicemen that city jobs were open to them, and Eggers boosted the city payroll 15 percent. Hague, who held onto his titles as head of the county and state Democratic organizations, found an equal number of county jobs for the men and women who wore the "ruptured duck" pin.

But Italian and Polish leaders protested the appointment of McGovern—an Irishman again! And why recognize the veterans' vote by naming *another* Irishman?

The two factions looked about for a knowledgeable, popular leader who could spearhead a drive against Hague and Eggers in the 1949 election. They found one almost immediately.

His name was John V. Kenny, and he would take his place in the political history of Jersey City, New Jersey, and the United States as the man whose election truly marked the defeat of the Hague machine.

Kenny, who had served as leader of the Second Ward for roughly 35 years, was a small man who could not see eye-to-eye with Frank Hague unless he stepped up on a stool. But he was a big man to his supporters. He had built up a loyal following in his ward by such acts as paying daily visits to the sick at Saint Francis Hospital and serving as a pillar of Saint Michael's Church. If a favor was forthcoming to a party member, "Johnny" was the man to see about getting it done.

Loyal to Frank Hague as long as he was in office, Kenny grew angry when the blatant nepotism that moved Eggers into the mayor's office was displayed. He made no secret of the fact that he thought that he should have been allowed to take over the job of party leader. Next, he backed a dissident faction in the longshoremen's union that was challenging the longtime Irish leadership there.

Word came north from Frank Hague: "Kenny's out." As the official reason for deposing the popular ward leader, the Democratic party heads noted that Kenny's son-in-law, a deputy warden at the county penitentiary, had turned in his boss for possible prosecution on delinquency-of-duties charges. The warden, of course, was a Democrat; and Hague could not tolerate one member of his family acting against another.

If John V. Kenny had followed the traditional path of those men and women who had annoyed Frank Hague, he would have dropped from sight; after all, none of the party faithful would associate with him any longer, lest they too feel the wrath of the boss. But Kenny had made long-lasting friendships, and he continued to show up at political dinners, wakes, and other gatherings where he could gauge whether or not an anti-Hague feeling was in the air. He sensed the unrest among the Italians, the Poles, the veterans, and other groups. Slowly, he began to gather names of supporters who might help mount an assault on the Hague stronghold.

The names included a smattering of Irish—Larry Kelly, Barney Doyle, Jack Deegan, Jimmy and George Creegan, and John J. Kenny (no relation)—but unfamiliar names and nationalities appeared, too. Joe Michalski, Mike Grabowski, Angelo Bevaqua, Frank Esposito. Several leading black figures nodded to Kenny: Dr. Marcus Carpenter, attorney Louis Saunders, and police officer Felix Isom. And such black women as Lucille Wallace and Dr. Marie Carpenter.

The small group of insurrectionists bided their time as the Democratic party pulled together to help Harry Truman win New Jersey and defeat Thomas Dewey in the 1948 presidential election. But then it decided to emerge from the shadows and challenge Hague directly, in the 1949 commission election. Hague, of course, had already told the voters he wanted them to reelect the current Jersey City commission: Mayor Eggers, his nephew; two Irish ward leaders, John Prout and Philip McGovern; Daniel Casey, another Irishman who was commissioner of public safety, the job that Hague had held so long ago; and Arthur Potterton, a Protestant, who helped balance the slate.

Feeling that the time was ripe for a frontal attack, Kenny's forces borrowed their theme from the idea of the Freedom Train, a traveling exhibition of important documents from America's history. The "Freedom Ticket" took its campaign song from a popular wartime recording, "Now Is the Hour," and the lyric was changed from "Now is the hour when we must say goodbye" to "Now is the hour when Haguey has to go."

Each passing day brought new recruits. William Flanagan, a young WWII vet who wrote a political column called "Voice in the Crowd" for the *Jersey Journal*, accepted a $15 weekly raise from

Kenny and his backers and turned the column into a paid political ad, "Choice of the Crowd." Edward Stevenson, known as "The Silver Fox" and newly elected as county Republican chairman, came aboard after Kenny agreed to try to swing Democratic votes to Alfred Driscoll, the Republican gubernatorial candidate in the November election. When he was assured that Kenny's ticket would be a fusion one, Jacob Levey, the diminutive Republican city chairman, also climbed aboard the onrushing Freedom Train.

Aware that Hague's control over the unions depended on keeping the leaders happy, Kenny went after the younger workers who were hungry for better jobs and more freedom. A number of youthful workers—Pat Mullane, Joe Connelly, George Kane, and Steve Wilson—promised support and began talking up Kenny's chances to others around them. Harold Krieger, a young labor lawyer, worked to convince state and labor leaders that Kenny could take Jersey City.

The growing list of Kenny supporters began to worry some members of the Hague camp. Secretary John Saturniewicz, for one, tried to talk Hague into balancing his ticket with more non-Irish candidates. "Saturday-Night" made it known that he himself would be available, and so would the respected Peter Artaserse. But Hague protested that old-time loyalties prevented him from making changes.

Kenny, however, had an open mind. Louis Messano, a former assistant prosecutor under Hague's administration, joined the Freedom Ticket. So did ex-football player Charles S. Witkowski, a local football coach. Insurance executive Donald Spence, the son of a famous Jersey City physician and a Williams College classmate of gubernatorial candidate Driscoll, clambered aboard to strengthen the idea of a true fusion ticket. Then, with the addition of James F. Murray, Sr., who had fought Hague for 20 years while Kenny had basked in Hague's largesse, the ticket was completed.

It would be Kenny, Spence, Witkowski, Messano, and Murray. Now all it had to do was win.

Small in stature, Johnny Kenny outlined his platform in high-pitched tones and staccato cadence at a rally at Public School No. 11. His commissioners, he promised, would do more for Jersey City schools, taxation, veterans' housing, transportation, industry, civil liberties, planning, labor, police and fire departments, and the abolition of political tributes. As candidate after candidate and supporter after supporter strode to the platform, each with two fingers raised in the "V for Victory" salute popularized by Winston Churchill in World War II, the cheers became deafening.

The Republicans had toyed with the idea of mounting an all-GOP slate against Hague's, but Truman's resounding victory convinced them to accept the idea of a fusion ticket. Nevertheless, old Hague foe John Longo decided to enter his own slate of candidates in the war on Hagueism.

Suddenly besieged from several sides—with dissension splitting their own ranks—the Hague forces sought to strike back early. Mayor Eggers demanded a probe into the fact that greater numbers of citizens seemed to be registering than ever before, causing a Kenny spokesman to compare the request to "Al Capone yelling for a cop." The Hague team next tried to make capital of the fact that Longo twice had been jailed on fraudulent voting charges. Longo, fearful that Kenny's team would simply repeat many of the abuses that the Hague administration had foisted off on Jersey City residents for three decades, distributed miniature brooms as he promised to "sweep out the old regime" and "clean house."

As time passed, however, Longo's supporters began to drift toward the stronger, better-financed Kenny camp. John Brandle, the son of labor leader Teddy Brandle whom Hague had destroyed years before, made the jump. So did Frank "Elmer" Russello, Longo's First Ward leader; he ended up on the Kenny payroll.

To liven up the contest, a local lawyer named Nicholas D. Introcaso, Jr., entered as "The Yankee Doodle Candidate." Dressed in an Uncle Sam costume and riding in a cart pulled by a donkey, he entered as an independent, got his laughs, and then threw his support to Kenny. A patrolman, James Higgins, who served as president of the Policeman's Benevolent Association, abandoned his plans to try for the commission and also backed Kenny.

Things were beginning to look grim for the Hague slate. Mayor Eggers, aware that something drastic was needed to counteract the

"Kenny in '49" buttons appearing everywhere, sent out a cry for help. Hurrying north came the boss, the king, the big man—Frank Hague. And with him, his old pal, A. Harry Moore, the former governor.

The setting was the Hotel Plaza, and Hague wasted no time making his feelings known. Kenny was characterized as "this despicable person and betrayer, who owes everything he has to the Democratic party." To prove disloyalty, the Mayor put on display letters Kenny had written in which he said he would consider himself a traitor should he ever run against Hague.

A Kenny rally a few days later brought a rebuttal from Witkowski, who said that since Mayor Eggers had served in the Coast Guard during the war, he was only a "synthetic veteran." Francis X. Burke, one of Jersey City's two Medal of Honor winners, had similar barbs tossed his way.

Much more tangible were missiles thrown at Hague when he spoke at an outdoor rally in the Horseshoe shortly afterwards. From somewhere in the crowd came a barrage of eggs, and a furious Hague—pointing wildly into the throng—yelled, "Get that sonuvabitch!"

No one moved, perhaps because the culprits could not be identified, perhaps because there were too many of them, perhaps because the police officers ringing the platform themselves were uncertain how much authority Hague still retained. Knowing, however, that only a few years before, his shout would have been enough to send his cops wading into the crowd with billy clubs whirling through the air, Frank Hague sagged visibly on the platform. Something new, something serious, was happening in Jersey City.

Hague found little solace the next day when his nephew announced that an investigation had shown that the egg-throwers were not loyal residents of the Horseshoe: "They came from Hoboken."

A similar reception, but larger and better organized, met a small band of Hague supporters who marched through the Gammontown section carrying red flares. They held them far in front of their bodies, possibly to avoid the heat of the flames but more likely to avoid being recognized. Their attitude was one of resignation rather than affirmation. Barney Doyle called the marchers "the bunion gang" and said their parade resembled a funeral march more than a rally.

Both factions scheduled closing rallies on the Sunday before the election.

To some 12,000 voters jammed into Dickinson High School, Hague shouted that "never in the history of any other city in the country have a group of men so demonstrated their anxiety to take over a city by gang rule." Charging that the Kenny campaign was financed by gambling interests, the old warrior said he could not believe "the people are going to turn over their city institutions and government to Kenny and his ticket." As his ward leaders led the applause behind him, he noted that former Governor Walter Edge, who had opposed him at times over the years, had recently written a book praising Hague's administrative ability. One by one, he put the spotlight on the notables sharing the platform with him: former Governor A. Harry Moore, Congresswoman Mary T. Norton, Assemblyman Peter P. Artaserse, State Senator Edward J. O'Mara, and numerous others.

And he concluded by noting that when he and former Governor Moore were first elected to the initial city commission under the Walsh Act, "we adopted a motto of 'good government.' And we have lived up to that motto."

The cheers were deafening.

Some two miles away, a crowd of 3,000 had gathered at Lincoln High School to listen to John Kenny. They heard how a Hague support group had tried to split the ticket by mailing thousands of postcards urging voters to vote for Kenny, but not for his running mates. "That wasn't my work," said Kenny. "We're like the musketeers—one for all and all for one."

He accused Hague, too, of having dredged up the fact that roughly 50 Kenny men who planned to act as challengers at the polls had criminal records—although they had long paid their debt to society and were "going straight." The egg-throwing incident in the Horseshoe, he charged, was staged by Hague to make it appear that the Kenny forces were hoodlums. James Murray, his face reddened with anger, backed up his leader and contended that Hague's slate "is so desperate they'd have their pictures taken with Al

Capone if they thought it would help in the campaign.'' The experienced campaigner and fiery stump orator brought the audience to its feet cheering time and again.

Kenny, as a longtime insider, had no trouble documenting the evils he had witnessed within the Hague regime, while Murray's own dossier on the machine's corruption was complete with names, dates, and places. And if the public grew too bored with details and facts, the Freedom Ticket provided plenty of amusement, too. As the crowd flowed out of the high school onto Crescent Avenue, it faced two live goats, one bearing a blanket labelled ''Hague's goat,'' the other was emblazoned ''Egger's goat.'' Members of Kenny's forces took turns shouting, ''We're going to get both their goats,'' while others directed people's attention to a jackass with a blanket showing a cartoon of the ''Royal Family''—Hague in a king's crown passing the sceptre to his nephew, Eggers, dressed as a court jester.

Hague's crowds were larger, the names of the platform speakers better known—but it was no use. His lengthy absences had made him almost a stranger in his old stamping grounds. Kenny dared to fly airplanes with banners touting his candidacy over the opening day baseball game of the Jersey City Giants. The Freedom Ticket charged that Hague, expressing puritanism in all things, was allowing selected gangsters and bookies to operate freely in Jersey City—and the charges hurt ''duh Mare'' and his successor, Eggers.

Importantly, the familiar Hague police tactics that helped him stay in power when voters went to the polls were greatly weakened by tightening of the state's Corrupt Practices Acts in 1948. And large groups of policemen, finally fed up with forced donations to feed the machine, decided to keep an eye on the voting machines.

Urged on by ''Now Is the Hour'' blaring from soundtrucks parked just far enough away from the polling places to be legal, the voters turned out. And by ten o'clock on that evening of May 10, 1949, it was all over.

At the Kenny clubhouse on Pavonia Avenue in the heart of the Horseshoe came the word: ''Eggers concedes victory to the Freedom Ticket.'' The announcement set off the scene of pandemonium referred to many pages earlier in this account. Borne into City Hall on the shoulders of his admirers past a symbolic coffin with a sign reading, ''Here lies the remains of the Hague machine, 36 years of age,'' John V. Kenny made his victory statement:

''This has been the hour. Tonight Jersey City's people have had their government restored to them after 36 years of one-man domination. My colleagues, at this hour of triumph, can never forget the citizens who rallied to our side and our gratitude to them can only be expressed in our determination to bring decent, orderly, efficient government to the people of this city.

''To our friends and supporters, my colleagues and I pledge our every effort to restore Jersey City to its rightful place in the economic, moral, and social life of New Jersey.''

Then, with his fellow commissioners flashing ''V for Victory'' signs all around him: ''Let us walk forward now as free men and women. May our waking moments be now devoted to the welfare and prosperity of this city that all of us love.

''Let us bid farewell to fear. Let us say goodbye to corruption.''

Standing in the awed throng, I tried to realize what Kenny's words meant. It seemed incomprehensible to my youthful mind that Frank Hague, the all-powerful politician whose name and methods had been part of the lives of everyone I knew in Jersey City for as long as I could remember—incomprehensible that he was no longer in a position of power. I could not grasp it, not from mere words.

A few months later, however, the meaning hit home in a graphic way. For some reason—I don't recall the exact circumstances—I was engaged in a conversation with an elder member of the congregation at Saint Peter's Church. His name was Joseph McDermott, a pillar of the church and a once-powerful political patron in the Hague machine. He had been a prominent aide for years to ''Honest John'' Coppinger, leader of the Fourth Ward. A meticulous dresser, conservative in the Hague style, ''Mr. McDermott'' (as we called him at all times) had long carried himself with the prideful air of a wealthy political figure.

But now Eggers was out and Hague's leadership, although still influential in county and state Democratic machinery, was waning rapidly. Mr. McDermott was sitting in a chair by his election district on Montgomery Street just opposite City Hall when an elderly woman approached him.

"Hello, Mrs. Foley," he said as he recognized the woman as someone he had helped with political favors in the past. The woman, wearing torn stockings that drooped over her ankle-high oxfords, stared at the politician.

"You dirty bastard," she screamed. "Drop dead." And she spit in his face.

Mr. McDermott, perhaps crying inwardly, pretended to take no notice of the insult. As the woman moved on, he calmly dabbed at the spittle with his handkerchief and resumed the conversation with me.

In a flash, I understood the "before and after" effects of politics.

12

In his effort to win, John V. Kenny had made a lot of promises—
"Promising Johnny" he would come to be known—to a lot of people, to numerous ethnic groups, to women, labor, and (if Hague's
and Eggers' allegations were to be believed) known criminals and
other unsavory characters.

His immediate problem was to try to make all of his supporters
happy.

To clear the route for jobs for his backers, he dismissed 350
employees—causing Eggers and other ousted commissioners
to accuse him of backing down on a pledge of "no retalia-
tion" against workers who were in favor with the previous
administration.

Short of city funds, "the Little Guy" forced through a slight increase in the city tax rates, angering citizens who recalled that lower
taxes had been part of his platform. And, still short of funds, he
worked against raises for police and firemen although he had pledged
to support them.

Obviously, running Jersey City wasn't as simple as Kenny had
thought. He announced early on, shortly after trying out the huge
chair in the mayor's office, that he planned to "turn the impossible
job over to someone else" after a short time. But turning the job over
and having it *taken away* were two quite different things, and Kenny
discovered quickly that Frank Hague and his nephew had already begun maneuvering to regain power.

Hague, still controlling county jobs, found places for his fellow ex-commissioners and gave a $500 bonus to all county employees. Patronage coming into New Jersey from the Truman administration still flowed through Hague, and the Democratic leader seemed in a good position to help elect a Democratic governor to unseat Republican incumbent Alfred E. Driscoll (allowed by the new constitution to succeed himself). Hague decided to put the weight of the County Courthouse and State Capitol behind State Senator Elmer Wene, with Wene promising in return to appoint a new Hudson County prosecutor, election board, jury commissioner, and others if he won the election.

The move put Kenny on the spot. As a Democrat, he did not want to seem to be approving Hague's choice, but could he back the Republican Driscoll and alienate his fellow Democrats? He announced, "I'm still a Democrat. I'll back Wene." But he let people know that there was no lingering friendship between Hague and himself by summarily firing Medal of Honor winner Francis X. Burke from the city clerk's job. He replaced the war hero with a lawyer and close friend, James A. Tumulty (not to be confused with the ponderous and witty T. James Tumulty), who proved to be a man with total disregard for the rights of Jersey City citizens. When he later was given the post of Hudson County prosecutor, he showed an almost insatiable desire to get personal revenge on his enemies and went about the business of probing the evils of the Hague regime with unparalleled determination.

Asked how he could simply discharge Burke, a man who had received his nation's highest honor, Kenny shrugged. "I think we'll let Francis X. fight his case in court."

Rumors persistently surfaced about Kenny's lack of enthusiasm for Wene as the gubernatorial hopeful, and grew stronger when candidate Driscoll promised that if elected, he would name Kenny Democratic leader of the state. No one questioned how a Republican governor could appoint a Democratic party leader, but the promise was enough to cause Kenny to back off from overtly supporting Wene's hopes. He endeavored to take a stance on both sides of the fence by holding a rally for Wene at Public School 11—but the assignment of stirring up the crowd went to T. James Tumulty, who had willingly jumped from Hague's side of the fence after Kenny's slate was elected.

The huge speaker was introduced to a crowd that greeted him with a chorus of catcalls and booing, for during the mayoralty campaign he had once expressed his faith in the Hague team by publicly blowing his nose in a Freedom Ticket flag. Holding up a cautioning hand, Tumulty shouted, "You're right. I deserve to be booed. But let's get it over with. All together now, give me one big enormous boo. Ready? One, two, three . . . "

A gigantic onslaught of booing and laughter washed over the 350-pound politician. It was followed by an enormous cheer. Tumulty, it was obvious, knew how to handle the public.

While Kenny, it became obvious, knew how to handle his difficult balancing act. On election eve, he told the regular Second Ward Democratic Club, "We are 100 percent behind State Senator Elmer H. Wene for governor, and for every other Democrat from top to bottom. Leopards don't change their spots. I'm a Democrat; therefore, I'm for a Democrat."

But such platitudinous statements did not make up for previous weeks of inaction, or for the fact that Kenny had left the job of pushing Wene to the 74-year-old Hague, whose fading leadership was virtually enough to insure a Driscoll victory.

When the votes were counted, the incumbent Republican governor took Jersey City by a margin of 18,000 and carried the state by a scant 80,546. It was enough.

Said Driscoll: "The returns in Hudson County bring to a conclusion an era in the history of the Democratic party. The books of the Hague machine are closed once and for all."

The defeated candidate's supporters were irate. "Kenny knifed Wene," charged former Mayor Eggers, and Wene's campaign manager, Jim Bishop—who would go on to national fame as a syndicated newspaper columnist and author of numerous best-sellers—sent Kenny a symbolic gift: a knife smeared with a reddish substance.

Said an unabashed Kenny as soon as the news of Driscoll's victory reached him: "I'm going home to bed." His face displayed no emotion.

Already stunned by the fact that not one of nine freeholders placed into power by Hague had cast a negative vote against Kenny's payroll slashes—and these were men who owed their summer homes and their children's fine schools to the former mayor—Hague was further shocked by the news that a Republican had carried Jersey City. He announced in a few carefully chosen words on the morning after the election that he was stepping down as party leader for the state and county. The mayor of Union City, Harry Thourot, was furious at his abdication. He called in the other Democratic leaders of Hudson County but the group ended a meeting with the news that John V. Kenny now headed the party.

Left absolutely out in the cold was Hague's longtime buddy, John Malone. Kenny turned loose an investigator to probe the city's finances under Hague over the previous three decades, and the inquiry produced thousands of signatures testifying to the ongoing practice of "rice pudding day" or 3 percent kickbacks. Indicted on charges of corruption, "Needle Nose" pleaded illness and poverty, and then pleaded guilty. He received a suspended sentence.

But Frank Hague remained untouched, living high and handsome.

Those close to Kenny were impressed with the way he had handled the precarious situation of seeming to back Wene and supporting Driscoll at the same time. "It wasn't that Kenny showed overt support for Driscoll," his public relations man, William Flanagan, told me a few years ago. "It was just the way that Johnny *said* he was for Wene," he explained.

Although the new mayor of Jersey City proved adept at walking a tightrope, he increasingly found it difficult to juggle his numerous friendships and obligations. Commissioner Witkowski, for example, initially given power over the police, placed Detective Joseph "Buddy" Brooks in charge of the department's gambling squad. Brooks became an overnight sensation by raiding previously sacrosanct gambling dens.

Rumor had it that Kenny had made promises to certain gambling interests and was unhappy with the raids. Shortly afterwards, Witkowski was stripped of his supervision of the police and put in charge of the city streetlights. Similarly, after Commissioner Murray, in charge of parks and public property, declared his independence of the administration, Kenny applied the screws: Murray was given a new jurisdiction; he was put in charge of the Jersey City bathhouse.

Such open dissension was certain to cause trouble within Kenny's upper, lower, and middle echelons. Unknown informers began feeding investigators data that tied the mayor to such gangsters as Abner ''Longie'' Zwillman and Anthony ''Tony Bender'' Strollo. Rumors? Innuendo? Perhaps—but Kenny would be sentenced two decades later to jail amidst charges by U.S. Attorney Frederick Lacey that corruption under his regime in Hudson County paralleled that under the Tweed Ring in New York at its worst.

Small wonder that several groups were collecting petitions to have the mayor recalled by the time he prepared for the Freedom Ticket's 1950 primary campaign.

If ever a ''free for all'' took place, the battle could be classified as one. Kenny went along with the regular organization candidates, but brought in two new names: Joe Connolly, a freeholder, and Alfred D. Sieminski to replace Mary T. Norton as the congressional candidate from the 13th District. When Congressman Edward J. Hart managed to convince the elderly Mary Norton not to seek reelection to congress and fade into obscurity with Hague, he was again nominated for his congressional seat from the 14th District. Meanwhile, ten Democrats began to vie for the Norton seat.

Despite a straw poll by the ever-present John R. Longo that showed a close race between Commissioner Murray's son and Sieminski, the latter came out on top by a two-to-one margin. Hart, for his efforts, chalked up a three-to-one win, and several other Kenny choices emerged on top in their races. The victory was nothing like the overpowering sweeps that Hague and his machine had put together so frequently, but it was good enough.

How long it would be good enough was problematic. In Washington, D.C., Senator Estes Kefauver's investigations into political crime were making headlines and causing nervous citizens to point fingers at suspected wrongdoers everywhere. Looking around him at the winners and losers in the 1950 primary, John Longo made a statement that should last through the ages: ''Politics is selfishly dirty and infested with phonies.''

"I can go out on the streets," said James I. McIntyre, a leader of one of the groups seeking to recall Kenny, "and pick any five men to run the city better than this commission." The investigative pressures began to mount. And some Kenny supporters began to jump ship.

James J. Creegan, credited as the founder of the Freedom Ticket movement, said he had worked for twenty years to get Kenny into office—and Hague out—but that conditions in subsequent months were so deplorable that he was compelled to quit in order to maintain his own dignity. "John Kenny has proved himself a total failure, incapable as a party leader," he said. "But he is expert in undermining and tearing down." Creegan formed a new independent political club, while another new Democratic group began backing Joe Madden, a powerful labor leader.

Oh, some business got conducted in the meeting rooms at City Hall. Responding to pleas by veterans returned from the wars, the city regulations that Hague had imposed to forbid dancing in restaurants were rescinded. The first black, Dr. Marie Carpenter, was named to the board of education. Even sound trucks with their blaring speakers were banned from city streets.

But the spirit of Frank Hague hung over everything that took place in Jersey City. The wily "Mare" had trained those who worked under him well, by merely setting the example, and it was obvious that the citizenry was in for more of the same form of "good government" they had long enjoyed. Clearly, those who had been "out" for so long now felt that their "in" position entitled them to the same sort of benefits others had gotten before them. Kenny's payroll began to grow, like Pinocchio's nose, longer and longer. And its growth was just as mysterious.

Take the case of Thomas Lolly, for example, hired as a public relations liaison between City Hall and the press corps. Given to spending his working hours mingling with the newspaper reporters at the Hotel Plaza bar during the day and joining the political night owls at Bickford's Cafeteria, he was carried on the city payroll as a "swimming instructor." Twice a month he was instructed to go to a public school in the Lafayette section of town to pick up his paycheck, but after losing his way several times, he arranged to have his checks mailed to him.

His name joined the "honor roll" of colorful Jersey City political figures when he was called to testify during a state-ordered investigation of Kenny expenditures. After admitting that he did not teach swimming, the Irishman was asked by a smirking investigator: "Isn't it true that you don't teach swimming because there's no pool in the school you're assigned to?"

"That's a damn lie! There's a pool in that school," Lolly exploded.

"Then why don't you teach swimming there?"

Rising indignantly from his chair, Lolly shouted in exasperation: "How the hell can I? There's no water in the pool."

When the hearing room quieted down, the city employee admitted that the "swimming instructor" title had been given him merely because the personnel clerk who filled out his employment card once had seen him splashing in the ocean at a Jersey beach. His real labors, he said, involved doing promotional work for the school system and he had spent an entire year working on a booklet extolling the merits of elementary education in Jersey City schools. Asked for a copy of the booklet, he confessed that it was never published.

"Could you show us your manuscript?" asked the prober.

"I don't have it. After I worked a whole year on it, I showed it to my boss—and he didn't like it." Lolly's voice took on a note of despondency. "He didn't like it, so I burned the goddamned thing." Shaking his head sadly, he left the stand—and walked into Jersey City folklore.

If such stories warmed the heart of Frank Hague more than the Florida sunshine, they did not do as much for the editorial writers at the *Jersey Journal*. The newspaper began urging a new form of municipal charter that would weaken Kenny's grip on city government. Nearly 3,000 supporters jammed the Hotel Plaza ballroom to cheer former mayor Eggers when he showed up to announce that he favored the proposed change, and a roar of approval met representatives from the Republican party who also spoke in favor of it.

Kenny, borrowing a trick from Hague's stable, used his majority on the city commission to put through a resolution calling for a *complete* study of a charter change. It required the voters to first choose a five-member commission to conduct the study in the November election—thus delaying any action for months—and then allowed the study group some nine months to complete its work. Thus, Kenny effectively bought himself two years of time. The opposition challenged his move in court to no avail.

There was much that the mayor could do in two years. Although he was bothered by phlebitis and an attack of pneumonia, causing him to set up a private political office at Pollack Hospital where he was accessible only to a chosen few, Kenny seldom failed to attend a wake for departed friends. With a pint-sized companion, Louis Pandolphi, whose proximity made Kenny himself appear taller, he showed up at numerous funeral homes to pay his respects. (After Kenny's death, "Little Louie" continued to sign his friend's initials, JVK, in the register books of deceased acquaintances of Kenny's who were on view for the last time.)

Of course, when business demanded that he be on hand, Kenny took time off from the racetrack or his vacation retreat.

He was, for example—and according to a statement by Eggers—in the right place at the right time to receive a contribution of $100,000 from notorious gangster "Longie" Zwillman, the last of the Newark "beer barons" fraternity from the Prohibition era. Zwillman made the payoff, Eggers charged, because he was a partner in a firm given a piece of a $77 million sewer contract by the city—an award that was made after only one bid was received. and that bid was $3 million higher than the estimate of the cost by city engineers. Underworld czar Gerald Catena, said Eggers, also was part of the contract.

Kenny also found time—according to the testimony of his First Ward women's leader, Mary Berkheimer—to collect $40,000 from gambling interests in Bergen County and distribute it to voters one election day. He also found opportunity after opportunity to provide "no show" jobs for anyone who was owed a favor or who promised loyalty. Charged by labor leader Joe Madden with being anti-union—"Kenny is a millionaire ward leader, the only one in the country, who never employed union labor in his railroad car cleaning contract with the Pennsylvania Railroad"—the mayor sometimes went out of his way to quiet the opposition. As an investigative probe would later reveal, two workers—Richard Dunn and Peter A.

McEnea—were provided with "soft jobs" in an apparent attempt to mollify the ironworkers' union. As a team, the men were to inspect various pieces of ironwork on school buildings. Although they were paid to look at fire escapes, hand rails, fences, and grille work, they furnished no reports, written or oral, of any needed repairs or modifications.

The probe, begun just as Kenny's term as mayor was ending, was prompted by a petition action of some 49 taxpayers. Acting on the petition, Judge Hayden Proctor named Samuel Larner, a Newark lawyer, to look into Jersey City expenditures, and Larner called on two other attorneys and a team of accountants to aid him. The proceedings were not to be adversarial, but the Kenny faction called on rotund, glib T. James Tumulty to serve as Special Attorney for Jersey City. He was to act as a sort of defense counsel. When Larner appointed lawyer Joseph Nolan of Newark as probe counsel, the stage was set for a repeat of the Case-McAllister investigation and the others that had preceded it.

Far from the heat, Frank Hague might have let a grin spread from ear to ear as he followed the revelations in the newspapers.

Joseph Brady, acting Third Ward leader, admitted to the investigators that he had taken law courses at night for two years while he was paid by the city Recreation Department for ostensibly working during the same hours. Did his superior know that he was going to school while he was supposed to be working? "He must have known," was the reply, "because his son Bernard Harnett, Jr., was a classmate of mine."

Another witness, Mrs. Eleanor Viola, women's leader of freeholder Joe Soriero's Seventh Ward, testified that she was assigned to Columbia Park to carry out her duties for the Recreation Department. Those duties? "I walked around and saw that none of the children were hurt, and I spoke to the children." She had no supervisor, she stated, and reported to no one. "I was on an honorary basis," she said, explaining that it was entirely her own decision to report—or not report—for work at the small neighborhood park each day.

"The leader of the Democratic party gave me my job," proudly stated another "outdoor baby sitter," Mrs. Josephine Monahan, who was 86 and a bit hard of hearing.

"Is that Mr. Kenny?" she was asked. "John V. Kenny?"

"Yes, he called me up on the telephone."

"Had you any experience in recreation work?"

"No." But then, she explained, the job did not really call for much training. Or much effort. She only showed up for it—although she drew her salary regularly—when her supervisor sent her a postcard, perhaps five or six times a month.

The supervisor whose duty it was to oversee the efforts of Mrs. Viola and Mrs. Monahan, along with dozens of other city employees, was the incomparable Barney Doyle, who once was described by the *Jersey Journal* as "sometime pro boxer, truck driver, salesman, bartender, photographer, ward leader, and Young Democrats chieftain." At the time, "The Barn" was getting $5,200 a year as "manager of special activities" and supervisor of recreation for the city's housing projects.

Back from military service after graduating from Saint Peter's College, and working toward a degree in educational psychology at Fordham, I had gotten to know Barney Doyle through my growing interest in Democratic party activities in my neighborhood. His cockiness, his unshakeable nerve, and his ability to uncover humor in the most dire situations never failed to impress those who got close to him. In the Larner probe, while others replied to questions with nervousness and trepidation, Barney piped out his answers with an aplomb worthy of movie star Jimmy Cagney's portrayals of tough guys of the 1930s.

Asked who appointed him to the various city jobs he had held at different times, Barney declined to name any individuals. "Some citizens," he answered. "Or maybe it was someone interested in my behalf, or mutual friends."

"Political friends?" asked Larner.

"Civic-minded friends," Doyle corrected him.

Asked another counsel: "Is this the only city job you have now?"

"I didn't know you could have *two*," Barney replied quickly with a gleam of interest in his eye to draw a laugh from the spectators.

Describing his work for the recreation department before he got the title of manager, he explained that at one city section, "I walked

up and down, sat down once in a while—in and out of buildings—
and supervised the children playing around the area." He started
games, he added in response to a question, "if there were enough
kids around." When a prober bore in, trying to get Barney to come
up with the names of some of the children he supervised, the best
Doyle could offer was: "There were a lot of little Johnnys and little
Mickeys and so on."

Larner observed that Doyle seemed to have a bad memory, opening the way for another laugh.

"Mr. Larner, sometimes I have trouble remembering what I had
for breakfast."

And when Barney defended some of his absences from work on
the ground that he had been in and out of the hospital with various
ailments, he noted that he was due for another operation shortly. He
wasn't able to be specific, however, about the illness the operation
might correct—"It's not Larner-itis, I know," he said—and he
could not provide the name of his doctor, either. "I haven't
consulted him yet."

The evident enthusiasm of the spectators for the beloved Doyle
caused the probers to turn to witnesses who might be a bit more serious in their responses. Norbert Rekuc was asked to explain how he
managed to hold down three—not two—jobs at the same time, working a full day in private industry for the Crucible Steel Co. in
Harrison, N.J., and also serving days as a bus inspector for Hudson
County and nights as a member of the Jersey City Recreation Department. Carolyn Reidy, Twelfth Ward leader, picked up a bimonthly
check from the Board of Education although she did no work for
more than four years. There was no point, she said, in showing up at
an office if there was no work for her to do.

As often happens when the investigators swing their nets into the
political waters of Jersey City and Hudson County, some surprising
fish turned up along with the ones expected to be snared.

George Langrehr had been one of the 49 taxpayers who had peti-
tioned some time earlier for a probe that eventually became the
Larner inquiry. Anti-Kenny at the time, he subsequently had been
given a job in the Recreation Department. Now he found himself
quizzed as to what were his duties after he was assigned to an empty

lot on a streetcorner. "Watching bocci games and preventing arguments" was the best he could offer.

The *Jersey Journal* discovered again—as it had found during the Case probe in 1929—that one of its reporters was also on the city payroll as a "public relations" worker. The miscreant was Thomas Lolly, whose father, as Hudson County Treasurer, had given John V. Kenny his first political post as his secretary. Suspended by the paper after telling the investigators, "what I did was nothing you can put your hands on," Lolly noted that his paid publicity work had not required him to be "any particular place at any particular time."

As witness after witness appeared for questioning, it became obvious that virtually every employee of the city's Recreation Department was someone who served as a Democratic committeeman (or woman) or a pollwatcher on election day. It was quickly evident why the department's payroll came to a staggering $600,000 a year. Because the evidence was so overwhelming, the job of T. James Tumulty became that of the court jester who attempts to inject a measure of amusement into the day's happenings in order to draw the attention of onlookers away from the matter's seriousness.

Faced with a witness named Feury, for example, who became confused as he tried to explain why city hospital costs were written off as losses even though many patients were able to pay, Tumulty interrupted Larner's questions. "For Christ's sake, judge, no wonder he can't speak," he said, pointing to Feury. "You have him in a fury."

In another instance, another witness, Deputy Mayor William Flanagan, defended the hospital's practice of "killing" a bill if the patient was a faithful party member or was someone who was otherwise owed a favor by the Kenny administration. Shouldn't everyone be required to pay his or her medical bills? asked Larner. "Well, in this case, where the patient died," replied the witness, "since the work at the hospital ended in failure, the wife wasn't sure if she had to pay."

Tumulty clambered to his feet as quickly as he was able, to help explain things: "Like the famous animal trainer, Frank Buck, the woman believed in 'bringin' 'em back alive!' "

The jests of T. James momentarily proved to be distractions, but the probe ended with a handful of indictments. Barney Doyle and Lou Lepis, chief of the Recreation Department, along with a few others were scheduled to undergo trial. Virtually all of the charged individuals were cleared long before a jury had a chance to decide their fate. Doyle, Lepis, and other Recreation Department personnel saw the trial judge dismiss the prosecution's charges for lack of sufficient evidence. One or two minor figures who pleaded guilty were given suspended sentences.

Along with others who knew Barney Doyle, I cheered the outcome of the case, just as I cheered when he later encountered one of the defense attorneys who was a recent appointee to the Jersey City municipal bench, "Bobby" Wall, in Bruno's, a popular restaurant on Fairmount Avenue. Perhaps because they looked at the world from different perspectives—Wall from the judicial bench, Barney from the streets and tenements—the two men never got along with each other, and friends made sure they kept well apart. For, like Doyle, Wall was known to be physically tough. (Once, perhaps after having had a few too many beers, Judge Wall had distinguished himself by hitting an irascible defendant on the head with his gavel.)

Meeting in Bruno's, the two confronted each other at the crowded bar and began trading abuse. Wall grew angrier as the flippant Doyle tossed barbs his way. Finally, declaring that he'd "had enough out of you," the legal expert whipped off his eyeglasses and passed them to a friend to hold. What Wall failed to realize was that he was practically blind without the glasses—and when he snapped out his fist, it landed on the jaw of an absolute stranger having a casual drink. The man dropped to the floor as Wall turned, recovered his glasses, and strode out the door without a backward glance. As he left, he passed Doyle's brother, who was just entering the restaurant.

"Pick up your brother," Wall said, "I just flattened him."

His brother hurried to the bar to see Barney doubled over with laughter, while several hangers-on helped the bewildered and bruised stranger to his feet.

The rumors of blatant favoritism and worse that would precipitate the Larner probe troubled Mayor Kenny's administration more with each passing week—and humorous incidents such as Wall's "kayo" of Barney Doyle did not serve to distract the attention of opponents and critics. The *Jersey Journal* contended that the docks of Jersey City had come under the control of gangsters, and in 1951 a new Democratic group calling itself Regular Democrats for Clean Government began to mount an anti-Kenny campaign. It was easy for Kenny, however, to point out that the RDCG roster included ex-mayor Eggers and some other former Hague supporters. Crying "Hagueism" at the top of his voice, he hoped to convince the voters that the seemingly immortal Frank Hague was still trying to regain control of Hudson County.

It was time, he realized, to sever all ties with anyone left on the payroll from the Hague days. He would put up a slate of new names, new faces, in the April 1951 primary. Out went such erstwhile Hague stalwarts as Peter P. Artaserse, Mrs. Eugenia Urbanski-Courtney, and several others—who promptly began fighting for their political lives on an RDCG ticket headed by labor leader Joseph Madden for sheriff. "Beat Kenny, Smash Gangster Racketeers" was the group's slogan. The new organization got added support from James J. Braddock, the popular former heavyweight champion, and from the two Freedom Ticket commissioners whom Kenny had downgraded: Witkowski and Murray. "The issue," said Murray in his endorsement, "is misrule, incompetence, and bossism." And Eggers denounced a recent crime spree of "two bombings, stabbings, racketeering, shootings, and wide open gambling in our city."

Kenny fought fire with fire. Under Hague, he said, racketeers had been protected, horse rooms had been allowed to operate in the old Chamber of Commerce Building, and a lottery had been held in the Second Ward. The ex-mayor had even allowed a brewery to operate in Greenville during Prohibition, Kenny told a huge rally in Bergen Square. Although Charles Witkowski tried to tell the citizenry that Frank Hague was no longer a threat, the voters turned back the RDCG candidates by a scant 14,000 votes out of some 165,000 cast in Hudson County. And the question of charter change, three out of five voters agreed, was to be placed on the ballot at a special election.

The Kenny victory did not cheer the mayor to a great degree. His health was not good—the phlebitis had left him somewhat lame—and growing intimations of criminal investigations were surfacing to plague him. But, despite a waning personal popularity, Kenny was still the Freedom Movement's strongest candidate and virtually was forced to announce that he would seek reelection with his fellow commissioners Messano and Spence. The death of James Murray solved the problem of having that longtime foe of Hague (and now Kenny) on the ticket; the spot that might have gone to him was filled by a newcomer, Bernard J. Berry. To provide the semblance of ethnic balance, the recalcitrant Witkowski was replaced with another new name, Matty Czacharowski.

Putting together a rival slate, ex-mayor Eggers turned to three dyed-in-the-wool Hagueites: Thomas Gangemi, Ezra Nolan, and Eugenia Urbanski-Courtney. To ward off the charges of "Hagueism" that were certain to be levelled at the ticket, he added Republican Joshua Ringle, who long had opposed Hague and all that he stood for. In the light of the eventual voter turnout, Eggers might have done better if he had tapped Kenny-foe Witkowski for the fifth slot, but Gangemi reportedly did not want to run with the ex-football hero. Gangemi was close to First Ward leader Bill McGovern, whose philosophy was that a commission slate should be comprised of people whose loyalties are not divided. (Eggers thought that Ringle, the man who had lost more elections than anyone else in Jersey City history—going back to 1929—would be so grateful for yet another chance that he could be easily controlled.)

Witkowski decided to run for a spot on the commission by himself. "I stand alone," he declared in a rain-soaked rally in Journal Square, and he proceeded to make no bones about the close links he observed between John V. Kenny and the underworld. Joe Madden, the popular labor leader who had run so well in the 1951 primary, grew angry with Eggers for not including Witkowski on the ticket, and let it be known that he himself would have been available to help defeat Kenny. Madden contended that Frank Hague was still calling the political shots in Jersey City, and charged that it was the aged politico's decision to keep both Madden and Witkowski out of the picture.

As the campaign began in earnest, the Zelinski brothers of Gammontown—only two of the three were alive at this point—decided to support the Eggers ticket, but their support seemed somewhat half-hearted.

When Kenny called for the city's employees to turn out for a parade on his slate's behalf, the RDCG took the opportunity to point out the payroll padding that had become so obvious. The organization's chairman manned a huge spotlight at McGinley Square, and as the line of marchers went by, the blinding light was focussed on the faces of numerous individuals. Over a loudspeaker, the chairman's voice boomed out to identify each person.

"There's Mae Reilley," he shouted through the electronic amplification. "That's right, Mae. Go ahead and smile. We'd be smiling, too, if *we* were on the pad at $10,000 a year."

Or, "There goes 'Sis' Gifford. Sure, she's waving. She has to be part of this 'bunion parade' to keep that fat county check coming."

A groan or chorus of booing greeted each revelation.

Kenny realized that his ticket needed a more exciting and positive come-on for the voters. Rallies and parades were not enough—not in a period when the new wonder of television was keeping people at home to watch the antics of Milton Berle, Jackie Gleason, and Sid Caesar. It fell to the redoubtable Barney Doyle to devise an idea to lure the citizens away from that magic box and its flickering black-and-white pictures.

Doyle proposed a gigantic Bingo game. Gambling, of course, was strictly against the law in Jersey City, but there was plenty of flexibility if players were offered a chance to vie for prizes of merchandise—such as TV sets, used pianos, cooking utensils—without any charge at all. Admission, it was advertised, would be absolutely free, on a first-come, first-served basis. More than 2,000 people showed up at the Jersey City Gardens, with hundreds waiting in line to get their Bingo cards and try for the prizes. Calling out the winning numbers was none other than the man responsible for the largesse: John V. Kenny. He concluded the evening with a brief speech urging everyone to vote "line B—that's B, like in Bingo" for his ticket.

Watching the progress of the various campaign efforts with great interest, I had asked Barney Doyle who would get the female vote in Jersey City. Would lingering memories of the free turkeys and other "gifts" of the Hague years cause the women to choose the Eggers slate? Barney smiled as he looked at me. "Just wait, Smitty," he said. "You will see where the girls are when we run the Bingo."

As the campaigns wound up, with election day looming just ahead, it was felt that Kenny had lost his zest for the mayoralty. He hinted that he would prefer to operate behind the scenes, running the party in the way that Boss Bob Davis had done so many years earlier. Despite a decline in his popularity, Kenny was still the best vote-getter in "the organization," and he could keep control over the positions on the county ticket whatever his title was. But, with strong opposition from Eggers, he was compelled to stay in the race or risk letting the Hague forces regain control.

Both camps were predicting victory the night before the election on May 12, 1953. But no one forecast that control of the city government would hinge on 327 votes cast out of a total of some 133,000.

When the dust cleared, the Republican on Eggers' ticket, Joshua Ringle, had accumulated the largest number of votes—a surprise almost beyond belief. Eggers himself came in second. Then came Kenny's new face, Bernard Berry, followed by Kenny himself, and Kenny's old friend, Donald Spence.

The result was a split commission, with the Kenny side holding a three-to-two edge over the opposition. It was obvious that the power of the Kenny machine was seriously eroded.

Ringle, however, soon demonstrated that his loyalty to the RDCG for helping him win his post was a sometime thing. After siding briefly with Eggers on a number of issues, he moved over to the Kenny side when a controversial $77 million sewer contract was under discussion. Eggers found himself a minority of one. Still, his continued opposition—along with the increasing number of investigative looks into Kenny's underworld connections—helped prompt a surprising and cryptic message from John V. Kenny at the December 15, 1953, meeting of the commission:

"Please accept my resignation from the office of City Commissioner of Jersey City, to which I was elected by the people of Jersey City on May 12, 1953."

John V. Kenny, the man who had led the onrushing Freedom Ticket to eliminate Hague's hold on Jersey City government, had said, "I can't take it any more."

In retrospect, it appears that Kenny may have decided that he had taken as much as he could from the pockets of the city's citizens—as much, at least, as he could get away with, without leaving plenty of evidence for the authorities. He went behind the scenes, acting as party boss for Hudson County and living like a millionaire while his battery of lawyers worked to fend off investigations that threatened to send him to jail. It would be 1971 before the overwhelming evidence of the corruption present during his regime would finally cause a federal grand jury to indict the 78-year-old politician for conspiracy to commit extortion.

Looking on from his own millionaire's mansions, Frank Hague could only shake his head in a combination of admiration and bewilderment. He obviously had taught his longtime follower how to get the rewards of power in Jersey City, and had taught him well.

But he had not taught him how to bear up visibly under the attacks, the pressures that are part of the job. Maybe such men as Kenny and Eggers, he may have mused, just were not strong enough—*tough enough*—to merit the positions they aspired to.

Maybe—probably—*certainly* there was only one Frank Hague.

13

T. James Tumulty, who died shortly before Christmas in 1981, was quoted in *The New York Times* on the kind of political genius that John V. Kenny brought to his role as ruler of the Hudson County political machine:

"He ruled by division. He kept factions within the organization fighting with each other, knowing that both sides would come to him to straighten things out. This constant recognition of him as the leader was his source of strength."

It was a different technique than that used by Hague—who gave the orders and expected them to be obeyed without dissent—and it was effective. T. James was in a position to observe how effectively it worked, because Kenny permitted him to stay close to him. The political boss owed the jovial lawyer a debt of gratitude: It had been T. James who saved the mayor from a possible jail sentence early in his career. Testifying before the Waterfront Commission of New York Harbor, Kenny had denied meeting with underworld figure Anthony "Tony Bender" Strollo to try to arrange labor peace on the Jersey City docks.

The only problem was that the meeting had taken place. T. James knew it. Kenny knew it. The commission knew it—and was about to present evidence that would cause Kenny to be indicted for perjury. Putting all of his considerable weight against Kenny's obstinacy, T. James convinced the mayor to hire a prominent New York lawyer (who lived in New Jersey) and to ask for a return appearance before the commission to correct his "lapse of memory." When called before another investigatory agency—this time in New Jersey—Kenny brought T. James along with him. Then the heavy-weight lawyer put on a display of verbal pyrotechnics laced with anecdotes that made the commission members forget they were supposed to be angry with anyone.

The mayor's decision to step down in 1953 caused several members of the Jersey City commission similarly to forget that they were supposed to be angry with him. Frank Hague Eggers suddenly found himself with no single focal point for his enmity and charges of malfeasance, and his zest for public office waned sharply. He had counted on his running mate—Ringle, the Republican—to support him in deciding on a new mayor, but Ringle decided instead to vote for a Kenny choice, Lawrence A. Whipple, to fill the now-vacant seat on the commission. If Eggers and Ringle had teamed up to oppose the Kenny-controlled votes of commissioners Berry and Spence, the two-against-two split would have required a special election. In that event, it seems certain that another member of Eggers' slate, Tom Gangemi, would have joined the commission and the Eggers forces would have had a three-to-two majority.

Then, behind the scenes, Frank Hague might once more have pulled the strings in City Hall.

Anthony "Ike" Venutolo, a former football star at Ferris High School who had gone on to achieve celebrity status at Columbia University, expressed concern to Kenny that Ringle might withhold his vote for Whipple, but Kenny waved him off with a shrug. "Don't worry," he said, "I can get him for a ham sandwich."

When the commissioners met and decided that Bernard J. Berry would serve as mayor, Eggers looked at his position and realized that he stood at a one-against-four disadvantage. The realization, combined with the tremendous amount of energy he had expended in trying to hang onto the reins of authority handed to him by his uncle, Frank, left him weak and powerless. The effect on his health was almost visible, and he died of natural causes the following July—barely seven months after his arch enemy resigned from the commission.

Another tie to the era of Hague was broken.

With each passing day, my own awareness of the local political scene was deepening. Hoping to capitalize on my basketball prowess at Saint Peter's, where I had captained the team and been named a member of the All-American Catholic Schools squad in my senior year, I had tried for a berth on the professional New York Knickerbockers—and had made it. But a disagreement with the coach as to whether I was good enough to play on the first team resulted in my leaving the Knicks. I mean, a kid from "Joisey" City sitting on a New York bench: Never!

Anxious to be of service to the city my dad Jimmy Smith had diligently served for 40 years in the police department, I began keeping an eye on the merits and demerits of the numerous political figures all around me. My athletic background helped get me a Recreation Department job, and a family relationship with the surviving Zelinski brothers—Charles and Teddy—helped me gain admission to certain inner circles. Although they had sided with Eggers against Kenny, the Zelinskis' control of much of the Polish vote in the Gammontown neighborhood made their support of considerable importance to anyone even remotely considering running for office.

I was given a quick example of how persistence could pay off in obtaining employment—in addition to the earlier instance cited of making oneself highly visible, as T. James Tumulty did when he repeatedly berated Frank Hague at budget meetings. In this case, Mayor Bernard Berry, who was serving as president of the Board of Education at the time, was continually asked for a job by a small fellow known as "Hymie" Wanzer. Giving in to the entreaties of chronically unemployed Hymie, Berry finally helped arrange a job as a watchman at a school not far from the board president's home. Soon afterwards, the sensitive fire alarms at the school went off and several fire engines raced to the scene. There was no sign of smoke or fire, but the firemen found the front gates secured by huge chains and a giant padlock. Rather than force their way in, they summoned Berry from his warm bed nearby, and the sleepy executive located a custodian who came scurrying with a key for the massive lock.

When the gates were opened, firemen, newspapermen, and the angry Berry hurried into the school. The alarm, it turned out, had been triggered by an electrical malfunction—but there was no sign of the new watchman. As the group of men were about to leave, someone opened the door to a classroom and Hymie was discovered fast asleep, oblivious to the sirens outside and the pounding footsteps all around him. Flashbulbs began popping as the embarrassed Berry rushed to wake his sleeping subordinate.

Violently he grabbed Hymie by the shoulders and shook him until the man's eyes opened wide in surprise. "What the hell's wrong with you?" he screamed. "Didn't you hear the fire engines?"

"Of course I did," was the calm reply. "But I was overcome by the smoke!"

It was soon going to be obvious to the voters of Jersey City that Mayor Berry would have plenty of opportunities for embarrassment during his term in office. The mood of the nation had swung to Republicanism in 1952 when Dwight David Eisenhower, with 442 electoral votes to Adlai E. Stevenson's 89, had been named the 34th President of the United States—and it suddenly made little difference to the party in national power that Jersey City remained in the control of the Democrats. Within the city itself, the ethnic mix of the voters continued to change: More blacks and Hispanics arrived, as more prosperous Irish and Italians moved beyond the city limits to the suburbs. The mood of optimism that surged forward at the end of World War II had twice been blunted—once by the fearful rise of a Soviet Union armed with atomic weapons, then by the spectre of the Korean war that caused thousands of people to consider building bomb shelters in their basements and backyards. Many voters readily accepted the idea that such local figures as a ward leader, city councilman, or even the mayor really had little say-so over their futures. Not when matters of life and death were involved!

Although a new form of city government—the Faulkner Act of 1950—was under study, the commission system still was the order of the day. And without a strong leader among the five members, the evils of the system readily came to light. Each member set out to build his own fiefdom, building up a payroll that included friends, hangers-on, and the party faithful who eventually could help him gain control (or so went the thinking of each commissioner). As a result, taxes spiralled ever higher, and—with each member concentrating on a payroll "arms race" of sorts—not a lot was done for the citizens of Jersey City.

There was little unity among the various political factions fighting for control of the Jersey City and Hudson County "pies"—not until the last weeks of the year 1955 when the news spread like wildfire through every ward and district:

"Hague's very sick . . . very, *very* sick . . . not going to make it . . . *dying.*"

During the year and the one that preceded it, the near-immortal politician had seldom been part of the local scene. Major rallies and important events had taken place without his physical presence— oh, at times a telegram of congratulations would arrive from a resort where the sun was shining and the healthful baths were steaming hot—but Hague's name more and more was raised only occasionally by a platform speaker to remind voters that things "used to be better" in Jersey City. Usually, the speaker would be a member of the "outs," and his words might have been drawn from an editorial in the *Hudson Dispatch* that ran when Hague retired:

"Unlike so many of the old time bosses, Mayor Hague . . . believed in giving the people a city and county administration from which they received *direct benefits.* The Medical Center is his outstanding monument . . . He also cleaned out the houses of ill fame *and kept them out.* Of all the things they say about Mayor Hague, they never accuse him of making a fortune out of vice, as so many old-time political bosses used to do. . . . Mayor Hague, a recognized genius in politics, also proved to be a progressive . . . municipal executive, who *did things* rather than just talk about them."

Now the man who did things instead of talking about doing things was unable to do more than barely lift his head to swallow a mouthful of water. Nearing 81 years of age, his tall and once-powerful frame ravaged by a succession of illnesses, he lay on a bed in a private room in New York City's Presbyterian Hospital. His longtime associates came, one after another, to visit the dying man, and try vainly to bring a smile to his lips by recalling the old days, the days of victory and fiercely fought battles. Scattered fragments of conversation could be heard drifting through the drawn curtains around the mayor's bedside . . .

"A long, long way from the Horseshoe, eh, Frank?"

"Remember when—guess it was about '19, hmm?—when we pushed Edwards in over Bugbee for governor? The whole damn state went against him, but we got him in!"

"Nobody in the whole country's ever gonna forget the way you took on Case and that goddam investigation, Frank. You made 'em look like fools."

"Hey, what about the time Chief Walsh arrested those cops who showed up to arrest *you?* God, people are gonna laugh at that forever!"

Occasionally, a cackle of laughter escaped the Mayor's lips as John Milton or "Needle Nose" Malone or another crony dredged up a memory from the past. But on Christmas Day, the respected Dr. Thomas White paid a visit to Hague's room, taking time out from his own duties as a heart specialist at the Jersey City Medical Center.

Recalling that sad scene, Dr. White later told me, "He asked that I summon an ambulance and let him go home to die."

On his deathbed or anywhere else, Frank Hague was the boss. Dr. White did as he was bid. It would not have been unusual, either, if Hague had clocked how long it took for the ambulance to arrive—as he used to do when he ran Jersey City, to make sure his emergency services were operating efficiently.

From the viewpoint of an historian or dramatist, it would have been appropriate had Frank Hague died in the Horseshoe section where he had begun his life and long political career—or even if he had died in the city or state that served as the base of his power. But, after speaking that typical last line—"I never thought you two bastards would outlive Frank Hague"—to his closest friends, Frank Hague slipped into a coma at his luxurious apartment on New York City's Park Avenue. Death came on New Year's Day, 1956.

And the city of Jersey City, which so often had found New Year's Day the occasion for celebration at City Hall—when the party faithful flocked to shake the hand of "duh Mare"—this time went into mourning. Flags slid slowly to half-staff at City Hall and the Medical Center.

When the funeral took place, of course, not a single politician would have dared utter the smallest, faintest word that could be considered critical of the Hague reign or the man himself. Thousands of ordinary citizens lined the streets as the Mayor's hammered-copper casket was borne in a solemn procession from Quinn's Funeral Home, through Bergen Square to Summit Avenue, and then along Mercer Street to Saint Aedan's Church, which the mayor had once gifted with an altar costing some $50,000.

In the procession were more than 100 members of the fire and police forces of the city. On motorcycles with their exhausts muted to a low murmur and on horses that were brushed until their coats gleamed, the uniformed workers paid their final respects. One went even further to show his devotion to his departed leader. Police Chief Michael Cusack momentarily broke from the ranks to rip a crudely-lettered sign from the hands of a woman at the fringe of the crowd. He tore the sign to pieces as the throngs looked on in surpirse.

On the disrespectful sign were the words: "God have mercy on his sinful, greedy soul."

It was the only jarring note, in a city of 250,000 people, to disrupt the solemnity of the occasion. In church, Monsignor Martin W. Stanton offered a solemn high mass for 1,500 mourners who filled the pews and stood in the aisles and rear of the edifice, while priests, nuns, and other members of the clergy prayed inside the altar rail.

When the will of Frank Hague was made known, there was little doubt that he had prospered mightily during his years in office. The exact amount of his estate—which was bequeathed in its entirety to his widow and, upon her demise, to his son and daughter—was never revealed. In 1951, the Mayor had acknowledged holdings of $2,049,000. But in 1954, T. James Tumulty had estimated Hague's fortune at $60 million. One of the Mayor's intimates guessed that it amounted to at least $8 million.

Whatever the amount, it was clear that Frank Hague's financial rewards testified to the truth of the saintly Dr. White's words about him:

"He had large vision and great ambition."

The massive doors of Frank Hague's costly mausoleum had scarcely closed when the wrangling combatants of Hudson County threw themselves back into the political fray. The continual findings of the Larner probe about "no show" jobs in various city departments, the upward trend of taxes, a rising crime rate, a decaying school system—these and other illnesses that were befalling many major American cities gave the "outs" plenty of opportunity to criticize the "ins."

All that was needed by the outs was a strong candidate, one who could ride over the weakening powers of the city commissioners and the stronger, behind-the-scenes manipulations of John V. Kenny in Hudson County.

Thomas S. Gangemi seemed to be the man who could walk off with all the political spoils in the 1957 municipal election. Handsome to a fault, and of Italian extraction, he had been largely educated on the streets during the Great Depression. Hard effort had enabled him to build a small fruit-selling business in the downtown section into a sizable industry that earned him the name of "The Watermelon King." He struck up a friendship with Hague's First Ward leader, the equally handsome Bill McGovern, and that contact brought him to the attention of the Irish members (Gangemi was known as Tom Reilly in those days) of the nation's most powerful political machine.

McGovern was gone now, however—as were Hague, Eggers, and others who might have been expected to support Gangemi in a battle against Kenny. But Kenny had one enemy ready to do battle: Former Commissioner Witkowski—still smarting after having been demoted by the former mayor from supervisor of the police to supervisor of the streetlights—was champing at the bit for a chance to challenge his old nemesis.

Another Kenny foe had also surfaced—the son of Commissioner James Murray, Sr., who similarly had been demoted by Kenny to look after the public bathhouse rather than Jersey City parks. The elder Murray made it easy for his son: he capitulated to Kenny. The once uncompromising Hague foe—perhaps sensing his end was near—surrendered. Murray jumped at the offer to run for county register, struck a deal for his son as president of the Tax Board, and accepted a promise that Kenny would run his son for the state senate in the future. In return, Murray agreed to give Kenny his coveted seat on the commission, and fight no more. The defrocked commissioner's death in August of '52 made his part of the bargain moot; Kenny kept his.

A lawyer and a dynamic speaker, the younger Murray had none of the rough edges that had characterized his father as a sullen and unfriendly person. James Jr.—or "Jim" to his close associates—had quickly learned the ins-and-outs of moving up the political ladder. After he had gotten an $8,000-a-year job as president of the Jersey City Tax Board, he ran against Kenny's choice, Alfred D. Sieminski, in the 1950 congressional election. Running against the organization, the youthful Murray was defeated, but his earnest efforts won him enough votes to impress Kenny—and the political leader kept his promise and supported the young man's successful bid for a seat in the state senate.

A united ticket headed by Gangemi, Witkowski, and Murray could easily best the organization's commission slate headed by incumbent Mayor Berry, it seemed. Gangemi had a large Italian-American following and plenty of money to mount a campaign. Witkowski, with Polish and Slavic backing, was experienced and known to be a fighting independent. And the polished Murray was looked on favorably by the intellectuals.

The task of the organization was simple: to keep the three men from forming a team. If each could be convinced that he was strong enough by himself, and the trio could be urged to form three separate tickets—the old "divide and conquer" principle would prevail.

While Jersey City's political matchmakers began to salve the egoes of the three contenders, others hurried to align themselves with one side or another. Increasingly playing a larger part in the political affairs of the city, I had my own first experience with "high level" political machinations when I accompanied the Zelinski brothers to meet Jim Murray. Having heard about the wealth and stature of this "well-known international attorney," I was somewhat surprised to find him working out of a small and rather lacklustre office in an old New York City building, although the Fifth Avenue address was impressive.

The conversation quickly turned to the favorite pronoun of politicians: "me." Murray wanted the Zelinskis' support to give his candidacy "major ticket" stature, and Eddie Zelinski wanted to join Murray's ticket in the event he formed one of his own and needed a Polish counterpart to Witkowski, should "Wit" decide to head *his* own ticket. Viewing himself as the potential "Irish" leader of Hudson County, Murray was careful to make no promises to the Zelinskis, but did his best to cajole them into supporting him—no matter who ran with him or against him.

Young Eddie Zelinski approached Tom Gangemi with a similar proposal, saying that he could get the Polish vote as well if not better than the procrastinating Witkowski—who weighed carefully the decision to run alone or with the fruit seller. One day "Wit" was "coming aboard," went the rumors; the next day he was "still thinking it over."

Eddie suddenly got a phone call from the Italian, whose mastery of English was extremely poor. "Go out and git yourself a new suit, kid," Gangemi said. "You's my Polish candidate." Eddie dashed out to buy a new seersucker for the coming campaign. A few days later, the phone in his home at 202 Warren Street rang. It was Gangemi again. "I'm sorry, kid, but you's out. It's Charlie Wit." A crestfallen Eddie was left with nothing but 24 months to pay for the suit.

Putting aside their own independent ambitions, the Gangemi-Murray-Witkowski trio formed "The Victory Ticket."

As the other candidates for a five-man commission slate, a career policeman and Irishman, William V. McLaughlin, was selected along with August W. Heckman, a lawyer who was both a Republican and a Protestant.

Kenny looked over his slate, called "The Winning Ticket." Along with incumbent Mayor Berry, who was a popular figure in Catholic circles, it included Joshua Ringle, the Protestant-Republican; Joseph Soriero, a longtime supporter; Joseph Michalski, a local undertaker; and Lawrence Whipple, a Kenny associate who was destined to become a future federal judge. To most observers, the ticket definitely had "underdog" status.

It did, that is, until April 2—when, with the campaign well underway, the *Jersey Journal* (which supported the Kenny-backed slate) front-paged a story that proved highly embarrassing to Gangemi. Commissioner Joshua Ringle, who had won in 1953 because of Gangemi's support, charged that the wealthy fruit marketer had actually been on Frank Hague's payroll at various times from

1938 to 1941 as "a non-laboring laborer." Supposedly, at the time that Gangemi was accumulating huge profits from his own business, he was being paid by the city's parks department.

The legacy of Frank Hague lived on—long after the man himself was dead and gone.

As might be expected, Gangemi denied the charges. He admitted that he had been on the city payroll, of course, as Frank Hague Eggers' deputy in 1953—but everyone knew that. Perhaps, he explained, the Kenny forces had confused him with his brother—or there was more than one Tom Gangemi living in Jersey City. The Winning Ticket responded with ads showing that the city records from the parks department showed paychecks made out to a Tom Gangemi who lived at the same address as the present candidate. Then, a respected city official who had been in charge of forestry projects told the press that he remembered Gangemi was on the payroll as a laborer—but that his actual "work" seemed to be merely to keep company with then-commissioner "Bill" McGovern. Gangemi decried the opposition for its lack of decorum when it trotted out the name of his dear departed friend. And he continued to deny the charges.

But the Winning Ticket had its theme now. The indomitable Barney Doyle hurried out to buy copies of all the recorded versions of a popular song of the day, "It's a Sin to Tell a Lie." Soundtrucks, although supposedly banned from the city streets, managed to play the record until the entire city was humming the melody and pondering its implications. "If we're lying," challenged the Kenny forces, "sue us, Tom. Sue us, and prove it."

Gangemi did not sue. Instead, his ticket began to issue countercharges. Mayor Berry, it said, had held a no-show job in the city's tax department some years past when he had been a clerk full-time for the Lehigh Valley Railroad. Ringle was accused by Eddie Zelinski of failing to show for work while employed by the bureau of elections. In the furor, the polished Murray lowered himself to contend that Berry's background as a railroad clerk left him unqualified to serve as mayor, and Berry countered with the rebuttal that Murray was two-faced in that he had previously asked Berry to join his Victory Ticket.

The raging debate over who *was* a no-show and who *wasn't* a no-show seemed to grip everyone in the city. But it was a little fellow named Joe Di Fabio who put the entire matter into proper perspective. Known sometimes as "Joe Mustache," because he sported one, and sometimes as "Joe D, Number Five," because he had an almost fanatical adoration of Yankee baseball great Joe DiMaggio (who wore number 5 on his uniform), the little political scrapper had a club supporting the Victory Ticket on the corner of Baldwin Avenue and Academy Street. One afternoon, he was addressing a small group of listeners in his best imitation of Jimmy Cagney's "tough guy" style:

"No-shows ain't no good! No-shows is killin' this city of ours!" He looked at the crowd, waiting for encouragement to lambaste Kenny and his cronies, and the entire terrible no-show system that they continued to support. "No-shows ain't no good," he repeated. "Unless you's one of them!"

Joe Mustache had the unhappy habit of saying one word too many, of putting his foot in his mouth over and over again. He had another problem, too. He continually chose the wrong side in elections, prize fights, horse races. Like Joe Bltlfsk, the sad little character in the *L'il Abner* comic strip who walked around with a cloud of misfortune hanging over his head, the scrappy little guy seldom came out a winner. The fact that he was backing Tom Gangemi in the 1957 campaign should have told everyone what would happen once the votes came in.

Other voices, though, were making themselves heard about the evils of no-showism. Gene Scanlon, a *Jersey Journal* reporter covering City Hall, was fond of telling about the time he had been asked by a nephew of John V. Kenny to accompany him on a brief trip. The young man had been given a job in the city school system and was supposed to drop by his assigned school to pick up his paycheck.

"I thought they delivered the check to you," Gene remarked. (Relatives of Kenny and others very close to City Hall got such preferential treatment.)

"Usually they do," the nephew said. "But the guy didn't show up today."

Scanlon picked up the angry young man in his car and headed in the general direction of the school building. Both men, it turned out, were unfamiliar with the neighborhood—and it took the two of them more than an hour to locate the school where the nephew "worked."

Sensing an all-out battle shaping up between Kenny's Winning Ticket and the challenging Victory Ticket, a number of other contenders threw their hats in the ring. If the two major slates divided the voters, they reasoned, there was always the chance that someone else could walk off with the spoils.

Nick Introcaso, who enjoyed dressing up as Uncle Sam in a red-white-and-blue suit of tails, claimed that his "Yankee Doodle Dandy Ticket" was the only one made up of "real Americans," since it included such challengers as Dominick "Pep" Simonetti, a street cleaner assigned to garbage duty, and Michael Urban, a bartender.

Daniel Marino's "All-American Ticket," however, was given a better chance. Called "The Rake" because he frequently used a garden rake to reach high enough to tear down the opposition's political signs, Marino first supported the slate headed by Mayor Berry, but then decided to use his popularity in the Marion section of town—heavily populated with Italian-Americans—to try for all the marbles. His ticket included Michael Arnone, young Sal Cozzetta (who would support my candidacy two decades later), and two others whose names plainly told their heritage.

Perhaps sensing the dangers inherent in a divided voting public, Witkowski charged that incumbent Commissioner Joe Soriero had asked Marino to enter his Italian-accented slate for one purpose: To draw Italian votes away from Tom Gangemi and help the incumbents retain power. Marino, claiming that he did not want to affect the votes that might go either to Soriero or Gangemi, withdrew his entire ticket. Then, in a complete reversal of form, he endorsed the Victory group. One of his chosen five, Mike Arnone, refused to quit and stayed in the race.

James J. Creegan, who, with his brother George, had been the first to support Kenny in 1949, decided to run for the commission, too. Once powerful politicians in the Junction Section of the city, the Creegans failed to realize how their hold had weakened on the area

John R. Longo (left), who twice defended himself against trumped-up charges while fighting the Hague forces, here pictured with his imported-from-New York City attorney, Vito Marcantonio. Marcantonio, a congressman accused of communist leanings, was chosen by Mayor Fiorello H. LaGuardia to defend Longo.

The candidates and their wives for the 1957 Victory Ticket. Missing is Charles Witkowski (who became Mayor in 1957) and his wife. On the extreme right is Thomas Maresca, who became a member of the Municipal Council in 1961. At the extreme left is August Heckman, next to him is William McLaughlin, and to his right, Thomas Gangemi. At the end is James F. Murray, Jr. Sitting in front are the wives of the respective candidates. Gangemi, the leader of the Victory Ticket, was the only loser. Four years later his dreams were realized when he became Mayor, only to resign less than two years later, charged with not being a citizen.

Charles S. Witkowski, then Commissioner of Public Safety, was stripped of his duties and his office denuded of all but a telephone. Several years later, Witkowski made a successful bid for the mayoralty.

Barney Doyle, ward leader and comedian par excellence, with then Mayor Thomas J. Whelan in 1964. They were discussing the distribution of dolls and other toys for Christmas. Whelan later served seven years in federal prison for extortion.

Campaign buttons for New Jersey elections, from 1901 to the author's try for the governorship in 1981.

Mayor-elect Smith is mobbed on election night, May 10, 1977.

Mayor Smith lifts a jubilant Governor Brendan T. Byrne to the cheers of Hudson County Democrats. Byrne credited Smith's endorsement as the turning point of his 1978 re-election effort.

The author is greeted by then President Carter at the White House.

The author landing one to the jaw of Muhammad Ali as they hype the crowd for their exhibition bout in the Jersey City Armory. The winner was the Jersey City Medical Center, which received the gate proceeds.

parade in Jersey City highlighting Daisy, an adopted pony who became the city's mascot. Enjoying the parade with Daisy are Regina Silver, Mayor Smith's daughter (in carriage), Carol Smith, another daughter (a medical student), and Smith's wife, Florence, on the extreme left. Also in the photograph are Governor Brendan Byrne, Senator Walter Sheil and Assemblymen Chris Jackman and Pat Pasculli, along with other Jersey City dignitaries.

DAISY
JERSEY CITY'S ADOPTE

Four mayors at a Pulaski Day Parade in New York City: Smith, Robert Wagner, Ed Koch and Abraham Beame, with Helen Poster, wife of the New York *Daily News* Columnist Tom Poster.

Members of the Mayor's staff paying their annual birthday visit to Miss Liberty. In the group surrounding the Mayor are Mary Ann Bauer, Joseph Bauer, Michael Bauer, Josephine Anzalone, Sondra Anzalone, Diana Anzalone, Lena Karlsson and Elizabeth Ranelli.

With Best wishes
(& Appreciation!)
to Mayor Timmy Smith
Jimmy Carter

Mayor Smith greeted by both President Carter and Vice-President Mondale at the White House.

St. Patrick's Day parade marching through Journal Square, heading for the reviewing stand. Left to right: Senator Walter Sheil, Governor Brendan T. Byrne, the author and Commissioner Paul Byrne.

Wearing an "I Love Jersey City" button, the author acknowledges the applause of the party faithful at a pre-election rally.

with its changing socio-economic makeup. An influx of blacks, an outflow of Irish and Slavic voters—and the Creegars became an anomaly.

Virtually every candidate on every ticket promised that a massive rally to be held in Journal Square on the Friday evening before the election would reveal who shortly would come out on top. The city's central shopping and amusement area was filled with more than 1,500 people long before nightfall, and when the huge searchlights began to sweep the darkening sky, a mighty roar went up. The people were there, waiting.

All that was needed now were the candidates.

Small groups of people, usually led by a gang of curious teenagers shouting and laughing, scurried from corner to corner. Then a band—six trumpeters and a bass drum—could be heard coming from the south along Bergen Avenue. "It's the Victory Ticket!" someone yelled, and a cheer went up. The happy supporters of Gangemi, Witkowski, and Murray rushed toward the band, looking for their heroes. Behind the musicians, however, came Nick Introcaso in his Uncle Sam suit. Riding in a pony cart, he waved magnanimously to the crowd, pleased that the spectators were enjoying his music.

From the other side of the square, a loudspeaker blared. "Here they *really* come!" shouted an announcer. And the crowd rushed to the north. It heard music, and the tune was hauntingly familiar. Then, suddenly, four soundtrucks rolled into the square, blaring out the melody that said clearly, "Be sure it's true when you say, 'I love you' . . . It's a sin to tell a lie . . ."

Frustrated at the raucous laughter and music of the Berry team, the Victory Ticket supporters whirled about in confusion. When another band came into the square—with 500 marchers carrying signs that said, "Monster Labor Rally—International Longshoremen's Association"—the still uncertain crowd cheered cautiously. When it realized that, yes, this *was* the heart of the Victory Ticket rally, its cries grew more enthusiastic.

The election itself would prove almost as confusing.

Certain of a Victory Ticket sweep, I hurried to City Hall as soon as the polls closed. All of the slate's candidates had won, I discovered immediately, with one exception. Tom Gangemi, the man who seemed most assured of victory, had gone down to defeat by an incredibly slim margin of 156 votes. Mayor Berry had bested him on the strength of a handful of absentee ballots, which traditionally are cast for the organization.

In a grim stroke of near-retribution, Gangemi's primary attacker—Commissioner Joshua Ringle—suffered a heart attack when he was told at the Masonic Club at Clinton and Crescent Avenues that he had lost the election. (The politician never completely recovered and passed away barely a year later.)

John V. Kenny took the news of his ticket's defeat in stride. Asked by a *Journal* reporter if he would support a change in the form of government, his reply was terse: "No. Let's give them a chance to see what they can do with the government as it is."

Present at the City Hall Assembly Chamber for the swearing-in ceremony, I immediately realized that the spectators were in an unpleasant mood. Their leader, Gangemi, would not take a seat on the commission—and the other four winners would have to put up with Bernard Berry instead. When someone in the crowd recognized a reporter from the *Jersey Journal,* which had front-paged Ringle's "no-show" charges against Gangemi, it took the intervention of several policemen to stave off a fistfight.

Repeated cries of "We want Tom!" echoed through the chamber as each new commissioner stepped forward. At the mention of Bernard Berry's name, a chorus of boos filled the room. The commissioner's 11-year-old son, standing at his father's side, looked upward, his eyes damp with tears, and said, "Keep your chin up, Dad." As the boy began to sob, the defeated Gangemi—looking handsome and sporting a red carnation on his immaculately tailored suit—stepped forward. He held up one hand to silence the crowd and placed his arm around the boy's shaking shoulders. It was an emotionally-charged picture, and an alert photographer caught the moment on film—in a scene that was displayed prominently in virtually every newspaper in the nation.

The commission members, in a surprise move, selected Charles S. Witkowski to serve as mayor. James F. Murray, Jr., who had polled the highest number of votes in the election, was appointed finance director. Longtime policeman Bill McLaughlin took over as public safety director, while Gus Heckman, the lawyer, became public works director. Minority commissioner Bernard Berry was named director of parks and public property.

The job given to Berry had a laughable—to some—payoff for the forlorn "Joe Mustache." As an employee of the parks department, Joe had supported the wrong man once again—making it well-known that he was backing Gangemi all the way. Now Berry was more than victor; he was Joe's boss. Shortly after the election, I was escorting a friend, Dave Jacobs, on a tour of the city and we visited Roosevelt Stadium to reminisce about the great athletic events that had taken place there. High up in the grandstands, we spotted a lone figure. It was Joe Mustache, cleaning pigeon droppings from the seats.

"Hi, Joe!" I shouted. "How're you doing?"

"No good," came the response, echoing over the rows of seats. "This job is shit for the birds!"

14

In Richard J. Connors' retrospective look at the career of Jersey City Mayor Frank Hague, *A Cycle of Power,* he notes in a brief epilogue that the period 1957–1961 "was one of low comedy or high tragedy depending upon one's point of view."

From my personal point of view—that of a young man struggling to understand the real workings of the political world while, at the same time, trying to hold onto my youthful idealism and adjust to the concessions that had to be made in order to support a growing family—the period was one of incomprehension, frustration, and constant surprise. As a supporter of the Victory Ticket, I was disappointed that my campaigning had not paid off for the likeable Gangemi, but was elated that four other Victory candidates would now be running things from City Hall. After all, I saw that they were men who had managed to forget their differences—in background, wealth, and education—to mount a successful crusade against the Kenny forces. Surely they would be able to grip the reins of power firmly, and solve some of the numerous problems that faced Jersey City.

Maybe, I thought, the quintet of commissioners would realize that there was much to be done; that it would take concerted action to do it, and that they had best get to work quickly.

I was considerably naive. Instead of adopting a Hague-like "Let's get things done" attitude, the commissioners behaved much as their predecessors had. Each endeavored to operate his own kingdom, with his own army of supporters. And the four-year term of the commission would prove to be among the most turbulent in the city's history. The disparity of the members themselves made teamwork virtually impossible.

Take, for example, the description of Commissioner Murray, as printed in the *Trenton Times*: "Murray, international lawyer and the Senate's foremost orator and self-styled intellectual, [seems] a little out of place in a Jersey City election. He held the job of tax board president in the city administration at the same time he was opposing some of Kenny's appointments in the Senate." Articulate and polished, with a burning desire to assure "greatness" for Jersey City, Murray had smoothly learned to play the political game. That ability made it almost a certainty that he would clash with "Gus" Heckman, a man of letters and culture, but one new to the rough-and-tumble world of local politics. Moreover, where Murray's legal-oriented mind was skeptical and probing, Heckman's was readily swayed by personal flattery.

Both men probably threw their hands up in despair when, out of gratitude to the defeated candidate, Mayor Witkowski tossed a bone to Tom Gangemi. The defeated candidate's son, Tom Jr., was appointed a deputy mayor. The young man's presence at meetings naturally gave his father entree, too, but Gangemi's thick dialect and poor grasp of English had to annoy the more eloquent commissioners. As in the case of several silent-film movie stars whose careers ended at the moment their voices were heard in "talkies," the elder Gangemi's matinee-idol appearance vanished when he opened his mouth. Out of the handsome face came such phrases as "Watch de udders an' see how dey do," "tree years ago," and "you got dat?" Or, in a reference to one of New Jersey's most famous centers of learning: "Dem wise guys from Ruggers ain't never worked like dis."

McLaughlin—perhaps because he had been a garrulous Irish cop for so many years—frequently delayed important meetings while he spun out verbose tales in polysyllabic language. And Berry, who everyone expected to repeat the moves he made while he had been a cog in the supposedly corrupt Kenny machine, now worked to change his colors by becoming a reformer. He frequently aligned himself with Murray on key votes, causing the other commissioners to suspect that he was up to something by abandoning his minority role.

Sensing that Commissioner Berry was sincere—and soon discovering that he was administering one of the most successful programs in the history of the Jersey City Parks and Recreation Department—I began to offer my help to his political career. Although he initially held my efforts for the Victory Ticket as sufficient reason to give me *persona non grata* status, my diligent work on his behalf soon earned me the post of a lieutenant in the "Berry Boosters." This was a political organization for recreation workers, who were primarily young, enthusiastic, and talented.

With so many diversified factions struggling to prove their superiority—to the other commissioners as well as to the individual groups of voters who had put them into office—all thoughts of teamwork vanished. Public meetings of the commission, notes Connors, "became public spectacles." Plots and behind-the-scenes maneuvering split the factions still further, until the city's collective head was spinning. Time and again the courts had to be called upon to resolve disputes.

By the time a year had passed, the *Jersey Journal* was reporting: "The Victory commissioners hardly are speaking to each other any more. Each has retreated into the confines of his own department, from which on frequent occasions can be heard noisy attempts to fabricate a working majority. . . . "

The disputes between Mayor Witkowski and the ambitious Murray soon developed into open warfare, with Murray frequently going out of his way to bait the short-tempered mayor into a public display of anger. The hangers-on began choosing sides. Others turned to man-in-the-middle Heckman and began to flatter him with the idea that his central position made him well-suited to moving up the political ladder. The department that he supervised for years had been the "dumping place" for ward heelers and doorbell pushers of the lowest class—men and women who were generally short on talent, long on chicanery, and committed to as little work as possible. One way to make sure that their new boss would not bear down on them, they promptly discovered, was to convince him that their support might make him the next governor of New Jersey. Although Heckman was a Republican, he knew that Kenny would not be adverse to supporting a "friendly" Republican if his other options were "unfriendly" Democrats. The commissioner gave a nod to some of the gladhanders around him to form a Heckman organization for the future.

While Jersey City services deteriorated around them, each commissioner wrangled and plotted his own career. Observers of the political scene had little to smile about—until one day when the always-impressive T. James Tumulty, in his role as deputy mayor, was "standing in" for Witkowski during the latter's brief absence for a vacation. Always eager to help a newsman in need of a story, Tumulty casually mentioned that he understood the city was thinking of selling off Roosevelt Stadium to private interests At the time, such a statement was comparable to Paris announcing that it was going to unload the Eiffel Tower. Tumulty was called on the carpet for his heretical announcement—whether it had been said in jest or not—and dismissed. As his last official act, he called in the newspaper photographers, settled his huge frame beneath a City Hall "Exit" sign and explained that his dismissal was "the greatest mass firing in the history of Jersey City."

No doubt the perpetually jovial politician kept his fingers crossed that his life would be long, "for when a Jersey City resident dies," he used to say, "there's only one sin he can be guilty of when he goes before Saint Peter—and that's not being on the city payroll. That's the only truly mortal sin!"

For the squabbling commissioners, the November gubernatorial contest between Democratic incumbent Robert B. Meyner and Republican State Senator Malcolm Forbes presented a dilemma of the worst sort. Meyner was running on the "Row A" ticket with the backing of Kenny's regular organization and looked exceptionally strong. But the Victoryites had gotten into power by opposing Kenny and all he stood for. At the same time, the commissioners had largely lost the support of the Victory Ticket workers who had helped them get elected, so they could not mount a challenge of sufficient size to challenge Kenny in the primary and he won easily. The Victoryites weakly came out for Meyner in the general election.

Wrote John J. Farmer in the *Newark Sunday News*: "The answers seem to lie somewhere between the desire of the Victory commissioners to scuttle John V. Kenny's County Democratic slate and their need not to incur Meyner's displeasure, especially if he is reelected."

John V. Kenny, sensing that an opportunity to regain full control of the political scene in Jersey City lay within his grasp, made a bold move: He began courting the elder Gangemi, who was still steaming over the cool treatment given him by the beneficiaries of his efforts to put the Victory Ticket into City Hall. If Gangemi helped produce votes for Meyner, Kenny promised, Gangemi could have the post of county supervisor and could name three other candidates on the November ticket. By September 30, Gangemi was responding to charges that he had fallen under Kenny's influence with a simple statement: "I am proud to be a 'puppet' of the great John V."

Gangemi's defection demoralized the Victory organization. Commissioner Berry, who had proclaimed loudly that his position alone gave Kenny a fingerhold on the reins of power to Jersey City, now found himself out in the cold. With Gangemi on hand to turn out the city's sizable Italian vote, Kenny no longer had to rely on Berry's popularity with the electorate.

The contest turned out to be no contest. Meyner was reelected with a statewide plurality of some 200,000 votes, and Hudson County's edge of 43,167 proved to be the largest county margin in the state. Despite efforts of dissident Democrats—the Victoryites and others—to stop the Kenny-Gangemi steamroller, the entire county ticket swept to victory. John R. Longo, never one to stop battling, waged a spirited battle for sheriff, but was defeated by "Bill" Flanagan, Kenny's nominee. The fact that Longo had long considered himself one of Frank Hague's bitterest foes, as had John V. Kenny also, meant nothing to the voters—the majority of whom undoubtedly missed the irony that was present.

An indication of the relative strength of the opposing political groups showed up in the vote on a proposal to build a low-income housing project in an area called Curries Woods. The lush, wooded section had long been used by Jersey City residents for picnics and outings and was considered by many citizens as extremely important for recreational needs. With Kenny and Gangemi urging the regular organization to back the housing project, the Victory Ticket candidates passed a resolution calling for a ''no'' vote on the proposal—and went down to defeat.

Despite Governor Meyner's boast that the Democratic party in New Jersey no longer had to depend on Hudson County, ''The Gibraltar of Democracy,'' to win the top post in Trenton, many Democrats were not so certain. And John V. Kenny was definite in his opinion that the governor was mistaken. Kenny's position was proved correct the following year when Harrison A. Williams (who, two decades later, would make headline after headline in the ''Abscam'' investigation) won his bid for the U. S. Senate by 87,000 votes across the state—with Hudson County supplying 75,000 of them!

In the April primary of that year, Harrison Williams and John V. Kenny both narrowly escaped political extinction, and were saved for a more serious fate years later.

The Victory Ticket forces were attempting to regroup and were enlisting as candidates people like ex-Kennyite Bernard Hartnett, Sr., and the former heavyweight champion of the world, James J. Braddock. They lured to their cause the still-impressive T. James Tumulty, who was always eager to change sides in order to be on the winning one. In this case, T. James did not have to switch sides: The Eisenhower landslide that saw a Republician win Hudson County for the first time in decades swept Tumulty out of congress after a single term. The oratorical talents of T. James, however, could still be counted on to win votes, and his ability to put humor into a campaign could do a lot to conceal the suspicions that Witkowski and Murray had about each other.

Kenny, meanwhile, recognizing the serious threat he was facing, reached back for a trick Frank Hague taught him and came up with a home town boy. (At any rate, the next best thing.) John J. Grogan, the popular Hoboken mayor and president of the Shipbuilders Union, was picked to oppose Williams, who had the support of the regular Democratic Party. Tumulty and Jim Murray were the Victoryites' 14th and 13th congressional candidates respectively.

Grogan did exactly what Kenny thought he would. He polled 82,080 votes in Hudson County, and carried the entire Kenny team to victory. True, he lost statewide by a mere 10,000 votes, but Kenny was again on top of the heap in Hudson County.

Except for the Democratic split in Hudson, Grogan would have beaten Williams. An Irish Catholic professor from Princeton by the name of McLean was placed in the race, some say by Governor Meyner, to cut the large Catholic vote that Grogan expected to get. McLean did just that. Although he received virtually no votes elsewhere, in Hudson County he collected 38,506, more than enough to defeat the fighting Johnny Grogan.

Tumulty, Murray, Hartnett and Braddock all went down for the ten count.

But those results were still in the future when, in 1958, a group of the city's concerned citizens once again decided that the commission form of government—which fostered divided responsibility and actually benefitted individuals who shunned teamwork in favor of independent action—simply could not solve Jersey City's growing problems. The Faulkner Act provided for changing the charter if voter approval could be secured for a study commission to analyze the city's needs; afterwards, an optional charter could be recommended and voted upon. Led by an independent thinker named Bernard Kaye, who had moved to New Jersey from New York, an organization called the Independent Voters Council was formed to lobby for the needed study.

The IVC—promptly dubbed "poison I-V" by the politicos in power who wanted to *stay* in power—soon was lost in a maze of similar groups that sprang up to try to lead a revolt and take credit for any change that might eventually take place. Of all the groups, one called the Community Charter Council (CCC) seemed to have the most strength. Its members included business groups, community-minded citizens, educators, and a number of politicians who realized the factionalized Victory administration was headed for defeat. Commissioner Bernard Berry, growing more confident as his administration of the parks department repeatedly drew praise, put his backing behind the CCC—to the dismay of his fellow commissioners and the regular organization. As a Berry follower, although I was now employed at Saint Peter's College as a placement officer, I decided to put my political muscle (not to mention my forceful voice and improving powers of persuasion) behind the new movement, too.

The influential *Jersey Journal* saw that the CCC was determined not to repeat the mistakes made by previous "change the charter" crusades in 1911 and 1950. It came out in favor of the recommended study. Under siege from all sides, the beleagured commissioners passed an ordinance in November, 1958, calling for a referendum to determine *first* whether there should *be* a study of the city's charter. The tactic delayed for a year the actual formation of a group to conduct the study, but at the end of 1959, a five-man charter study commission was elected.

Although he considered himself a political mastermind in the same league with the departed Frank Hague, John Kenny demonstrated in the election that he was a long way from filling the shoes of "duh Mare." In addition to voting on the question of whether or not a charter study group should be formed, the voters were asked to select the men and women to do the job. For some reason, Kenny failed to put up a slate of candidates. If he had, he might have emerged victorious in one way or another: If the citizens voted "no" against a study, the status quo would prevail, and he would retain control of the Hudson County reins of power; if the vote was "yes," the Kenny slate would have been elected to conduct the study—and could delay it or shape the new "changed" form of government to the organization's own wishes.

But the only candidates on the ballot—put there primarily by the CCC—were John Loftus, a respected lawyer and educator; E. Curtis Plant, a Public Service Company executive; Benjamin Michalik, a professor at Saint Peter's (as was Loftus); attorney Annette Brof-Quinn; and Patrick J. Baratta, a businessman.

It would take nine months and 58 meetings before the group finished interviewing scores of past and present city officials, leaders of civic and religious organizations, political figures, and "ordinary citizens." During the period, Barney Doyle explained what charter change probably meant to the typical man and woman of Jersey City:

"Smitty," he said to me one spring afternoon, "the people don't know what the hell charter study is all about. They see it like the big carnival where blokes put their kissers through a hole in a sheet of canvas, and local hicks throw baseballs at 'em. Here, the people see the politicians as the blokes with their kissers stickin' out—and the 'Joisey" *Journal* has pulled up a wagon of horseshit for 'em to throw instead of baseballs. And the knockers can't wait to hit the 'pols' in the puss with the horseshit.''

While the study was underway, bizzare things began to happen on the political front. Perhaps sensing that change was imminent and wishing to appear respectable enough to hold a post in a new, more effective form of government, or perhaps thinking that past misdeeds might soon be uncovered by a new administration, several major political figures began speaking openly about "errors" long concealed from the public. One of the most notable occasions occurred at a forum at Saint Peter's College in which County Supervisor John Deegan, leader of the Tenth Ward and a man extremely popular with the rank and file, began confessing his proclivity for "double dipping"—or operating on the familiar formula of "One for the city, and one for me." Seemingly in a trance as he addressed the stunned auditorium, Deegan appeared to realize only belatedly the consequences of his admissions. Long known to intimates as "Double-Dip Deegan," the nattily-dressed official that day lost his mystique as the people's choice and was never again seriously considered for the post many thought he was destined for: Mayor of Jersey City.

"I dunno," said a bemused Barney Doyle afterwards. "It was like old Double-Dip had a double dip of truth serum."

The words of the report issued by the charter study commission in July, 1960, were unmistakeable—and clear even to the citizens who thought the idea of charter change was simply to let one group throw mud (or worse!) at the politicians. "The commission form of government is the underlying cause for the failure of Jersey City to meet its problems," said the study group. "The divided responsibility; the concentration of administrative and legislative powers in individual officials, with virtually no checks and balances; the inability to consolidate, coordinate and modernize administration; and the conflict of ambitions which are inherent in the commission plan make it unworkable in a complex city such as ours."

In place of a commission, the study group recommended that there should be a system that allowed a strong mayor to work with a nine-person city council, three members of which would be elected from the city as a whole, the others named by the voters of their respective wards. The administrative and executive duties would belong to the mayor; the council would have legislative responsibilities. (The recommendation—except for the judicial functions which are administered by municipal judges—was much the same as that made by H. Otto Wittpenn in 1911, a half-century earlier. If Wittpenn's proposal had been adopted, rather than the commission system which the *Jersey Journal* said meant "an end to bossism," the emergence of Frank Hague on the scene—as the most complete political boss in our nation's history—might never have come to pass.)

Bursting with ideas, filled with enthusiasm, the CCC seemed in a strong position to force the election of those candidates who were dedicated to a new form of government. John F. Loftus seemed the ideal candidate for the mayoralty. He was a "new face," highly respected, devoted to reform.

In my office at Saint Peter's, the two of us frequently discussed his chances of winning the election, should he choose to run. He began to look into his chances of raising campaign funds, however, and soon discovered what others had learned before him: Corporations in a position to make sizable contributions did not want to make them to an independent, a reformer—a man who could not promise favors in return for the money. There was, of course, the oft-heard statement that "We just don't want to get involved in local politics." Many contractors who worked for city, county, and state—and who also were in a position to provide a huge influx of campaign funds—were not interested in supporting a professor of business law with a reputation for honesty.

There was another obstacle worrying Loftus. He was well aware that Commissioner Berry, who had virtually severed all ties with the regular organization, was interested in running for the mayor's job. Loftus told me privately that he admired Berry and now considered him an independent—but he declined to endorse the commissioner publicly. I sensed that the respected professor was twice wounded—first by the lack of financial support from the local captains of industry, and then by Berry's unwillingness to put his political power behind a "Loftus for Mayor" effort. For whatever reason, Loftus let it be known that he should not be considered a candidate for the city's top spot.

(Shortly after the election, the learned educator left Saint Peter's to become Dean of Seton Hall Law School. Wiseacres in the Kenny organization boasted in overly loud whispers that Kenny had "arranged" the appointment with the archdiocese to make sure that Loftus withdrew from the Jersey City campaign!)

Without Loftus to lead them, the remaining powers in the CCC decided they had to align themselves with Berry in order to defeat the entrenched strength of John V. Kenny. Frank Guarini, who would become my campaign manager in 1977, was serving as president of the CCC, but was said to be maneuvering behind the scenes to help Berry get elected. (Frank had a reputation for surreptitious maneuvering, as I would learn first-hand two decades later.) When the spotlight turned in Berry's direction, it caused a split in the CCC ranks, with a minority demanding that the voters should be offered a slate of wholly new faces.

The people of Jersey City got nothing of the kind.

In addition to Berry, who was nominated for mayor, the CCC slate for the nine council positions included four men— Thomas McGovern, Thomas Maresca, Fred Martin, and Michael Esposito—who were professional politicians and friends of Berry. The other "Clean City Candidates" for council spots were Anthony DeSevo, a dentist; Joseph Swierzbinski, a New York attorney who was active in local Polish-American organizations; George Clott, an attorney well known in Jewish circles; and two members of the charter change study group, Annetta Brof-Quinn and E. Curtis Plant. Only the last two were considered as true-blue CCC members.

If John V. Kenny was dismayed that Berry had forgotten the allegiance once owed him, the county leader gave no indication of it. Undoubtedly he was familiar with a saying that I first heard from the lips of Barney Doyle: "The patron saint of politicians is Judas Iscariot."

Besides, Kenny had his candidate for mayor close at hand. County Supervisor Gangemi had money, the appeal to ethnics of an Italian's becoming the city's first "strong" mayor, and a handsomeness that was plainly evident. Taking a page from the book of tricks used by their Democratic forebears to snatch the "reform" label from Republican Mayor Mark Fagan at the turn of the century, the two erstwhile antagonists decided that they would be the ones to offer voters some "new faces." They lured to their slate James C. Rochford, a New York businessman and a former high officer in the Knights of Columbus; Thomas M. Flaherty, an insurance broker and Saint Peter's College graduate; Thomas J. Whelan, an executive of the telephone company, and Theodore Conrad, a maker of architectural models.

To give an impression of political savvy, the Kenny-Gangemi axis proposed for other council slots Dr. Paul Sinclair, a physician and the first black to win election to office in Hudson County; Jack Kelaher, a popular clubhouse figure; John J. Kijewski, a member of the state assembly; and Mrs. Evelyn Holender, a committeewoman in the regular Republican organization.

The Irish Kenny and Italian Gangemi clashed over only one council candidate. William P. Boyle—son of the late Tom Boyle, who had been Kenny's closest friend and the Second Ward leader—was eminently acceptable to Kenny for the remaining opening on the council slate. But Gangemi wanted the spot filled by Joseph T. Connors, a popular Kenny organization man who was the leader of the Fourth Ward. Connors was a former Air Force pilot and policeman who enjoyed a close rapport with the city's downtown section. Kenny argued, but eventually agreed that Connors should get the nod, and he suggested that young Boyle run as an independent.

Incumbent Mayor Witkowski, of course, declared himself ready for reelection, but veteran observers of the political scene felt certain that the only thing voters would remember about his campaign would be his theme song. A popular march from the Broadway show *Best Foot Forward* had had its lyrics altered from "Buckle down, Winsocki," used to cheer on a football team, to "Buckle down, Witkowski, buckle down! You can win, Witkowski, if you buckle down!"

Obviously over-inflated from the applause of the sycophants around him, Commissioner Heckman entered the race. Sporting a derby and looking dapper, he was certain that the mayoralty was simply a stepping-stone to the governor's mansion.

The campaign got off to a fast and furious start. Barney Doyle told a newsman that one of the candidates for mayor was a "cement head." When the reporter printed the remark—without saying whom Doyle had referred to—the candidate called the paper to complain.

"But we never identified anyone as 'cement head,'" protested the editor.

"Yeh," grumbled the candidate, "but everybody knows who he meant!"

The fine hand of "The Barn" was also felt when Mayor Witkowski ordered a helium-filled balloon floated over Journal Square with a banner promoting his reelection. Within hours, it seemed, someone had untied the rope holding the flying campaign sign and let it go sailing off into the blue. Shouting "Sabotage!" was not enough for the angry mayor. He ordered a second balloon sent aloft and posted a guard on it around the clock. Within hours, the buoyant gas was leaking out of several punctures in the balloon and it was sagging sadly. "Barney Doyle got it with a high-powered rifle," I heard.

The air was hissing out of Witkowski's hopes, too. And "Gus" Heckman was no threat (he would wind up with only 3,748 votes out of a total of 112,049 cast in the election). The battle quickly narrowed down to Berry vs. Gangemi, and the two foes started trading punches in earnest.

If Berry's presence on the commission had been good for Jersey City, Gangemi asked in his heavy accent, why were there so many things wrong in town? Why were streets so dirty? Why was nothing done about crime? Why were taxes going up and services going down? Why weren't schools and playgrounds kept open after school hours for recreation? And why weren't streets cleaned up after a snowfall? (A paralyzing winter snowfall gave birth to the slogan of Gangemi's slate: "Remember the snow! They all must go!")

Feeling that he was being unfairly tarred with the sins of all his fellow commissioners—who had responsibility for police protection, the street cleaning system, and other areas—Berry struck back to show that Gangemi's term as county supervisor was rife with scandal and impropriety. Among other things, he charged that Gangemi had been behind the county's purchase of expensive marble-topped desks and specially designed chairs for offices in a new building—desks and chairs that cost more than some purchased for President Eisenhower by the federal government.

After the headlines from the furniture deal died down, the Berry forces pointed out that the county was asking $6.2 million rental on a building assessed as worth only $125,000. The structure was a defunct nightclub, the Top Hat, that was to be converted into a hospital for geriatric patients. That attack was followed with one accusing the county of agreeing to the $350,000 purchase of a piece of property that had been assessed at $90,000.

On the streets of Jersey City, however, it was soon apparent that Gangemi and Kenny were not in mortal danger, even though wounded. I was working harder for the Berry slate than I had ever worked before, and opened a Berry club next to Public School 11. A huge red-white-and-blue banner with *Thomas F. X. Smith* on it stretched from the roof of the building to the street, and "Berry for Mayor" signs were visible at every window. But when I spoke to friends, strangers, and longtime political-scene watchers, I heard the same responses:

"Berry's been in office for eight years and Jersey City has gone downhill."

Or, "What did he ever accomplish when he was mayor?"

Or, "Maybe a businessman—like Gangemi—can do more in office than a politician can."

The idea of Kenny hanging onto power was repugnant to me, but it wasn't so for everyone. Barney Doyle, wise in the ways of politics, was 100 percent behind Gangemi.

"Barney," I said, "I can't figure it. You're a friend of Berry's and an enemy of Gangemi's. But you're working to get Gangemi elected. I don't understand it."

"The Barn" looked me straight in the eye. "Smitty," he said, "Berry was the commissioner of parks for four years and I didn't get a bag of grass seed."

Despite the outlook, I and other Berry supporters increased our efforts to get out the vote. The night of a major rally we had scheduled at the Moose Lodge Hall, a tremendous thunderstorm broke over the city. It seemed unlikely that a crowd would show up, and I kept my fingers crossed that the reporters would not ask embarrassing questions about the seeming lack of support for the Berry slate. As the rain fell in torrents, my mood became more somber as I waited for the phone call that would signal a successful or unsuccessful rally.

I paced the floor at home until 10 o'clock, and suddenly the telephone rang like an alarm bell. I was afraid to answer it, but then lifted the receiver.

"Tommie, what a crowd!" shouted Dr. Vincent Krasnica, who had been a friend since our days together as altar boys and who would not lie to me for the world. "Hurry up, get here right away! It's mobbed."

In the background I could hear the noise of the crowd and the blaring of our theme song, urging voters, "Hey, look me over! Lend me your ear!" Our efforts had paid off, encouraging people to turn out for Berry in the most adverse weather conditions imaginable. Smiling, reassured that we had a good chance for election, I hurried to the hall to thank the mob for showing up.

Our elation was short lived, however.

When the final ballots were tallied, Gangemi led the mayoralty candidates with just under 50,000 votes. Berry trailed, some 18,000 votes behind. Witkowski was further back, and Heckman ended up a distant—and disappointed—fourth.

The terms of the Faulkner Act required a candidate to be elected with 50 percent of the total vote, plus one more. Since no candidate had reached such a total, Gangemi and Berry were required to have a head-to-head runoff election five weeks later. The situation was the same in regard to the three at-large council seats and in all but one of the wards. Joe Connors, the World War II bomber pilot, destroyed his opposition and claimed the Downtown seat. For the rest, a runoff would be needed, and it was obvious that with the Gangemi candidates generally ahead of the Berry names, we had our work cut out for us.

Five weeks. That was all the time we had to erase the lead of the Kenny-Gangemi forces. Could we do it, or would we be hearing the victorious rivals taunting us with a chorus of "Bye, bye, Berry" to the tune of "Bye, Bye, Blackbird"?

Gangemi did his best to help us at times, it seemed. His difficulties with the English language required his speechwriters to simplify the words they put into his mouth. Still, he made gaffe after gaffe. Once, for example, proudly telling the story of the four clergymen who had died when a U.S. cruiser had been torpedoed during World War II, he referred to the men as "a Catholic priest, a Protestant minister, a Jewish rabbi, and a Quacker."

While sophisticates snickered, however, Barney Doyle was emphatic in his belief that Gangemi's man-on-the-street vocabulary and dialect would only endear him to the hearts of the voters. "Go ahead, you silly bastard, laugh," Doyle once snapped to a man sneering at Gangemi's pronunciation. "Everybody I know in Jersey City talks like him!"

With each passing week, the attempts by the Berry forces to sway the public grew more desperate. Referring to Kenny's connections with underworld figures, ex-Mayor Berry said that the election of Gangemi would be a prelude to the "arrival of gangsters" in City Hall. Gangemi decried his opponent's "frenzied smear campaign," and even the *Jersey Journal* censured Berry for stooping so low. Noting that one Berry campaign slogan urged the voters to "Clean up the mess in City Hall," the 380-pound T. James Tumulty asked a reporter to print the fact that he was no longer connected with the city administration. "Nobody said you were," the newsman replied. "Oh," said T. James, grinning widely from ear to ear, "I'm sorry. I thought they were saying, 'Clean up the mass in City Hall.'"

The lighter moments did not conceal the fact that as the inevitability of a Gangemi victory loomed ever nearer, more CCC and Berry supporters were "jumping ship" to align themselves with the man who shortly would be in power. One after another, the independents came out for Gangemi. Only John R. Longo, still a political heavy-weight after three decades of activity, stood his ground. In a stirring speech, he conceded to an awed crowd that it was an "uphill fight," but promised that "if we stand on our own feet, no Kenny—or group of Kennys—can stop us." Then, referring to Harry S. Truman's sur-prise upset of Thomas Dewey, who had been called a "sure thing" in 1948 by political pundits, Longo proclaimed: "Bernie Berry will pull another Harry Truman!" Time and again the crowd came cheering to its feet.

Only a few days remained in the campaign, and although Berry seemed to be gaining, it was evident that Gangemi still held a wide lead. Then, Berry obtained some information that—in view of later events—might well have given him the mayoralty if he had dared use it on a "no holds barred" basis.

Someone—no one ever knew who started the rumor—suggested that Tom Gangemi, the man fighting to be elected mayor of a major metropolitan city in the United States of America, was not a citizen of the country in which he lived.

It was incredible, unthinkable, almost beyond belief.

Berry was reluctant to make an outright charge. But he began ask-ing cryptic questions during his speeches. "Tom Gangemi," he would suddenly say, "who are you? Where were you born?"

Gangemi, obviously puzzled, shook off the questions. At this late date, he was not about to engage in a debate as to whether he was legally qualified for the office of mayor. Berry later contended that he worded his accusations carefully so as not to embarrass Gangemi's family with an outright statement, but there was also the possibility that he feared a lawsuit charging libel, slander, defama-tion of character, and the like. At any rate, his last-ditch effort failed.

Gangemi took the runoff election, 57,927 votes to Berry's 43,164.

On the council, only Tom Maresca and Fred Martin of the Berry ticket managed to beat their opponents on the Gangemi ticket. De-spite the controversy over charter change, despite the cry for "new faces," the people of Jersey City looked to the future with their government in the hands of wise old professional politicians—most of whom had played a part in ruling the city's destiny for a long time.

Kenny, the "little leader," had managed to hold on long enough for the tide to turn once more in his favor. And it was unlikely—charter change movement or not—that things were going to change much in City Hall to improve the lot of Jersey City residents. The people could only hope things would improve under their new president, John Fitzgerald Kennedy—a man who seemed genuinely concerned about improving the roles of blacks and other minorities, establishing a "New Frontier," providing medical care and other help for the aged, and cutting taxes.

Things, of course, changed hardly at all. Along with others, I wondered if there would have been noticeable improvement if the wise John Loftus had decided to run for the mayor's post. After Gangemi won the title, Loftus told newsmen that a "new face" in the race could have been victorious because many voters stayed home rather than cast their ballots for any of the three familiar candidates. He called the campaign "uninspiring, with too much name-calling, too many appeals to the standard blocs of votes, and not enough effort to bring out those voters who vote only every four years." As much as I admired the man, I was saddened by his remarks—because those of us who really cared about a change of government in Jersey City had been working diligently for it, putting our efforts on the firing line to bring it about. Loftus had pondered, wavered, and finally declined both to run himself or even voice support for Berry.

"Berry doesn't have a chance to win," Bill Flanagan told me before the election, in an attempt to further open my eyes to the realities of politics. Flanagan, who had tied his future to John V. Kenny in 1949 as a speechwriter for the Freedom Ticket, was a power in Hudson County circles in 1961. He had climbed from a job as a low-paid reporter on the *Jersey Journal* to master the art of public relations, a skill vitally important to any ambitious politician, and he had become John V. Kenny's alter ego. Later he became executive director of the New Jersey Turnpike Authority, holding down one of the most desirable jobs in the state; but in 1961 he had sufficient time on his hands to put his cool, analytical mind to work on matters of the day. In simple matter-of-fact statements, he pointed out that

Gangemi had the support of the very large bloc of Italian voters—
"The Italian-Americans are coming out for Tom like he's Joe
DiMaggio," said a lifetime friend of mine, Joe Georgia—and that
vote, when combined with the ballots of the patronage-rich Democratic organization, simply was too much for Berry to overcome. His
only chance, if any existed at all, would have been if Witkowski had
withdrawn and tossed his support behind the former mayor. But neither "Wit" nor Heckman were about to admit that they could not
carry off the big prize.

If, in the aftermath of the fierce election, I and many other Berry
supporters seemed exhausted and less interested in the goings-on in
City Hall, it was understandable. The split caused by the rivalry of
the various groups that opposed the Community Charter Council, the
warfare of those pleading for "new faces" and yet putting their support behind old ones, and the fact that Kenny-backed candidates
controlled seven of the nine council seats—well, it left those of us on
the outside with little more than hope.

For a while, it looked as if our hopes would be answered with action. Mayor Gangemi investigated an idea used successfully in New
York City—alternate-side-of-the-street parking for cars on different
days of the week—and put it into effect in Jersey City. As a result,
the sanitation trucks could make their way through crowded thor-
oughfares and collect trash—and there was a marked improvement in
the cleanliness of the streets. He also managed to add some 500 new
streetlights, brightening the avenues and helping reduce crime, and
he set about towing away abandoned cars, obtaining federal grants,
and speeding up local building projects. But the tax rate continued to
climb, too.

And suddenly, just when it seemed that the strong mayor and a
cooperative city council were really the answer to Jersey City's
troubles, a new political bombshell exploded to produce both
dismay—and laughter.

Mayor Thomas Gangemi announced that, just 26 months after his
tumultuous election, he was resigning.

It seemed that the voters of Jersey City *had* elected a mayor who
was not a citizen of the United States.

Probably it could not have happened—could not *happen*—in any other American city, but in "the Mecca of politics"—well, what else was new?

The surprising announcement came, ironically, out of the idea of one of the mayor's public relations men for a special celebration for Columbus Day. The aide suggested that Jersey City should invite an Italian with the name of Christopher Columbus to visit City Hall and "rediscover" America. A suitable businessman bearing the distinguished explorer's name was discovered living in Genoa, Italy, and Mayor Gangemi prepared to fly overseas to extend the invitation personally. But—so the story goes—when he applied for a passport, the discovery was made that he had no birth certificate or other proof of his U.S. citizenship.

Rather than leaving for Genoa, Gangemi entered Harkness Pavilion of Columbia Presbyterian Medical Center in New York City and his public relations staff issued the bulletin that his overseas innoculation had made him ill. When the entire city council was summoned to his bedside, however, speculation naturally had it that he was *seriously* ill. But, with tears streaming down his face and his voice breaking with emotion, the one-time fruit peddler who had climbed high in the world of politics said he was stepping down.

To finish his term, which still had nearly two years to run, the mayor proposed a candidate who was quite ready to sit behind the big desk: His son, Thomas "Buddy" Gangemi, Jr.

He probably expected a battle when he looked around at the astonished faces of the councilmen clustered in his room. One face was missing.

Councilman Thomas J. Whelan was elsewhere.

Plotting?

15

Suddenly—as if everyone in the entire nation had opened their eyes one morning and found that they had gone blind—it did not matter who was mayor of Jersey City, who ran Hudson County, who sat in the governor's chair in Trenton.

John F. Kennedy, barely a thousand days into his term as President of the United States, lay dead on a stretcher in a hospital in Dallas.

And nothing mattered.

A country, however, cannot mourn forever. In time, the explosive thrust of a bullet into the brain of the 35th president and the subsequent murder of the man who allegedly had slain him merged into historical incident—one of many that increasingly were brought instantaneously to the attention of millions through the fairly young medium of television. In an era when the latest news flooded into everyone's home with an unparalleled urgency, and when crisis followed crisis after crisis, people began to grow immune to the effects of shock on a national scale.

After all, said wise and sober heads, in the past 18 months or so look what we've come through: A humiliating defeat at the Bay of Pigs in Cuba; a feeling of helplessness as the Russians divided East and West Germany with a wall of concrete and barbed wire; civil rights upheavals in the South; the Cuban missile crisis that had the entire world trembling on the brink of nuclear war; and several faltering half-steps as we tried to catch up with the Soviets in a leap into space. With such worries, such seemingly unsolvable problems confronting us, what else *is* there to do but cross our fingers and hope for the best?

And, once it was said—once it had been gotten out into the open that life had to go on—only then did Americans begin to look once again at the problems close at hand. After all, they reasoned, there are things taking place hundreds of miles away, thousands of miles away, and—where space is concerned—millions of miles away, that we can do nothing about.

But in City Hall, in the polling place right down the street, or in a political debate in a neighborhood bar or at the family dinner table, a person still could make his or her voice heard. And maybe, just maybe, a person could do *something* about what was happening.

And so, for the people of Jersey City, the focus swung once more to local politics. The question of who was mayor was again important, and would continue to be important despite (or because of) the national phenomena capturing the public's attention throughout the balance of the 1960s. Somehow, adjusting to the "future shock" that was part of their lives, men and women everywhere managed to concentrate on protests against the burgeoning war in Vietnam . . . the murder of three civil rights workers in Mississippi . . . a blackout of eight northeastern states . . . and other events that *should* have meant paralysis—all the while retaining their ability to stay tuned in to what was happening close to home.

And close to home, Thomas J. Whelan was Mayor of Jersey City.

Why the members of the city council ignored Mayor Gangemi's request that his son be named to succeed him will never be known, any more than it will be known why Tom Whelan was given the nod. In retrospect, and in light of subsequent events, it seems certain that the firm hand of John V. Kenny, "the Little Guy," was resting on Whelan's shoulder. It also seems obvious—from a story told me by Fred Martin, the councilman from the predominantly black Bergen-Lafayette ward—that Whelan felt certain of his imminent appointment.

According to Martin, the council members had spent long hours and days wrangling over who among them should get Gangemi's title. The argument had reached the point where it seemed that a fistfight was about to break out, when someone noticed that Whelan was not even present to take part in the discussion. Martin went looking for him and found the Journal Square legislator stretched out on a sofa, relaxing with his shoes off and his hands linked behind his head. A contented smile was on his lips.

"Tom, are you crazy!" Martin shouted. "You're out here, like this—and they're getting ready to make a mayor in there!"

Whelan's smile turned into a grin, and he waved his hand in a gesture of dismissal. "Fred," he said, "just let 'em go at it. They each just want the chance to get in there and rob the city."

Martin returned to the council chamber, perhaps impressed with Whelan's apparent honesty and lack of interest in the role of the chief city executive. He thought it over.

And then Fred Martin cast the deciding fifth vote that made Thomas J. Whelan Mayor of Jersey City.

A veteran of more than sixty combat missions as a pilot in World War II, Whelan stood tall at six-foot-one-inch. His greying hair and military bearing gave him an undeniable appearance of power and authority. Barney Doyle, one of the few people who could make the new mayor laugh, often said, "He looks like he should be commanding a U-boat."

Quickly grasping the reins of power in a fist that was not to be unclenched for eight years, Whelan jumped into a municipal crisis. At the time of Gangemi's resignation, the mayor had been in the throes of a controversy with the Jersey City police and fire departments. The hard-working members, still trying to recover from the decades of 3-percent kickbacks under Hague, were demanding salary increases. Gangemi had resisted, pleading that the tax burden on the city's residents had been climbing inexorably to speed the departure of more and more financially responsible citizens to less demanding neighborhoods. The question of raises finally showed up on a referendum, after Kenny's organization went from door to door to gather petitions for the vote—and, probably, to urge residents not to vote in favor of the pay raises.

When the police and firemen saw their increases turned down at the polls, they grew emotional. The Democratic organization lost the members' support overnight, and irate cops began issuing tickets for illegal parking and other "violations" to anyone suspected of having voted against the pay hikes.

Whelan saw immediately that something had to be done. Despite the defeat of the measure at the polls, he announced raises for all members of the police and fire departments. But where would the money come from, if not directly from the taxpayers? He took care of that question by summarily dismissing 500 employees of the Medical Center—a move that undoubtedly caused Frank Hague to spin like a dervish in his grave. Another 100 employees were relieved of their responsibilities at the city Board of Education, and the angered electorate was further appeased by a Whelan announcement that all city employees would have to work longer hours—at the same pay—from now on.

The public outcry that might have been expected to materialize over the pay increases for the policemen and firemen did not grow beyond a murmur, even though the bulk of terminated employees were promptly absorbed into Hudson County's government under Kenny's directives. Whelan had demonstrated that—like Hague had been—he was a "take charge" mayor who was not afraid to make a decision even if it went against the wishes of many voters. In the eyes of many Jersey City residents, the new mayor would pay those who produced and somehow would cut the fat out of the city budget.

Because he was named to serve only for Gangemi's unexpired term, and because the city faced a number of serious issues at the time, Whelan was spared the customary in-fighting that had characterized Jersey City government from the days when Frank Hague's hand first began to loosen on the throttle. Hardly had he solved the police and fire pay raise crisis when the explosive summer of 1964 was upon the new mayor—and upon all America.

The panic, the terror came suddenly, almost without warning. Sociologists looking back on it later would lay some of the blame on unemployment, rising inflation, and various economic causes. But to many of the nation's black population, the death of John F. Kennedy—who had championed black causes—and the assumption of the presidency by Lyndon Baines Johnson, whose very voice signified "Southerner" and all that the word stood for in regard to civil rights—well, the combination, of course, played an important role in what happened. In June, when three young men named Schwerner, Goodman, and Cheney were murdered in Mississippi as they tried to help black voters there—was it odd that rioting seemed to be the only natural response?

Suddenly flames were racing through huge sections of Detroit, Newark, and other cities, and the cry, "Burn, baby, burn!" was echoing everywhere.

While people in Jersey City trembled, looking in horror at the television pictures of fiery fury so close at hand, Mayor Thomas Whelan once again "took charge." He issued shotguns to patrolmen of the Jersey City police force and ordered that the barrels of the guns should be plainly visible at the open windows of patrol cars cruising the city streets. He called rioters in other areas "punks" and criticized mayors of other cities for their temerity in dealing with lawlessness. Overnight he became a nationally-known figure, appearing on network television as a man signifying "law and order"—and enforcing order at gunpoint.

It was probably enough to set the whirling spirit of Frank Hague at rest again.

The nationally syndicated newspaper columnist, Walter Winchell (who once had been a confidante of Franklin Roosevelt and J. Edgar Hoover), hailed Whelan's leadership in hundreds of papers throughout the country. "Whelan sent steel-helmeted cops to trouble spots and ordered them to meet force with force," wrote the still-influential newsman. "Anyone who attacks a policeman in Jersey City better be prepared to come off second best."

The mayor's tough-minded image was reinforced by statistics that showed major crime on the rise by 12 percent in cities all across America, but in Jersey City it had plummeted by 14 percent. Not unexpectedly, white voters agreed with Winchell's appraisal of the mayor as "a man of exceptional leadership ability and courage." What was surprising, however, was that blacks also seemed to appreciate the fact that he had kept the city "cool" during the troubled summer. And, somehow, he had managed what seemed a small miracle while actually cutting taxes almost three dollars per each $1,000 of assessed valuation. During the terms of his immediate predecessors, Witkowski and Gangemi, the tax rate had increased $11.58 and $15.24, respectively.

As 1965 dawned, there was little question that Whelan could mount a campaign for a full term as mayor of Jersey City and win easily. The *Jersey Journal* was behind him, praising him for continuing Gangemi's street-cleaning and streetlighting programs. And Whelan could boast that the city had allotted some $18 million worth of new building permits, had removed some 3,000 abandoned cars from the streets, and had received more federal grants than ever before. The rioting—so fearful to peaceful citizens who had seen the horrifying results in neighboring Newark and in the New York boroughs of Brooklyn and the Bronx—had shifted to the West Coast, some 3,000 miles away, to the Watts section of Los Angeles. As people read the *Journal's* reports of 1,000 injured, 34 dead, and $175 million in fire damage, they could look to Mayor Whelan with growing appreciation.

In Jersey City, of course, no candidate—no matter how strong or how good a job he is doing—can run unopposed. That would be unheard of, impossible. But Whelan must have chuckled as he looked over the list of contenders willing to challenge him.

There was former Mayor Thomas Gangemi—now a naturalized citizen and the winner in a court case to upset a law that would have prevented him from running for elected office. His platform was a simple one. He contended that Whelan's greatest successes occurred because the new mayor had simply followed the plans set in motion by his predecessor.

There was former Mayor Witkowski, still tall and intractable, but without the devoted band of spirited followers who had helped him earn third place in the balloting just four years previously.

There was Joe Connors, a WWII bomber pilot, who had made something of a name for himself as a councilman by splitting politically with both Gangemi and his one-time mentor, Kenny, and then consistently turning out the largest numbers of marchers in the parades celebrating Columbus Day and St. Patrick's Day. He was extremely popular from a personal standpoint, and had the support of such notable citizens as Dr. Kenneth Brophy, businessman Edward Robinson, and Michael (Mickey) Barrett of the Greenville section.

And there were others—Cornelius Givens, Edward F. Zampella, Michael J. Bell, among them. As to myself, now employed as placement director of Saint Peter's College, but very active in political circles, I had given thought to projecting a friend named Wally Sheil into the arena as "Mr. Clean." But the idea had died aborning when it became clear that the evils so evident under previous regimes were not all that apparent under Whelan.

We would learn—along with millions of others—that the rulers in power at the time were simply better at covering some of their lapses of honesty than their predecessors had been. But, in the meanwhile, the effort for Sheil was aborted, and a close friend, Tom Flaherty, enlisted my support for the Whelan cause.

The world of politics was rapidly growing much more scientific. For the first time, the Kenny forces turned to professional pollsters to assess their chances. In short time, the Kenny-Whelan backers were willing to bet money that the total number of votes cast for Whelan would be greater than the votes of any other two candidates added together. And the gamble would be even money!

As a schoolboy in the 1940s, I sometimes took part in a popular betting game that called for the bettor to choose any three baseball players who together would collect a total of six hits on a given day. The schoolboy bookies went out of business one season when the bettors consistently chose Ted Williams, Joe DiMaggio, and Stan Musial. Recalling how easy it was to win, it now seemed incredible that no two candidates opposing Whelan could muster enough votes to entice bettors on the outcome. But there was little "action," and when the votes were in, it was easy to see why.

Whelan pulled 57,610 ballots. His closest competitor, Gangemi, drew fewer than 23,000, and Joe Connors in third place pulled just over 11,000. The next three names—Bell, Givens, and Zampella—divided fewer than 10,000 votes among them. Zampella's total of 419 led to one of those amusing anecdotes that are so much a part of Jersey City's political lore. The personal and popular candidate, who went on to serve as a judge for 15 years, charged fraud in the counting of votes, noting that in his own election district only one ballot had been cast for him as mayor. Pointing out that he lived in the district with a wife, two sons, a mother, and four other relatives, the defeated Zampella angrily shouted: "You mean my own mother didn't vote for me?"

The overwhelming victory produced another surprise. Cornelius Givens, the first black to run for mayor of Jersey City, was trounced by Whelan by almost a 20-to-1 margin in his own ward, the Bergen-Lafayette section. Of course, Whelan had the support of Fred W. Martin, the most popular black leader in the city's history and a man who would have a school named after him as the decade of the 1980s dawned.

In all, Whelan and seven of his nine running mates were swept into office on the first ballot. Only Jack Kelaher, an incumbent from the West Side, and newcomer Anthony Peduto of the downtown area required a runoff election. Both then were victorious to complete the sweep.

The *Jersey Journal,* in a story by-lined by Lois Fegan, wife of the newspaper's editor, told its readers about Whelan's victory in jubilant prose: "Brown eyes flashing, bright smile spreading, her left hand nervously crumpling a scrap of paper, Eileen Whelan picked up the telephone in room 407 of the Hotel Plaza to inform her six children that Daddy had won." The story revealed Tom Gangemi's disappointment, too: "The city forgot what I did for it!"

If it is true, as has been said, that power corrupts and absolute power corrupts absolutely, there is probably a sound explanation for what transpired in Jersey City during the subsequent years. Tall, self-assured, non-political Thomas Whelan now had been firmly placed into power—not by a vote of his fellow members of the council, but by the votes of nearly 60,000 residents of the city. And, hand in hand with county boss John V. Kenny, he embarked on a program of corruption that—in the words of a United States attorney—"paralleled Boss Tweed's swindles in New York a century before."

The citizens—both those who had placed Whelan into power and those who had opposed his election—were largely unaware of the kickback schemes and payoffs that were to come to light a half-dozen years later. They observed a kind of "division of power" between the city leader and county boss. Whelan began to put on weight, seeming to be stuffing himself with too much pork roll in the comforts of Asbury Park, and Kenny (as Hague had done so often during his reign) began to winter more frequently in Florida. Some political observers contended that a state of "cold war" existed between the city and county forces, and it was undeniable that Jersey City entered into a period of physical deterioration as it received less aid from the county.

Writer Gene Scanlon, who was working as a public relations man for Whelan, once told me with a sarcastic grin that the mayor's sole accomplishment during his term in office was the alternate-side-of-the-street parking regulations that helped the sanitation department. But there were a few other moves that benefited the citizens—chiefly the construction of five new schools, including the first high school built in the city in 50 years.

Such efforts, however, were barely more than minimal and did not go far toward correcting the evils that had been allowed to accumulate over a period of almost a half-century. If the era of Hague had taken a toll on Jersey City, the Kenny period virtually finished it. A number of autonomous agencies were introduced into city government during the late 1940s and early 1950s in an effort to halt the mounting problems—"no shows," kickbacks, nepotism, soaring tax rates (a large part of which was caused by the "free" services of the Medical Center). But the establishment of a Sewerage Authority, Redevelopment Agency, Parking Authority, and Incinerator Authority only appeared to give additional politicians the power to grant construction and service contracts. After World War II, federal funds had been provided to build low-income housing under the aegis of a local Housing Authority, and the first tenants—elderly, for the most part—found their new homes eminently satisfactory. In time, though, the initial tenants died off or moved into nursing homes or into the homes of their children, to be replaced by poor, indigent tenants with large families. Not only did the highest-taxed city in America have to subsidize housing for these residents, but it had to provide accompanying food, school, and public safety services for sizable dependent families.

Perhaps Mayor Whelan, as other city leaders had done before him, looked at the problems and decided it was hopeless.

And, in such a situation, shouldn't a person contemplate that old saying, *Charity begins at home*? Whelan began to look after his own interests. More and more, he seemed to leave the operations at City Hall in the hands of his best friend, Tom Flaherty, president of the city council. Anyone who wanted to see the mayor on business was told to "see Tom Flaherty." Having known Flaherty since my own days in high school and college—he was a year behind me both at Saint Peter's Prep and Saint Peter's College—his rise to authority seemed to me a case of "local boy makes good."

Whelan needed friends. John V. Kenny, now well into his seventies, was concerned with his own failing health, and Kenny's number two man—Democratic County Chairman John J. Kenny—had split with his boss on a number of issues, including the continued support of Whelan himself. The two Kennys were also battling over whether or not to back former governor Robert A. Meyner in a new try to match A. Harry Moore's record of three terms as the state's chief executive. John V. Kenny had literally "made" Meyner governor after the Phillipsburg attorney lost a bid for the state senate, but once in power Meyner had turned his back on the county boss. He had even gone so far in his 1957 election speech to point out that the returns proved that a Democratic candidate no longer needed Hudson County's votes to win in the state. Now, getting even, John V. Kenny rejected Meyner's bid for his support and threw his weight behind former State Senator William Kelly in a field of six primary candidates. Deciding to display his own strength, John J. Kenny backed Meyner and claimed the former governor would capture 30,000 Hudson County votes.

Kelly, who had served as president of the state civil service commission, was not well known and lacked the stamina for a wide-ranging campaign. Nevertheless, John V. Kenny felt confident of his own power in the county and said his man would get 60,000 votes there. He was off the mark by only a slight bit: Kelly beat out Meyner in the primary, 54,684 to 21,707. Statewide, however, the results were quite different, and Meyner scored a three-to-one victory over his opponent in the primary.

Obstinate and angry, Boss Kenny let it be known that he was not about to change his mind. In the November election, he backed Republican nominee William T. Cahill over Meyner for the gubernatorial post—and saw Cahill win easily. John V. Kenny had his revenge over John J. Kenny and proved once more who was in command in Hudson County.

It was a lesson that John J. Kenny would remember. And pay back.

Before the gubernatorial contest took the spotlight, however, the focus was entirely on the local politics in Jersey City. The 1969 mayoralty race took place in May and it had become obvious to me—keeping an eye on things from my office at Saint Peter's—that Whelan had some opposition forming against him if he decided to seek another term. The opposition was still in its early stages, but it was plainly evident that the citizenry was almost crippled by rising tax rates. In the space of six years during which Whelan had been in office, taxes had climbed from $113.37 per $1,000 of assessed valuation to $152.94—a rise of nearly 30 percent. In 1968 alone, crime had risen by some 30 percent from the previous year, and the cost of water had climbed 100 percent.

There were unsettling and unwholesome charges, too. Julian Robinson, who had been the first black appointed as a department director, had joined the Whelan administration as director of health and welfare, but had resigned after a short stay. Now he was hinting at dark things in the administration, using such words as "kickback" and "payoff."

By this time, I had managed to build a loyal group of friends and supporters who appreciated my honest efforts on behalf of past candidates devoted to clean government. After the Wally "Mr. Clean" Sheil campaign, the Whelan team had more or less ignored me and those who listened to me—even though we eventually had supported Whelan. Now, late in 1968, my phone rang. On the other end of the line, Tom Flaherty's voice boomed out a hearty cry of recognition.

I was not surprised at the call. During the Whelan years in office, I had grown close to "Buddy" Gangemi, the former mayor's son. I had met several times with the elder Gangemi, who was still smarting over his defeat and who was more than willing to help finance his son's try for the mayoralty. I had also grown quite friendly with Julian Robinson. At the time of Flaherty's call, I was weighing an offer from both Gangemi and Robinson to run on their tickets as an "at large" candidate for the city council.

It was obvious that Whelan and Flaherty were anxious to reduce any opposition as quickly as possible. "Smitty," Flaherty said almost as soon as I answered the phone, "how'd you like to come on board as a campaign manager for the mayor?"

The offer was too much to turn down—not for a youngster raised in the heart of the city known as "the Mecca of politics," not for a student of the mayoralty wars of the past century. I briefly pondered some of the accomplishments of the Whelan administration—such beneficial moves as Grandview Housing for the elderly, the Montgomery Street low-to-moderate-income housing development, and the Port Jersey Marine Terminal on the waterfront in the southernmost part of the city that meant jobs and tax revenues—and I told Flaherty that I'd be glad to lend whatever assistance I could to help Tom Whelan gain reelection.

As things turned out, it did not matter which Gangemi ran, nor that a black—Robinson—ran, nor that candidates named Bell, Yengo, and Maresca ran. Still admired for his "law and order" stance during the riot days, and swept up in the same kind of fervor that grew around anti-integrationist Governor George Wallace of Alabama, Tom Whelan garnered 43,105 votes in the contest. It was more than double the total of his nearest competitor, but less than the 50 percent plus one necessary for a first ballot victory. Only the popular Greenville councilman on Whelan's ticket, Tom McGovern, won without a runoff. All the rest had to run again against their nearest rivals.

Whelan collected more than 50,000 of the 84,065 votes cast five weeks later, to end the political career of Tom Gangemi by more than 16,000 votes.

I thought, as the victory celebration raged around me, that my suggestions had played a part in the triumph. While other candidates concentrated on the data and statistics of tax increases and construction permits (and generally confused the voters), Whelan was presented as a human being who understood the problems confronting people everywhere in the city. We featured old photographs of the mayor at the throttle of the fighter plane he had flown during the war, giving him an image of heroic stature. Although Whelan had been less than a spectacular football player during his Dickinson High School days, photographs of him in his old football helmet in the familiar defensive-tackle pose showed that he was ready for action. And there were shots of Tom "Man on the Job" Whelan—in the white helmet of a fire chief, with a sooty face—and Tom "The Family Man" Whelan, walking arm in arm with his wife and children on Easter Sunday.

The mayor's victory was marred only by the surprise upset of two council candidates who were defeated by independents. William J. Thornton, opposing the administration, scored a 12-vote victory over incumbent councilman Fred W. Martin, who had cast the deciding vote that had put Whelan in the mayor's office in 1963. And incumbent councilwoman Evelyn Holender was soundly whipped by Morris Pesin, an activist who had helped bring Liberty State Park into being and who had said that, if elected, he would act as a "watchdog" against wrongdoing by other members of the administration. He had campaigned feverishly, racing from speaking event to public appearance in an automobile that had a small doghouse mounted on its roof.

With seven Whelan-backed members on the council and two opposition newcomers, I was surprised—and delighted—to learn that in the wake of the successful campaign, I had been elected unanimously to serve as city clerk of Jersey City. My first duty, after taking the oath of office myself, was to administer the oath to the reelected mayor, Thomas J. Whelan, who was prepared to serve for another four years.

He would not serve that long as mayor. But he would serve more than seven years in a federal penitentiary.

16

There had been plenty of political surprises in the several months before one Thomas F. X. Smith found himself strolling the corridors of City Hall as a person who belonged there, rather than as a visitor. On the national front, Lyndon Baines Johnson had told a disheartened nation that he would not stand for reelection in 1968, and Richard M. Nixon had edged Hubert H. Humphrey for the country's topmost job. Trying to wage a double war—against inflation on the one hand and the persistent North Vietnamese on the other—Nixon and his vice-president, former Maryland Governor Spiro T. Agnew, found themselves so busy that a state of suspicion and confusion began to hold sway over all of Washington. It would culminate in the exposures of Watergate less than five years later.

There were exposures that would come sooner from the deeds and misdeeds within the Whelan administration. Newly arrived on the scene, however, I looked around at the team the mayor had put together over the years and once again felt a feeling familiar to anyone who has ever been close to the world of politics: With so many different personalities, so many different temperaments, so many different nationalities and backgrounds, how in the world will *anything* ever get decided? Ever get done?

There were the councilmen—Whelan's selections, William A. Massa, Frank J. Quilty, Neil Pecoraro, Thomas M. Flaherty, John Jaroski, Jack Kelaher, and Thomas McGovern; and the two ''opposition'' members, William J. Thornton and Morris ''Watchdog''

Pesin. As Director of Public Works, the group appointed an old friend of mine, Morris Longo—yes, he of the famous name in Jersey City politics and the same enthusiastic campaigner who had devised "Buckle Down, Witkowski" for that candidate's unsuccessful 1961 try for the mayoralty. And the job of Democratic County Chairman, formerly held by Kenny's nemesis, John J. Kenny, was now in the hands of Walter Wolfe, a man who had been a boyhood hero to hundreds of Jersey City youngsters in the late 1930s and early 1940s.

Wally Wolfe.

It was difficult for me not to feel proud that I was a small part in the governing mechanism in which this legendary figure also worked. To many of the city's residents, Wally personified the idea of serving both God and Country. A tall, handsome young man with dark hair and shining blue eyes, he had earned himself a niche at St. Peter's Prep as one of the finest athletes ever to attend the school. An outstanding player on the football field, he had been an obvious star on the baseball diamond—one of the greatest produced by the state's scholastic athletic programs. But before the Boston Red Sox could sign him to become a professional with skills that seemed certain to earn him an eventual place in the Hall of Fame, the drums of war sounded.

And as the fine American he was, Wally marched off to battle the Japanese on an island that few people in "Joisey" had ever heard of. Giving up a precious piece of safety in a small foxhole to make room for three of his Marine buddies, the young hero felt a fragment of an enemy shell burrow deep into his skull. He survived, but afterwards wore a steel plate in his head. His dreams of starring as one of the finest third basemen in Boston history—perhaps in the World Series!—ended in an instant of pain and flashing light and blood. Returning to his hometown, Wally Wolfe married one of the prettiest young women in town—as destiny seemed to rule that he would—and began to devote himself to serving his fellow citizens.

And I, who admired him so much, was working with him.

I found that I was working hard, too. I had to—because the entire Whelan administration suddenly faced what appeared to be an almost insurmountable crisis.

Whelan's position as a "take charge" executive had tarnished considerably, while his "law and order" posture had been diminished after President Johnson's refusal to run for reelection defused the anti-war strife that had plagued many urban areas. The citizens' minds were firmly fixed on local problems that concerned them: rising unemployment, rising taxes, and deteriorating services. So when Whelan proposed that the city's budget for 1970 be set at a record level—and that the increases would be financed by a staggering jump in taxes—it would be putting it mildly to say that the public reaction was one of fury. Under the terms of the Faulkner Act, the voters could recall an elected official after the official had served one year in office. Almost as soon as the new budget and tax increases were announced, the word "recall" began to be heard throughout the city.

At the budget hearing in mid-March, a record number of citizens jammed the assembly chamber, overflowing into the hallways and down the staircase to the first floor. Angry voices, one after another, spoke out against the increases. A final count showed that more than 140 people, most opposed to the budget, made themselves heard. At times tempers flared and, as the council members grew tired, the shouting matches threatened to become a riot. It was two a.m., some three days after the hearing began, when the municipal council passed the new budget by the expected seven-to-two vote. But then a court ruled that the members had acted too soon, that they had not given everyone a chance to be heard, and the list of speakers was lengthened. Finally, the budget was approved once more, after Whelan had gone on record as refusing "to cut a cent" from it.

Now recall appeared inevitable. Several groups began racing the clock, hurrying to get the proper number of signatures on petitions that would allow a new election to be held. July 1, 1970, was the cut-off date. An organization calling itself the Community Action Council (CAC) sprang up under the direction of a telephone company executive, Jack Finn. He was joined by Father Francis Schiller, a religious activist; Dr. Paul Jordan, a young physician; and Bernard M. Hartnett Jr., a veteran politician whose father had broken with John V. Kenny in the 1950s. Although most of its leaders were political neophytes, the CAC attracted numerous seasoned veterans from several political groups. Jack Finn's wife, Mary, along with a number of irate homemakers—Mary Ann Bauer, Lois Shaw, Charlotte Haley, and Loretta Kelly among them—jumped in to help gather the signatures of thousands of female voters.

If the kind of dissension that had prevented other political achievements in Jersey City over the decades had not once again surfaced, Mayor Whelan and his associates might have been more worried about their political futures. But a rival group rose to oppose the CAC. Calling itself the Citizens Independent League, the organization was all in favor of recall—but it wanted to be the group credited with achieving it. The CIL was headed by Thomas "Buddy" Gangemi, son of the former mayor and one-time deputy mayor in 1957. Backed by longtime supporters of the Gangemi family's political ambitions, the group saw recall as its stepping-stone into City Hall once again.

Both the CAC and CIL fanned out across the city in a frantic rush to collect the 28,670 signatures that would be needed to recall Whelan. The same number was required to remove from office three of the council members, while four others could be removed if the petitioners provided 4,000 to 6,000 signatures each—the exact number depending on how many voters were registered in each councilman's ward.

While each organization predicted that it would be first to show up at the city clerk's office with the required 100,000-plus signatures, it was "Buddy" Gangemi who got to bask in the flash of the photographers' bulbs when he duly presented—on January 11, 1971—some 7,000 pages, each bearing 20 signatures.

Under the law, my office was required to check the validity of the petitions within ten days, then schedule a new election between 60 and 90 days after the date of verification. Although we worked frantically, it soon became obvious that the huge number of names made it impossible to complete the checking process in time. An extension was granted by Superior Court Judge Samuel A. Larner—the celebrated investigator who had earlier sought to rid the city of Mayor John V. Kenny. After several more extensions and days of feverish activity, I announced that the CIL had failed to effectuate an election by some 11,406 names. With my aides, Helen Kozma and Ed Hart, I informed former judge Edward Zampella (legal representative for the CIL) that 5,953 of the names on the petitions were not those of registered voters. And 6,961 were invalid because of duplications or because the signatures did not match those in the election registers.

A handwriting expert had been hired to investigate many of the signatures that seemed to be forgeries. Upon receiving certification, thousands of suspect signatures were forwarded to the office of the attorney general for possible fraud action.

Stunned and angry, Gangemi threatened to file a legal challenge to our findings. But he was spared the trouble when Jack Finn swallowed his pride and said that the CAC would combine its 22,000 signatures with those of the CIL. Perhaps more worried now than he made evident, Mayor Whelan asked the court to invalidate all the petitions on the ground that they were "permeated with fraud." His argument was rejected, and my aides and I set to work to examine the combined petitions.

Going over each name with painstaking attention to detail, it became obvious that while enough names were now present on the petitions—there were 782 more than necessary, in fact—forgeries by "phantom" signers reduced the number below the required amount. As if that were not enough to stop the recall movement dead in its tracks, a judicial ruling from the appellate division of the superior court did the job. It upheld a Larner opinion that the affiant to a recall petition (the individual who swears to the validity of the signatures) must be both a resident of the city and a registered voter. In the case of a councilman, the affiant must be a resident of the particular ward in which the councilman lives.

The date was May 4 when I, in my role as city clerk of Jersey City, ruled that the mayor and assorted councilmen had escaped the threat of being forced into a recall election. In perhaps any other American city, it might have been a time for the political figures who had been under attack for so long to breathe easily.

Not in Jersey City.

Even while the recall movements had been forming and gathering steam, the mayor and his close associates had been deluged by a torrent of subpoenas. The United States government was probing the activities of the Jersey City administration since 1965. Whelan and seven other top officials were summoned before a federal grand jury meeting in Newark, and I—still learning the details of my new job—was ordered under a subpoena to bring all documents and records that concerned construction contracts amounting to more than $100,000 awarded by Jersey City after January 1, 1965.

At a meeting called by Mayor Whelan to learn who in the administration had received subpoenas, those whose subpoenas hinted of wrongdoing seemed surprised that they were being called to the inquiry. I remember turning to Moe Longo, who also was still feeling his way in his new assignment, and saying, "Gee, Moe, if everyone else is innocent, I guess you and I are the ones the government wants."

I was making light of a serious matter, and it turned out—to my relief—that Moe and I were not on anyone's "target" list. The grand jury handed down a number of indictments—for Mayor Thomas Whelan, Business Manager Philip Kunz, Purchasing Agent Bernard Murphy, Councilman Thomas Flaherty, former county chairman John J. Kenny, County Auditor William Sternkopf, County Police Chief Fred Kropke, Kenny aid James Corrado, County Engineer Frank Manning, County Treasurer Joseph B. Stapleton, and county "boss" John V. Kenny.

And County Chairman Walter Wolfe!

A cry of rage came immediately from 77-year-old John V. Kenny, who had learned from Frank Hague that the best defense was an instant, furious, all-out attack. "We took on the biggest, the best, and most vicious—Frank Hague!" shouted the "little leader." He waited for the assembled newsmen to nod their recollection. "And we beat him! Hague was ten times tougher, and we wouldn't back down. Well, we're not backing down now."

John V. Kenny had an explanation to suggest why the government was after an innocent man: "They're trying to frame me."

If the government was out to frame anyone, it seemed to be doing a good job. Its basic charges were that Whelan and enough associates to make an even dozen defendants—they were immediately dubbed "the Hudson 12" by the newspapers—had prospered to the tune of some $3.5 million by awarding construction contracts to companies that paid kickback money for the assignments.

Within a few days, it became obvious that Whelan was in huge trouble. One of the dozen, James Corrado, a close confidante to John V. Kenny, quickly pleaded guilty to one of two counts of conspiracy in his indictment. Then, in a stunning move, John J. Kenny—who had long been a favorite of John V.—"made a deal" and had himself severed from the trial. Another defendant, Frank Manning, joined him. The two men, a government attorney jubilantly announced, would be witnesses for the prosecution.

If Whelan had hopes that the U.S. attack might be weakened by trying to prove the guilt of a dozen men at one time, he saw the odds turning against him as the number of defendants dwindled—first to 11, then to nine. And when the aging John V. Kenny, whose health was failing rapidly, was given a severance from the trial by a sympathetic judge, the Hudson 12 had become the Hudson 8.

The trial took two months, during which the jury heard scores of witnesses but undoubtedly was most impressed by the testimony of John J. Kenny. The former Democratic county chairman readily revealed everything he knew about who had paid what to whom in exchange for what—and his years in local government had made him an extremely knowledgeable witness. At one point. he claimed that John V. Kenny was so fearful of his misdeeds being exposed during the trial that the county boss had given him—John J. Kenny—$50,000 in cash to bribe a government witness not to testify in the case. John J. admitted that he had accepted the money and had hidden it away in a garbage can in his basement. On cue, the government prosecutor wheeled a trash can into the courtroom and showed the jury $50,000 in bills.

Another witness, introduced by the prosecution as a "respectable" businessman, testified that he had been given $50,000 by his employers after the company won a contract to construct a bridge. The money, he stated, was a payoff for various politicians who had decided which firm got the contract. As if to prove his allegation, he admitted that he had personally pocketed $5,000 of the money before passing the rest on as ordered. "I knew the bastard was crooked," said a voice on the defendants' side of the packed courtroom.

Helping to turn the tide further against Whelan and his co-defendants were the huge sums of money that the government was able to show the men had amassed during their relatively brief terms in office. Federal agents had swooped down to confiscate $700,000 in bearer bonds owned by John V. Kenny, along with $20,000 in cash obtained from ticket sales to a Democratic party fund-raising dinner at $100 a plate. Government exhibit 2214 was a cancelled bank book that showed $1,231,000 had been stowed away in a Florida bank account jointly owned by Thomas J. Whelan and Thomas M. Flaherty. The mayor's chauffeur, a former police officer named Mickey Atchinson, testified that he had taken the money out of the account at Whelan's direction shortly before the federal indictments were handed down. The subsequent whereabouts of the $1.2 million were unknown.

Bolstering its charges that an organized scheme of kickbacks had existed from November 1963 onward, the government produced numerous contractors, engineers, suppliers, and others who had done business with Hudson County and Jersey City during the period. Testifying under immunity from prosecution—as did John J. Kenny and Frank Manning—many in the parade of witnesses admitted having made kickbacks, while others stated that they had refused to do business in the city or county rather than make the payoffs. Several contractors said that if they had agreed to return 7 percent of a $40 million contract to "the boys," they could have gone to work but had turned down the deal. John J. Kenny promptly proceeded to identify who "the boys" were.

It took the jury only four hours to reach a verdict. The foreman, Mrs. Ruby McCullough, announced in a firm, unwavering voice that the defendants—all eight of them—had been judged guilty on all counts of conspiracy and extortion.

All eight defendants. Including Wally Wolfe.

I could not believe it. If my heart had been sickened when I had first heard the words, "The United States Government versus Walter Wolfe," the anguish doubled when I heard the jurors' verdict. It couldn't be true. Not Wally; not the beloved, handsome man who had fought so hard for his school, his country, his dream.

Happily, Judge Robert Shaw felt much the same way that I did. He looked at the marine hero, who had been charged with 27 counts of extortion and two counts of conspiracy in the $3.5 million scheme. With but five dollars in his own bank account, Wally had contended that he was simply a victim of circumstances. Taking note of his past stature and present situation, the judge passed a non-custodial sentence on the proud wearer of the Purple Heart. Although he was not sent to jail, the still-youthful Wally Wolfe was forbidden from ever taking part in politics again. (He eventually proved his leadership abilities anew, by being elected president of the Iron Workers Union in Jersey City.)

Judge Shaw was nowhere near as lenient with the other defendants. Both Whelan and Flaherty received sentences of 15 years in federal prison and, unable to post $400,000 bail, they began to serve their terms at once. (Each was freed after spending one-half of the proscribed term in jail.) Murphy, the city's purchasing agent, received a similar sentence; Sternkopf, the auditor, got 10 years, along with a fine of $20,000; and the others received jail sentences ranging from two to five years.

With the outcome of the case making headlines across the nation, the image of Jersey City as a hotbed of corruption and bossism was further enhanced; but the immediate problem facing the citizens was to choose a new administration that could find solutions for the problems of today and tomorrow. An outsider, viewing the situation, might have thought the new mayor would be chosen from among candidates who could show a clear division between the former administration and themselves.

Not in Jersey City.

John V. Kenny, now 79 and ensconced in an "office" in Pollack Hospital, had pleaded guilty to the government charges and had been officially given a jail sentence, which then had been rescinded because of his age and health. He had subsequently announced his retirement as city and county political leader, but, as the scholarly author of *A Cycle of Power* points out, "he had purportedly 'retired' a couple of times before and observers wondered whether this was indeed his swan song.'' They wondered even more when one of Kenny's closest friends, Charles K. Krieger, was named interim mayor of Jersey City by a seven-to-one vote of the city council.

The appointment of Krieger was one of the most bizarre occurrences in a city where bizarre political developments had become commonplace. The new mayor was a 58-year-old executive with a brokerage firm who had fled his native Austria shortly before the Nazi takeover some 33 years earlier. Compact, balding, and a veteran of World War II, he was fluent in German, French, and Spanish as well as English, and he held a doctorate in philosophy. Truly, he was unlike any other Jersey City mayor who had preceded him. His appointment, some said, was a ''miracle.''

With his wife Esther beaming at his side, Krieger took his oath of office on August 5, 1971—and promptly was met by a barrage of questions from such longtime mayoral hopefuls as ''Buddy'' Gangemi, John Yengo, Edward Zampella, and Michael Bell. The focus of their queries: Hadn't John V. Kenny stretched his still-powerful hand into city hall's coffers from his bed in Pollack Hospital via the appointment of his friend, Kreiger, as mayor?

The best they could get out of the diminutive new chief executive was an affirmation of ''personal affection'' for the retired Democratic political leader. But he promised that he would attempt to change the image of the city during his brief 90-day stay as mayor. To prove it, he announced that one of his first official acts was the firing of Warren Murphy, the personal secretary of the convicted Tom Whelan.

Obviously enjoying the job, Krieger gained headlines when he invited the mayor of Vienna to visit Jersey City, but as a special election neared—set for November 2, 1971—to let the voters decide on a mayor and councilman-at-large to fill the unexpired terms of the departed Whelan and Flaherty, Krieger reluctantly chose not to run. Perhaps he realized that his education, his status as a naturalized citizen, and his connection with Kenny might all combine to turn various segments of the Jersey City voting population against him.

His withdrawal in no way left the voters without a sizable field of candidates. Nearly two dozen people let it be known that they would be glad to enter the race, even if it meant serving only for 20 months initially.

From the beginning, it looked as if the "man to beat" was the 30-year-old physician, Paul Jordan, who had been one of the founders of the Community Action Council organized by phone company executive Jack Finn to bring about the recall of Mayor Whelan in 1970. Jordan, the crafty Finn knew, was the type of "new face" that could win support among business and religious groups as well as the electorate. With the aid of Father Francis Schiller, a youthful cleric, and veteran politician Bernie Hartnett, Finn and Jordan had already proved their strength by getting 22,000 names on the Whelan recall petitions, and had endeared themselves even to the rival Citizens Independent League (headed by "Buddy" Gangemi) by agreeing to combine their lists with those of the CIL to try to bring down Whelan.

Finn, however, was clever enough not to let Jordan's hat be tossed into the ring too quickly. Do that, he reasoned, and the opposition only had more time to present negative reasons why a man should not be elected. He let it be known that the CAC was considering any number of qualified candidates—an indication of the organization's depth and strength.

He dropped the name of one possible contender, Alexander Herrenchak, and smiled as one or another member of the entrenched machine made puns on the candidate's name: "The CAC's come up with a Herrin'—one of those Jewish fishes" or "I wonder if this Herrin' smells as bad as the church people with him" (this last from an old Horseshoe politician who remembered when "duh fodders [priests] was too respectable to start trouble"). Before long, the machine had probed into Herrenchak's background and felt that it had enough material to ensure his defeat in the election—but soon realized that its investigators had been wasting their time. Finn, it seemed, had tossed out Herrenchak's name only as a red herring. His candidate would be Paul Jordan, as had been expected.

Jordan won quick support from Father Victor R. Yanitelli, S. J., president of Saint Peter's College, which was reappearing on the Jersey City political scene after a hiatus of a decade. Tom Stanton, president of First Jersey National Bank, became the next prominent name to commit to the young doctor who had worked at Patrick House, a rehabilitation center for drug addicts, and whose father had been a teacher in the city's school system. The influential *Jersey Journal* came out in support of Jordan early on, and he was established seemingly overnight.

"Buddy" Gangemi, who had seen the CAC get off to a flying start (in the race for petitions to recall Whelan) and then had caught and surpassed them, decided he might do the trick again. With followers still on hand from his 1965 and 1969 efforts urging him to go for the nomination, the son of the former mayor said he would mount a winning effort this time. There was a problem, of course, that would have to be overcome. Where the elder Gangemi had been close to Boss Kenny, the son and Kenny had been distrustful of one another. "Buddy" could count on little help from the septuagenarian who still remained powerful within the Democratic machine, no matter how often he said he had retired from politics.

Besides, the machine regulars had been so occupied with the trial, outcome, and consequences of the Hudson 8 that they had little time to collect their differing opinions and choose a candidate. When they came up with a name—Morris T. Longo—even some old-timers in the organization were surprised. The brother of the courageous John R. Longo, Moe was a career public employee who was not well known on the political scene. True, he was a former all-sports star athlete at Lincoln High School and had served as a captain in the army—but over the years, the Longo family had earned a reputation for independent, "maverick" thinking. In other words, Moe Longo's "loyalty" to the machine was questionable.

Another cause of worry: With both Gangemi and Longo in the race, there would be a chance that the solid bloc of Italian-American voters would be split. Some regulars advanced the theory that Kenny had urged the nomination of Longo in a deliberate attempt to split the Italian-American vote and prevent Gangemi from becoming mayor. He would thus be in the position of helping Jordan, who might thereafter be in his debt. (I found the theory preposterous, but a friend, Willie Wolfe, one of the most loyal workers the Democratic machine ever had and a man I consider completely honest in his remarks, once told me that Kenny had given the word, "Go Jordan," on election day.)

Other candidates surfaced—until there were 18 in all, including Republican party hopeful Ed Magee and perennial hopeful Michael J. Bell. I knew many of them from past efforts, but got to meet even the least-familiar newcomers when the Chamber of Commerce asked all 18 to debate before an invited audience at the Hotel Plaza. Having gained a modest reputation as an apt public speaker, I was invited to moderate the program. There was a condition, however, which I laughingly accepted at once: I had to assure the business community that I did not intend to run for the mayoralty, and, therefore would be an impartial moderator.

That decision was easy compared to the legal question I had to resolve.

The city clerk normally examines the election petitions, conducts the drawing for ballot position and receives the voting returns. However, since this was a special election to be held at the general election, I contended that the county clerk was responsible for the conduct of the election. Supreme Court Judge James Rosen agreed, and I was reduced to an interested observer of history.

There was little time for any of the candidates to mount the kind of campaign that permits rebuttal of an opponent's arguments. Finn's contention—that the CAC and its candidate, Jordan, could cut out the disease that had infected the city for so long—was difficult to turn aside, especially by the veteran politicians who had been associated with previous administrations. When the polls closed, Jordan was victorious with some 26,771 votes—more than 5,400 above the total achieved by Gangemi. And the young doctor had beaten Longo by 14,000 votes. All in all, however, because of the large number of candidates, Jordan received only 32 percent of the total number of votes cast—one of the lowest pluralities in any mayoralty contest in the city's history.

There was speculation that Gangemi would have won if Kenny had supported him, or if Longo had dropped out of the race. But the doubts and "what if?" theories meant little. It was that Jack Finn had cleverly engineered a "new face" into the office of mayor of Jersey City. Patrolman Dominick Pugliese, Jordan's running mate for the office of councilman-at-large, was an easy winner, too. At the Hotel Plaza, as early as 9:50 on election night, the newly elected mayor flashed a victory gesture and shouted to the cheering crowd: "Thank God Almighty we're free at last." And he followed with a statement that sent his exhausted supporters into a frenzy: "John V. Kenny is through once and for all!"

Still, when the frail and once all-powerful former mayor and county leader died shortly after Jordan took office, the mayor ordered the flag on City Hall lowered to half-staff. The New York *Daily News,* pointing out that Kenny was a convicted felon, criticized the decision.

Proclaiming an end to bossism—"The dynasty of fear is ended"—the enthusiastic and energetic new occupant of the mayor's office made it clear that he expected the members of the city's autonomous bodies to submit their resignations. Corporation Counsel James Ryan, after some resistance, gave up his post. Finance Director Anthony Ferrara attempted to get the municipal council to veto the mayor's action, but failed—and was dismissed. The council's inaction towards Ferrara's plan showed plainly that it was not going to resist the new order and when Jack Deegan called for 16 county organization candidates to attend a meeting to plan an anti-Jordan strategy, only three people answered the call. One of those present, Assemblyman Joseph LeFante, blasted the tottering organization as "suffering from lack of leadership." More likely, it simply was a case of the members' knowing which leader they preferred to follow.

As if to prove that his "youth movement" could succeed where older and supposedly wiser heads had failed, Jordan began promoting the ideas that many argued were needed to revitalize Jersey City in 1972. He did nothing as dramatic, of course, as President Nixon's weeklong visit to Communist China that February, but what he did on the local front seemed every bit as significant to Jersey City voters. He put through one of the largest tax cuts in the city's history, added 200 policemen to help silence critics who were citing rising crime statistics, and opened nearly a dozen vest-pocket parks for relaxation and recreation purposes throughout the city (although the previous administration had laid the groundwork for the last program).

Perhaps his largest program—a $2-billion plan to develop a huge section of waterfront property into an area of housing, industry, and recreation—was not thought through carefully enough. It ran into immediate opposition and eventually became the target of a full legislative investigation. Assemblyman David Friedland, who had once been a Jordan supporter, instigated the probe when he questioned the legality of a contract awarded to two New York-based firms for construction on the waterfront. The awards had been given without the city asking publicly for bids. Friedland, a skillful attorney, tenaciously pursued the issue before the joint legislative committee. He predicted that Jordan's plan would eventually come to naught, and that the city would regret the contractual arrangements. (He proved prophetically correct, and almost a decade later Jersey City had failed to realize even one cent in taxes from what can be considered one of the finest pieces of waterfront property in the entire United States.)

Mayor Jordan also ran into trouble when the *Hudson Dispatch* printed a front-page report that claimed waterfront property would be used as the site of a new prison. The mayor quickly denied any such intentions; there were rumors that the story had been "planted" by one or another opposition candidate preparing to challenge him at the end of his brief elected term.

The incredible thing was that, once the mayor had settled into his office and put a handful of programs into action, it was time to start getting ready for the 1973 election—and, where nearly 20 candidates had run just two years earlier, only one rose to confront him now. The opponent was Thomas "Buddy" Gangemi, in whose breast hope appeared to spring eternal.

Gangemi took a direct attack, as might be expected. He charged that in 18 months in office, Paul Jordan had given the people of Jersey City little else but "public relations pledges." And, he added that Jordan, despite vows to the contrary, had embraced a number of old-line politicians.

Meanwhile, by diligently performing my duties as city clerk, and having established a reputation for honesty—so much so that my penchant to speak out led a White House spokesman to refer to me later in my career as "the mouth that roared"—I had developed a good working relationship with the mayor. Still, I was surprised when he asked me to run with him as a candidate for councilman-at-large. Surprised and delighted; honored, perhaps, might be a better word. I weighed my decision carefully, calculating how my entry into the political wars would affect my wife Florence and our daughters Carol and Regina.

At that time, I decided that it would be imprudent to run for the council, and I proposed that the offer be made to ''Wally'' Sheil, a boyhood friend.

If I would not run along with him, Jordan asked, would I serve as the keynote speaker at his major fund-raising affair? This time, my reply came much more quickly. As city clerk—a post in which I saw myself working for the people of the city and not for whichever administration happened to be in power at any particular time—it would not be proper to appear as an enthusiastic advocate of the mayor in public, no matter how fervently I believed in him. As a private citizen, I told him, I would be glad to tell friends and associates my opinion and would encourage their support for him.

But, I said, my chief responsibility—both to him and the electorate—would be to do something that few city clerks of Jersey City had concerned themselves with: Supervise an honest election.

17

To the political outsider, the office of city clerk in Jersey City or elsewhere might seem of little significance—a sort of routine job that involves issuing and accepting official documents, calling meetings to order, and so forth—but because of a number of quasi-legal factors and considerations, the man who holds the office frequently has power to affect the outcome of local history. For nearly seven decades, the office had been closely controlled by the incumbent administration in City Hall. One of Frank Hague's choices for city clerk, World War II hero Francis X. Burke, had publicly campaigned for and had been a significant vote-getter. For Mayor John Kenny, it was well-known that his city clerk, James A. Tumulty, would do anything short of murder—and there were some who said that the man might stoop to *that* if it became necessary.

It was, I soon found out, virtually impossible for me not to play a role—a minor one, but still a significant one—in Paul Jordan's battle with "Buddy" Gangemi. Aware that I had been a follower of the local political scene for more than 20 years, the mayor asked me to submit a list of men and women who might make good candidates for the council posts. It must be noted that I was not the only one asked to prepare a list, lest the reader sense that I am immodestly proclaiming myself as the mayor's closest confidante.

There were several men—Peter Zampella, from the Downtown section; Dominick Pugliese, at-large; and Morris Pesin, known for his efforts to make Liberty State Park a glorious recreational facility for New Jersey residents, from the West Side—whose names appeared on virtually everyone's list. But I confronted Mayor Jordan with several other names that he did not immediately accept.

William Massa, for example, from Journal Square. Bill Thornton, from Bergen-Lafayette, and Mrs. Lois Shaw, an original member of his CAC team.

Massa, the mayor pointed out, had been a maverick when he served as a councilman during the Whelan reign, and had been the only councilman to vote against the assumption of the mayoralty by immigrant Charles Krieger. Long considered to be a shrewd observer of the complex world of Jersey City politics, Massa had shed his reputation for political astuteness when he became one of the 17 losing candidates in the race that had seen Jordan come out on top in 1971. Of all the contenders, his vote total—a paltry 1,238—put him far down the list of also-ran's. Still, to the voters in Journal Square, the man remained popular, and I pointed out to Jordan that he was the only candidate faced with recall whose enemies had failed to obtain the needed number of petitions. Whether it was the strength of my arguments, or some other factor of which I am unaware, Jordan selected Massa to represent Journal Square.

There was a somewhat different problem with the consideration of Bill Thornton, the black candidate from the Bergen-Lafayette ward who wished to run for reelection. The mayor had been told by Father Francis Schiller, his old employer and political ally, that Thornton could not win. Father Schiller and the mayor were very close, and the cleric was willing to back Jordan's introduction of a methadone facility to combat the growing problems of drug use in the city. To further that cause, Jordan had named Father Schiller's choice as director of the city's Narcotic and Drug Abuse Program, displacing the former head, Anthony Amabile. ''The mayor has the right to name his man,'' said a meek Amabile, who possibly felt himself under fire because Jordan had hinted he might ask the public prosecutor to look into the way program funds had been handled previously.

Now, when Schiller reported negative feelings toward Thornton, it was natural that Jordan gave them consideration. I argued, on the other hand, that Thornton was an articulate, meticulously groomed individual whom black voters may feel should have another chance. And the fact that previous blacks who were elected had held little continuity in office in Hudson County could swing votes to the slate, I said, if Jordan stayed with Thornton. Again, the mayor made what I considered the right choice.

I can take some credit for Lois Shaw's selection. Initially Jordan's supporters wanted Ed Gaffney, a CAC stalwart, but that, I suggested, would give them an all-male ticket. I proposed Lois Shaw and impressed on the mayor how imperative it was to have a woman on his ticket. Jordan agreed with my assessment: Lois Shaw became his candidate.

Another potential candidate for the slate, Tom McGovern, had encountered trouble when a number of Jordan supporters attempted his recall, and when he was rushed into a local hospital—ostensibly because of illness—wild rumors began circulating that he had decided to run with Gangemi. We learned soon afterwards, however, that the illness was real, and that he would support Tim Hawkes, a Greenville neighbor and former football star who had been increasingly involved in our campaign. The young man, Jordan decided, would add a bit of youthful exuberance to our efforts.

It was vital to collect names for the nominating petitions as quickly as possible, because time was short. Despite the fact that City Hall employees were "released" from their work to assist in last-minute efforts to come up with the necessary number of signatures, it began to look as if Hawkes would not have the needed number by the deadline. His supporters began to race the clock, and in my role as city clerk I once again had to decide whether or not the petitions would be accepted. To forestall any claims that my watch or the City Hall clocks were fast or slow, I ruled that the four o'clock cut-off time would be determined by the mechanical voice of the operator giving the time over the telephone. The number was dialed, and the voice stated clearly, "At the tone, the time is three fifty-nine and forty seconds . . . three fifty-nine and fifty seconds . . . four p.m."

The hour had come, and I announced that the filing was closed. And it was evident that Hawkes did not have enough signatures to enter the race.

Telephones in my office and throughout the building were ringing. Other supporters were hurrying down with more petitions, more signatures. They would give Hawkes more than enough! Couldn't the time be extended—a few minutes, if not a few hours—to allow the petitions to be delivered? What if the petitions arrived momentarily, by 4:15 at the latest?

I was almost ill when the pleading voices beseeched me to "bend the rules a little, Tommie. It's been done before." I knew that the rules—the *laws!*—had been bent, or broken, frequently in the past. I knew the election cases by heart, and was aware that such actions had been sustained by court decisions. But I also knew that because I had openly supported the Jordan ticket, it would look extremely suspicious if I allowed the Hawkes petitions to be filed after the deadline. I refused to bend the regulations.

Jordan supporters were surprised by my action, openly suspicious of what they considered a display of disloyalty to "our" team. Although I did not know it at the time, the decision would be the first of several that would eventually drive a deep wedge between some Jordanites and myself.

At the time, my strong stance on the side of fair play and honesty was of great significance. But shortly afterwards, a court judge ruled that Hawkes' adherents could file the additional petitions. A fundamental premise of the election laws, as Hudson County Superintendent of Elections Joseph Brady often advised, is that they must be "liberally interpreted so that the will of the people is not thwarted," regardless of the literal reading of the statues. To some staunch Jordan supporters, the court had shown me who really was in charge in Jersey City.

I had little time to worry about any enemies that I might have created by my action. The Gangemi forces were welding together as strong a ticket as possible. "Buddy" offered as councilpersons-at-large Shirley Porte, a leading official of the Parent and Teachers Association, perennial GOP hopeful Ed Magee, and Frank J. Quilty, a Whelan holdover who was popular in the Hudson City area. Other candidates for the ticket from various wards included Henry Przystup of Greenville, Thomas Cowan in Journal Square, Anthony

Cucci from Downtown, Addison McLeon in Bergen-Lafayette, and the popular Thomas Maresca in Hudson City.

Maresca seemed such a strong favorite that few in his ward wanted to challenge him, but the CAC found a willing volunteer: Al D'Auria, a member of a family that long had been close to the entrenched Kenny machine—a posture that had earned him a place on the city "pad." Another CAC contender was Paul Cuprowski, who had served as the president of the Thomas Maresca Association and had received considerable publicity in that role.

The simple fact that there were only two candidates—the incumbent Jordan and the anxious Gangemi—made things relatively easy for the voters this time around. Both campaigns settled on virtually the same slogan, "Jordan, Yes, Jordan!" vs. "Gangemi, Yes, Gangemi!" But the mayor had the stronger platform when he urged the voters to "reject the 'Buddy' system," with its implications of cronyism and the return of City Hall to old-time political hacks. The mayor won the support of most of the area newspapers, and *The New York Times* summed things up by saying: "The overriding issue is simply whether the voters wish to restore their ties to the vaunted machine that ruled city affairs, or to reaffirm the break they made 18 months ago."

The speeches were made, the banners waved, and the money spent. And when the votes were totalled, Jordan had 48,845 to Gangemi's 32,364. Three council candidates—Pesin and Thornton (both with Jordan), and Maresca (nominally with Gangemi, but actually an independent)—were victorious on the first ballot. Five weeks later, the remainder of Jordan's candidates won their runoff elections. Zampella, who trailed by almost 1,000 votes on election day, May 8, turned the tables on Anthony Cucci, Gangemi's choice, in the runoff as large numbers of voters who had been disillusioned by the easy defeat of "Buddy" swiftly changed sides.

A dejected Gangemi told his disappointed and angry following that he had been beaten by "the liberal press." As he strode out of the room, downcast, a staunch supporter (and perennial loser) Mike Bell tried to cheer the crowd by saying that the courts would overturn the election results by upholding his charge that Jordan had used public funds in his campaign.

Such charges made the mayor state that his opponents would receive "no amnesty" from the administration. The line was once again clearly drawn between the "ins" and the "outs." If Jersey City were going to solve its problems of high taxation, rising crime, aging schools, and all the others facing urban America, it would solve them—Jordan said—by putting an end to the Hudson County political machine and developing the vast waterfront area that held so much promise.

As saddening as it was to me—to everyone—nothing changed, other than the leadership of the Hudson County Organization. Paul Jordan and Bernie Hartnett, Jr., were now the leaders. The grandiose campaign literature that pledged a new and revitalized waterfront area—"a city within a city"—proved to be little more than words and pretty sketches on paper.

The failures—and who doesn't have failures—of the Jordan administration did not capture the full attention of a public that had the daily revelations of the breaking Watergate scandal to feast upon. Suddenly, the unblinking eye of television and the excited voices of electronic newsmen were flooding Jersey City and the nation with word of seemingly traitorous actions of such men as Haldeman, Ehrlichman, and Dean. And then with news that the vice-president of the United States had evaded income tax payments . . . and resigned in disgrace. And then with the resignation of the president, of Richard Milhous Nixon himself! In, and around and between, there was word about Patricia Hearst and bloody shootouts in California, the massive war between the Arabs and Israelis, the seizure of an American ship, the *Mayaguez,* and its dramatic rescue from Cambodian forces by the U.S. Navy and Marines, and—occupying everyone's attention for month after month—the nation's glorious, fireworks-filled celebration of its bicentennial birthday on July 4, 1976!

While historic events raged around us on all sides, Jordan's squabbles with people near at hand seemed overwhelmingly inconsequential. Jack Finn, the vital force behind the CAC movement which had made Jordan mayor, sought the city chairmanship—but Jordan, wanting to run his own show, failed to support him for the position. An incensed Finn issued an ultimatum: Either he got the chairmanship or he would leave the CAC. Finn prevailed, but his relationship with the mayor became increasingly shaky.

Jordan needed as much continuing support as he could muster, because several of his "pet" projects were under fire from the citizenry. The planned network of methadone centers for drug addicts—to be built under the sponsorship of Patrick House, Jordan's former employer—met strong community protests when it was proposed. While citizens admitted that drug use was a growing problem throughout the city, few communities wanted a facility located where it would attract addicts to the neighborhood. The issue was exacerbated when Patrick House announced the purchase of two rather unusual acquisitions, a pair of bar-and-restaurant establishments. Despite the rising protest, Jordan refused to back off from his idea that the drug centers were needed, or from the belief that his former employer was the right choice to operate them.

He did, however, back down when a storm of protests met his proposal for a chemical tank "farm" on some waterfront property. The state's Natural Resource Council rejected the idea outright.

During his first full four-year term, Mayor Jordan could point to several not-insignificant accomplishments. He developed the first full-time municipal court in the state and could take credit for one of the finest screening clinics for child health in the nation.

And—as many of his predecessors could not—he could claim a "clean" record, a substantial achievement in the years that followed the "Hudson 8" scandal.

But viewing the mayor's actions from my close proximity to his administration, I increasingly found myself wondering about what he was giving the people of Jersey City—the "little guys," the men and women who had voted for him, and the children who would become adults to vote in future elections. Was the Office of the Mayor giving these people enough?

I wondered.

And the answer that came to me, time and again, was "*no.*"

No, it was not enough.

Now the mayor was faced with a decision. Unpopular at home—voters in increasing numbers were beginning to agree that the city administration was not productive enough—and yet looked upon by some voters elsewhere in the state as a youthful reformer, Jordan saw opportunity facing him. He had, he thought, a good chance to become governor of New Jersey if he mounted a strong campaign against the incumbent, Brendan T. Byrne. Byrne himself was battling a wave of unpopularity as a result of his misfortune to be in office when the state's first income tax law was enacted.

Jordan's decision to challenge the governor's attempt at reelection was ironic, for it had been Jersey City—during Mayor Whelan's term—that sued to require the state to provide each child with a "thorough and efficient" education. The need to finance the education program required funds, and one way to supply them was through an income tax.

The mayor began paying close attention to a series of statewide polls, and realized that he was not well known outside of the immediate area. Thus, his poor standing in the view of Jersey City residents would not hurt him overly much—and, besides, there *was* the fact that more New Jersey governors had come from "Joisey City" than from any of the state's other 576 municipalities. There was, of course, three-time governor A. Harry Moore, and Edward I. Edwards, and James F. Fielder. Jordan decided the odds were with him—and announced he would enter the gubernatorial race.

Once again, as had happened so often in recent years, there was a scramble among potential candidates for the office that the mayor would soon vacate.

Mayor Jordan, hoping to name his own successor, pointed his finger at Bill Macchi, who had served as his Director of Human Resources. But Jack Finn, in his role as chairman, determined that he would put the power of the CAC behind Arthur Cashin, who had been Jordan's campaign manager. Dom Pugliese, the councilman-at-large who had twice been elected with Jordan, saw no reason why he should not step into the mayor's role. When Macchi got Jordan's nod, the councilman was disappointed and angry.

Almost daily, it seemed, the list of candidates lengthened, until I began to wonder if the record of 18 that had been set only a few years earlier would be broken. Perennial office seeker John Yengo declared, and so did a local autombile dealer, Louis Campenni. Then

Bill Link, espousing black causes and interests, threw his hat into the ring.

Looking over the field, I saw that several of the five declared candidates had qualities that I had to view as negative. Either they represented a particular point of view that reflected narrow interests, or they had not shown a capacity for leadership, or they were tied to earlier administrations which had proved incapable of setting Jersey City on the path toward greatness that I—along with yesteryear's reformers, H. Otto Wittpenn and Mark M. Fagan—believed the city should tread. I had broken with Mayor Jordan openly and completely partway through his term. Now there was a growing question in my mind:

Should I—Thomas F. X. Smith, who had grown up in a "cold-water flat" like one of the city's most famous political figures—try to become mayor myself?

The more I looked at the other candidates and studied the failures of previous administrations—and the more I realized that Jersey City needed a leader with the qualities of honesty and consideration for every citizen—the more I concluded that my idea was no idle dream. But another question kept coming to me: Could I marshal the support I would need to win?

My speaking abilities had won me many adherents in political circles, of that I was certain. With a powerful God-given voice and a fervent style that often was compared to that of an old-style evangelist, I felt certain that I could get my ideas across to the voters in a convincing way.

"Tommie Smith delivers a message with the fervency of a Billy Sunday and Clarence Darrow combined; he's one of the great orators of our time," I remember John R. Longo saying once. And from his vantage point of having heard political speakers during a period of a half-century, he was not merely paying me a compliment, I knew. But, I asked myself time and again, was a voice and a firm conviction that I could handle the city's biggest job enough to beat five contenders for the mayoralty? Were they enough to overcome the fact that I would be running as an independent, running against the "organization" and its choice?

Again, I discussed the situation with family members—with my wife, my daughters, Regina's husband Mark Silver, and my mother and father. Their encouragement was so solid that I could almost feel it.

I began to sample friends for their opinions. May Ann Bauer, one of the stalwarts of the CAC and a devoted worker who helped carry Paul Jordan and his team to victory in 1971, said she would be on my side. Other women—Lena Karrlson, Karen Quinn, Viola Disbrow, Gail Ernst, Ann Minervini and Josephine Anzalone—said they, too, would help get out the vote. My boyhood pal, Wally Sheil (whom I had proposed that Jordan accept for the councilman-at-large post offered to me), agreed to help lay campaign plans. So did Stanley "Sparky" Stine, Bob Janiszewski, Ed Scala and John Romanowski. And a New York *Daily News* reporter who had recently become a friend. The *News* man, Dave Hardy, who closely resembles all-time prizefighting great Muhammad Ali, never failed to lift my spirits. One glance at his smiling face or a few encouraging words from his lips could brighten the day when things looked darkest.

With such brave men and women urging me on, my decision was made easier.

I gave the word that I would enter the race, and almost overnight there were huge red, white, and blue banners everywhere. "Thomas F. X. Smith for Mayor in '1977," they proclaimed.

There was no chance for me to win.

That, at least, is what the regular Hudson County Organization believed. It was solidly behind the mayor's choice, Bill Macchi, to succeed him, and was backing Jordan for the governor's job. Several of the other candidates seemed to have better financial backing than I did, or could make specific appeals to large blocs of voters.

I had primarily my reputation for honesty and independence.

And my vocal abilities.

To make the maximum use of my talents, I vowed that I would stage the same kind of campaign that Jeff Burkitt had waged in his continuing battle against the dictatorial Frank Hague. My studies of Hague's victories over the years had taught me that it often was possible for a single man, speaking loudly enough, to come close to defeating him. The way Burkitt had spoken on streetcorners and at open-air assemblies—that would be my technique. On the bed of a flatbed truck pulled up at intersections, I would raise my voice against the evils that administration after administration had allowed to flourish in Jersey City—and I would lay out my plans to remedy them, point by point.

Old fashioned? Yes, wise political leaders told me it was old-fashioned. This was the electronic age, and a campaigner had to use television and radio. So I was told, but I remembered that in the 1930s my Uncle Frank Kelly had raised his voice in a plea from a flatbed truck for someone to join Burkitt and him in fighting Hague. Few of the frightened citizens, of course, had responded to the pleas of "Kelly," and the taunts and jeers of Hague's cronies and support-ers would ring out from hallways or shadowed doorways, just out of my uncle's line of vision.

"Come on out, you cowards! You Hague monkeys!" He would cry. "Come out and fight like a man."

I was going to fight, I decided. Fight like a man for a better Jersey City. It would mean walking the streets, buttonholing people I met and shaking their hands, and talking, talking, talking continuously until I had made them aware of who Thomas F. X. Smith was.

And what he stood for.

Day after day, with a few close members of my political team, I walked the streets. And day after day, more signs bearing my name—and our freshly-minted slogan, "He'll Walk the Streets"—began to appear in windows, on walls, and on waving banners. My voice—which Governor Byrne once said could be used to address a crowd in Giants Stadium in the New Jersey Meadowlands without the need for a public address system—fortunately stayed strong, and small groups of people heard my views on the city's need for more police, the Medical Center's need for increased funding from the state, the citizenry's need for a lower tax rate, and on . . . and on . . . and on.

And the small groups of people, we soon noticed, were growing into larger ones.

Partway through the campaign, we got one of those "media breaks" that sometimes come to a lucky politician. While jogging along the waterfront one morning, I encountered a stray dog that had been wounded by a patrolman who thought the animal was going to attack him. Adopting the dog—which I named "Henry Hudson" to commemorate the river where we had met one another—I and my family nursed him back to health, and he soon began to trot alongside me when I took my morning run. Now, not only was I walking the streets. I had a steadfast and photogenic companion.

New companions were springing up alongside me as well. Political companions who began to think that maybe Thomas F. X. Smith did have "a shot" at the city's top job. Councilman Tom McGovern and black leaders Earl Byrd, John Stallworth and Bob Watson endorsed my candidacy. The regular organization began to crack when Freeholders Ann O'Malley and Moe Longo announced for me; and voters old enough to remember the strength so often displayed by John R. Longo came my way when that legendary figure, asked for his opinion of the various candidates, stated simply: "Smith can win."

Then, Warren Curtis, a "powerhouse" in the Jordan organization, announced that he was giving up his position as a ward leader to "join the man who's walking the streets." The Macchi-Jordan forces showed signs of panic when Anthony "Ike" Venutolo and Welfare Director Thornton Smith endorsed my candidacy. A masterful attorney, Harold Krieger, who had been prominent in the 1949 Freedom Movement, climbed aboard early. Through his efforts, Frank Guarini decided to forego his own ambitions for a try for the mayoralty and serve instead as my campaign manager.

It was impossible not to feel a sense of elation. As the son of a policeman who had worn the city's blue uniform for four decades, I began to get knowing smiles from members of the Jersey City police and firefighters. Ray Maloney, one of the city's greatest all-around athletes and a fellow graduate of Saint Peter's Preparatory School, spearheaded a drive to gain backing for me from other former athletes.

"Tom," businessman Joe Shaara had said to me, "you can beat Jordan. You both have contrasting styles. He's a fancy-dan boxer, and you're a streetfighter, a slugger. The city wants a streetfighter!"

Now people were coming up to the truck parked in Journal Square where I was speaking, and they were asking—*asking!*—for campaign buttons. Despite the long hours, despite the fact that I was speaking several times a day and for long stretches at a time, my voice actually was growing stronger. I was not worrying about using elaborate phrases or speaking with formality. And a brother of a close friend once expresed concern that my flying hair, rumpled suit, and Jersey City speaking style might alienate some voters.

"Uh-uh," argued Ralph DeRose, himself an unsuccessful gubernatorial candidate, "he *looks* Jersey City and he *talks* Jersey City. And, you want to know something, brother? The people see him *as* Jersey City." My appearance, voice, and manner, he realized (as Hague and other warriors had realized in the past), were all assets that the voters would appreciate.

And the support grew. Now Republicans were swinging my way, led by the Zelinski family, Viola Callaghan, Everett Warner, and Joe "The Irish" Galano. As the race entered its last weeks, it was obvious that I had taken a lead among the six candidates. What made it very obvious was that all five opponents were beginning to attack me rather than inform the voters about what they each could do, *would do,* for Jersey City. Meanwhile, I was getting across to ever-growing numbers of voters some of the things I believed in:

—That the federal government had to spend more money to help decaying urban areas revitalize and rebuild themselves, and that the money should come not by increasing the tax burden on the citizens but from reductions in our foreign-aid programs. Uncle Sam, I said, "should stop pumping so much money into countries that would destroy us tomorrow if they could."

—That the future of the nation is dependent on the well-being of its major cities.

—That street crime could be reduced both by increasing the size of the police force and taking officers from behind desks and putting them on the streets, and by reducing the number of plainclothes squads.

—That opponents to a waterfront revitalization plan which would include the demolition of Frank Hague's pride and joy, Roosevelt Stadium, were making a mistake. The stadium, unused for the most part and rapidly falling apart, was a costly relic of bygone days. Tearing it down would help Jersey City build for the future, not continue to live in the past.

—That the calm beauty of Liberty State Park, which Morris Pesin had done so much to improve and expand, should not be disturbed by allowing commercial developers to use the property for a "theme" amusement park.

There was more, of course; much more that I managed to tell crowd after crowd while I campaigned during those weeks of vacation time and a leave of absence from the city clerk's position I continued to hold.

Then, as if no time at all had passed since the day that I had made the decision to run, it was election day. Where had the days, weeks, months gone? I pondered the question as I paced back and forth, as I had done in locker rooms and dugouts during my ballplaying years, in one of the local political headquarters on West Side Avenue. The polls had closed, and the returns began to come in.

The first results came from the four Marion districts, where huge concentrations of Italian voters live. They were expected to vote—as they normally did—for a candidate of Italian extraction or for the choice of the regular organization. I was neither, and everyone was apprehensive about the initial numbers.

"It's a landslide for us, Tommie!" Charlie Free screamed.

Sure enough, we had swept all four districts. And, despite the number of candidates in the race, we had received better than 50 percent of the vote—necessary for a first-ballot victory. I knew that evening that I felt calmer than I usually appear, and I began to feel a smile curving over my lips. The smile grew as jubilant poll watchers came dashing in from other wards. The Journal Square ward had 30 districts. We took all of them, and again with better than 50 percent.

"Quiet, everybody," said a close friend, Bill Tremper, as he leaned into the telephone. "We're getting Hudson City." In the northernmost section of Jersey City, Hudson City has the highest socio-economic indices of all six wards. It is overwhelmingly independent as a rule.

"We won every district in Hudson City," Tremper proclaimed. "Big!"

Smiling, but dazed—we had taken 62 out of the first 62 districts—I looked at John Gillen, "Barky" Cioffi, Sal Mosca and Tony Lombardi, four men who had walked every Jersey City street with me. They were in the room, cheering wildly.

Lucy Falco called excitedly. She was waving a phone as her husband Frank shouted. On the other end of the wire was Pete DiNardo, whose wife Margaret was at my side. The DiNardos had worked hard for me in their Greenville ward. I grabbed the receiver.

"We got it! We got it! Every district, in a landslide," I heard Petey say over the din in his Greenville club.

Now the count was 92 straight districts. I could hardly believe it.

Paul Byrne, a 280-pound political pundit and loyal friend, was grinning and shaking his head in surprise. "It's all over now," he bragged.

I waved a protesting hand. From my days as a scrappy little ballplayer with the Saint Peter's altar boys, I had been superstitious, and followed the old adage of not counting your chickens before they are hatched. "Paul, there are three wards to go yet," I said. Under my breath, I said, "Damn, now I'll bet he's jinxed us."

But Paul's brash proclamation did not change the numbers that continued to flow in. "We took 24 out of 25 in E Ward," Chet Kaminski shouted, and I heard roars of jubilation and the excited voices of Tony Cucci, Frank Manzo, Dom Dellasandro, and Dom Amoroso.

"Hey," I yelled in mock despair, "what the hell district did we lose?"

Now everyone was laughing, cheering, applauding. And the Westside Ward numbers were in. It was the same story. We won 33 out of 34 districts. Then Bergen-Lafayette reported, and once more it was a landslide.

J. Owen Grundy, the city historian who has personally known every mayor from Mark Fagan onward over a period of five decades, later would compare the sweeping victory—and the outflow of public enthusiasm that followed—to the 1949 upset of the Hague organization by John V. Kenny, the "little guy."

On election night I had a taste of the mood of that earlier evening. Within moments of the final vote tabulations, several police cars came screeching to a stop in front of the headquarters building. Then with their red lights flashing, they sped with the mayor-elect to a victory celebration at the Lincoln Park Casino. The crowd outside was packed so densely that I almost felt compelled to use my athletic strength and agility to make my way to the door, and inside the Casino I found a mass of humanity packed almost as tightly, if not more so. A phalanx of officers had to clear a path, and I had to smile at the incongruity of the scene. Throughout my campaign, I had made a point of the idea that Jersey City's streets could be made safe for citizens—and I had walked miles of those streets without security men and policeman at my side.

"If I am elected," I had said, "I won't have to be surrounded by policemen—and neither will you."

Now here I was encircled by a ring of blue, not to provide protection from those who would do harm, however, but merely to help me battle through the hordes of well-wishers.

Strange things happen, I couldn't help thinking as I began my off-the-cuff victory speech. *Strange things certainly happen in the city known as the Mecca of politics.*

Afterword . . .

The incomparable Barney Doyle—may his soul rest in peace—would have a phrase for it, I am certain, if he were alive today. Looking at me, working once more in the city clerk's office in City Hall, rather than in the office of the mayor or the governor's office in Trenton, Barney would probably cock an eyebrow and let a grin flicker across his face.

"Smitty," I can almost hear him saying, "once I was boxin' a lug dey called 'duh Michigan Assassin' an' in duh toid round he lemme have one—a big righthand—right on duh old potato. I blinked a coupla times and went down. But duh crowd kept yellin' to '*Get* up, Barn, get up,' an' so I got up.

"And, Smitty, dere's folks out dere yellin' for you to get up, too. An' you will."

"The Barn" passed away midway through my term as mayor, in 1979, and the Hudson County Vocational School was ordered draped in black and purple mourning colors for a period of three months. It seemed small enough honor for the only person in the recorded history of the nation to hold simultaneously the position of head janitor at a school and that of president of the teachers' union. Reminded that mayors, governors, presidents, and popes had died in the past without the school entering into mourning, one of the administrators responded without hesitation, "Yes, but this was Barney Doyle."

Barney would have seen the humor, the irony in my unsuccessful bid for the gubernatorial nomination. He managed over decades to translate all the ins and outs of Jersey City politics into simple language, often putting complex issues into a few succinct words that made everything crystal clear. And he probably was chuckling the day after my election as mayor when the *Jersey Journal* began a story about the outcome this way:

> "City Hall today, the State House tomorrow!" That's the chant today of Thomas F. X. Smith's supporters. And, they suggest, they'll grab the Courthouse on their way to Trenton.

"Kid," I can hear Barney saying, "dem people can chant all dey want, but don't listen to 'em. It ain't dat easy. It ain't easy at all."

I am not sure which "supporters" were talking about my moving on to Trenton so early in my career as an elected official. I would later discover that several people closest to me certainly hoped that I had such ambitions—and they would encourage me to harbor them in order to move themselves up the political ladder. But in the flush of victory, I had only one thing in mind, and that was to develop a theory of leadership that would enable me to do the most for the huge and varied constituency that had placed me into power. To act effectively, I believed, I would have to tread a middle ground between the dictatorial rule of previous mayors and the weak, machine-dominated rule of others.

It could be done. I was certain of it. And only by doing so would I be able to remove from Jersey City the stigma that so long had made its politicians persons to be either laughed at or jeered at, either ignored or feared. That stigma had to be removed, thought one native son, for the city first to gain new stature in the eyes of its own citizens. And then, in the eyes of the state and the entire country.

There would be no recriminations, I decided. No "clean sweep" of all those who had opposed me. "Come, work *with* me," I urged. "Let's all work together."

Not everyone accepted the offer, of course. The overwhelming defeat of former Mayor Paul Jordan's hand-picked successor, William Macchi, dealt a serious blow to Jordan's ambitions for the gubernatorial post, and Jordan in fact withdrew from contention shortly after the election. When a pollster who had predicted a first-ballot victory for Macchi reported to Jordan that the numbers had been erroneous for the first time in years of poll taking, the departing mayor said in chagrin, "It's a hell of a time to be wrong."

As immodest as it may seem at this point, I could not lay claim to the mantle of a "professional politician" if I did not proudly list a few achievements that took place during my single term as mayor of Jersey City. After all, although my present plans about possibly running for office again are indefinite, it never hurts to speak out about your record while you have someone's attention. And, if I had chosen to run for a second term as mayor, I would have run on a record that included:

—Obtaining $30 million in sorely-needed funding from the state for continuation of the vital work of the Medical Center and another $30 million promised in the future.

—Making the Montgomery Gateway Project, an ambitious rehabilitation program for the area often first seen by visitors on their way to City Hall, into a reality.

—"Holding the line" on commercial development in Liberty State Park, chosen by Ronald Reagan as the site to announce that he would run for the presidency.

—Development of a 10-year, multibillion-dollar program of redevelopment for the city's northern waterfront on the Hudson River, and preliminary plans for a similar program for the western waterfront area that would include the demolition of Roosevelt Stadium (where a youthful Tommie Smith watched major sports events, and which an older and wiser Thomas F. X. Smith regretfully understands must vanish for the good of the majority).

—Attraction of a dozen new businesses to the area along Route 440 on the city's west side, where previously companies—including the giant American Can Factory—had closed down by the score.

The list could go on at length—to include the additional policemen put on patrol to make the city safer, the "Blitzsweep" effort to clean up the streets, reduction in the *municipal* tax rate (Does not include county or school budgets over which I had no control) to $47.30 per $1,000 assessed valuation in 1980 when I left office from $52.06 per $1,000 at the time I became mayor, and various budget-cutting measures that saved the taxpayers and the city millions of dollars without sacrificing efficiency and service. Yes, the list could be lengthened, but I am not asking for your vote.

Yet.

With your record, I can hear you thinking, *what went wrong? What prevented you from moving to the governor's mansion? A senatorial post? The vice-presidency? The White House? After all, isn't that every American politician's dream?*

A book could be written about what "went wrong" after I had decided, at the urging of "friends" (and the quotes *belong* around the word) to run as a candidate for the 1981 gubernatorial nomination in New Jersey. But that would be an entirely new story—one involving deception on the part of others, last-minute changes in the regulations governing the raising of campaign funds (changes which I endorsed, but which ultimately worked against me), and my apparent inability to prove to a majority of the state's voters that four years of honest, 12-hours-a-day and seven-days-a-week effort on Jersey City's behalf could overcome nearly a century of manipulation, pocket-lining, and ridicule.

No matter how loudly I spoke, no matter how forcefully I told people that Jersey City politicians had changed, that the city no longer deserved the reputation that it held for so long—no matter how often I *convinced* one listener, then another and another, and then an entire group—I found that I had to begin all over again at the *next* meeting. Undaunted, I would begin again . . . and again . . . and again . . .

But then, suddenly, it was time for the voters to go to the polls and choose the Democratic nominee for governor from nearly 20 candidates—and I had been able to reach only a small fraction of the state's voters. To hundreds of thousands of others, Jersey City was as it had always been: boss-ridden, machine-run, rife with graft and kickbacks.

During my administration, it was not so, and even the suggestion—repeated ad infinitum—sickened me. Someday, one day, I might try to win another opportunity to prove that Jersey City is not what so much of this lengthy chronicle reveals it once was; that today it is an urban community with the problems and promise faced by many others in this great country. That the people are the finest in the world and don't deserve the image that a few politicans gave them. I know that it will not be easy to prove it. I know that I will be knocked down more than once. By cynics, by enemies, by professional pollsters and advisors who will sneer that a loud-talking, honest and well-meaning, six-foot-two-inch Catholic from an impoverished part of "Joisey City" does not stand a chance in an era of smooth, well-dressed, wealthy politicians who glibly can fill a half-hour of *Meet the Press* or *Face the Nation* without ever saying what they really think.

Yes, I can expect to be knocked down.

But, blinking my eyes to clear my vision, if need be, and shaking my head to focus my thoughts, I intend to keep getting up—the way Barney Doyle did when the "Michigan Assassin" sent him to the canvas so many years ago—and I intend to go on fighting.

For a better Jersey City.

A better United States of America.

A better world.

The author wishes to express his gratitude to those who have assisted him in his political campaigns—some in his 1977 mayoralty victory, some in his try for the state house, and some who have been with him in all his political endeavors:

Roslyn Abraham, Arthur J. Abrams, Bernard Abrams, Mary Accurso, Richard Accurso, Harry Aceti, Peter Aceti, Jr., Mrs. Peter Aceti, Peter Aceti, Sr., Rocca Aceti, Edith L. Ackerman, Mrs. Ethel Ackerman, Phil Ackerman, George Adams, Don Addas, Joseph Adinente, Assemblyman Mike Addubato, Nilsa Aguiar, John Aiello, Rose Albatiello, Dr. B. Albers, Bill Albers, Harry Albers, Margaret Albers, Mickey Albers, Michael D. Albers, Dr. Edward Allegra, George Allen, Dean Allen, Mary Allen, Canty Alsten, Mary Amabile, Tony Amabile, Matthew Amato, Joseph Ambrose, Frank Ambrosio, Gabe Ambrosio, Richard Ambrosio, Mayor Paul Amico, Victoria Amodio, Dominick Amoroso, Sue Amoroso, Theresa Amoroso, City Clerk Tony Amoruso, Ivy Anderson, Helen Andri Joy, Stanley and Carolyn Anichowski, William Annese, Adele M. Annitto, Tom Annito, Salvatore Antinora, Michael P. Antonicello, Nicholas Antonicello, Josephine Anzalone, Jeff April, Anthony Aranscke, W. and E. Arcell, Mary Archibald, Frank Arnone, Joanne B. Arnone, Josephine Arnone, Michael Arnone, Nicholas Arnone, Louis Artificio, Anthony Artificio, Jr., Michael, Dorothy, and Joan Artificio, Lillian Ash, Pat Astolfi, Stephen Astolfi, John Aston, Philip Attanasio, Marie Austin, Peter Avagliano

Michael Baber, Jr., Michael Baber III, Peter Babiak, Ruth Babiak, George Babich, Patricia Backus, E. Bafano, Rozia L. Baisey, Jack Bakalian, Mary Bakalian, Joseph Balasco, Jr., Charles T. Balcer, Jr., Dolores Balesterri, Ellen Balesterri, Janet Balesterri, Lou Balesterri, Dorothy Baltarzuk, Edward Baltarzuk, Gene Bannon, Ted Barako, Rose Baratta, Guido Baratelli, Joseph Barbera, Sam Bardach, Spiro Bardis, Martin Barelli, Ruth Barmad, Howard Barmad, Bill Barna, Joseph Baron, Louis Barone, Carmela Barone, James Barratta, Agnes Barrett, Diane Barrett, Michael Barrett, John Barrett, Patrick Barrett, Emmett Barrett, Edward Barrison, John Barry, Joseph Barry, Laura Bartilucci, Susan Bartoszek, Florence Bartoszek, Mark Basile, Lorraine Batile, Frank Bassillo, Victor Bastek, Mary Ann Bauer, Joseph Bauer, Sr., Joseph Bauer, Michael Bauer, Mrs. Thomas Bauer, Burley Battee,

Mildred Bean, Edward Beards, Nancy Becker, William Becker, Walter Bednash, George Beese, Frank Beirne, James Bell, Pearl Bell, Rodes Bell, Armond Bellavia, Andy Bellezza, Adeline Bellizzi, Anthony J. and Catherine Bello, Richard Bello, Susan Belluci, Thomas P. Bellucci, Michael Beradino, Rev. E. Bennett, Theresa Beradino, Samuel Berger, Milton Berkowitz, Art Bernaducci, Janet Bernhardt, Dianne Berra, Angel Berrios, Joan Berry, Celeste and Gloria Bethea, Jenny Betlow, John Berwecky, Jack Bettinger, R. Betz, Clair Biasa, Stanley Biaszcyski, William Bilyk, Charles Bird, Kenneth Bird, Marie Bisanti, Richie Bishop, Mary Bishop, Alex Blahitka, James Blaney, Raymond Blasczak, Stanley Blaszyk, Charles Boas, Michael and Catherine Boccino, John Boehm, Joanne Bojar, Benjamin and Margaret Bokuniewicz, James Bolden, Margaret Bolden, Solomon Bolden, Harold Bond, Bill and Kathy Bondi, Santiago Bonilla, Joseph Bonjorno, John Bordak, Estelle Borowski, Felix Borowski, Jean and Michael Borseso, Bill Boseski, Mary Bosquett, John Bostwick, John Botti, Grace Bower, David Boyd, Thomas Boyd, Joseph and John Boyle, Dick Bozzone, Dr. Milton Blum, Loretta Bloomer, Bob Bracken, Joseph Bradley, Thomas Bradley, Joseph T. Brady, Joseph Brady, Jr., Earl and Sandy Brady, Pat Brady, Helen Branch, Harvey Braun, Florence Brescia, John Bresnock, Shella Bresnock, William Bresnock, John Brett, Michael Brett, William Briamonte, Neil Briody, William and Edith Broking, William Bromirski, Joseph T. Brooks, Shirley Brooks, Kenneth F. X. Brophy, Carolyn and Edmund Broslawski, Rev. Brower, Bernard Brown, Elaine Brown, Frederick J. Brown, Harold Brown, James A. Brown, John Brown, Kenneth Brown, Loretta Brown, Margaret Brown, Pearly Brown, Eugene F. Brunner, Jim Bruno, Debra Bryant, J. and L. Brzozowski, George Bucolo, Gerald Buccafusco, Ralph Bucci, Jimmy Buckowski, Mae Buckowski, Anthony Bufano, Jr., Surena Bulle, Carrie M. Bullock, Tony Bullock, Al Bundies, Louis and Mary A. Buondies, Deborah Burke, Frank Burke, Deborah Burke, William Burke, Ellison Burns, Michael and Louis Buscio, Millerdean Butler, Elizabeth and Donna Butler, Ann Butler, Anne Butler, Carl Butler, Fred and Dora Butler, Dr. Joseph Buttighieri, Earl and Joyce Byrd, Andrew Byrne, Cecelia Byrne, Kathy Byrne, Paul and Robert Byrne, Barbara Byron, Edward Byszanski, Capt. Edward Byszynski

Cesar Cabral, M.D., Victor Cabrera, John J. Cadden, Pat Cadden, Martin Cahill, Mayor Jerry Calabrese, Michael Calandra, Harry Calandrillo, Puella Caldwell, Frank C. Caleca, Paul Calefati, Dominick Caleo, Joyce and Harry Calfee, John F. Cali, Joseph Calianese, Marie Edna Calianese, Pamela J. Calianese, Patrick Callaghan, Viola Callaghan, Pauline Callahan, J. Callandeillo, Harry Callari, Frank Cangelosi, Pauline Cannon, Chris Cammeci, Benjamin and Millie Camilleri, Ginny and Frank Campanile, Patricia V. Campbell, Bill Campe, William A. Canfield, Phyllis Capelli, Ernest Capitani, Mary and Elaine Caporrino, Joseph A. Caporrino, Mayor Steve Cappiello, Frank Cappola, Julia and Lucille Cappoli, Peter Caravoulias, Thomas Carberry, Anthony Carbone, Casper Carbone, Joseph Cardella, Peter and Phyllis Cardiello, Fred Carlock, Sidney and Catherine Carlomagno, William Carlson, Alfred (Doc) Carmichael, Elaine Carney, Harry K. Carol, Louis Caroselli, Agnes Carr, Debbie Carr, Elizabeth Carr, John and Matilda Carr, Kenny Carr, Rosemary Carr, Vincent and Patricia Carrino, Neil Carroll, Donald Carson, Benjamin and William Carter, Edward P. Casey, Frank Casey, Tony and Alice Casino, Leonard Casner, Mariana Cassidy, Marietta L. Cassidy, Joseph T. Cassidy, Patricia Castagno, Martin R. Castegon, Marion Catanio, Joseph Castelo, Manuel Castelo, Juan J. Castillo, Philip F. Castoreno, Gabe Cataneo, Richard Catena, Alfonso N. Catrillo, Bob Catrillo, Gabe Cattaneo, Joseph Caulfield, Theresa Caulfield, Mr. P. A. Caulfield, Anthony Cavalier, Anthony and Anna Celauro, Adolph R. Cella, Jr., Kathleen Cella, Joan Cella, The Cella Family, Palma Rose and Salvatore Centinaro, Eileen Cermak, Joseph Cermack, Marge and Mike Cermack, Adele

Cerwinski, Tony and Frank Cevezo, Frank Chapel, George Chapin, Gene Chapoutot, Robert Cheloc, Charles Chimenti, Audrey Chiorazzi, Henry Chojnacki, Walter and Constance Chowanec, Alexander Chowanec, Andrew Chrisomalis, John P. Chrisomalis, Harriet Christensen, Richard Christie, Sam Christopher, Mary Christopher, Rose Christopher, Bart and Philomena Ciancrotta, Aldo Cianfanelli, Bernie Ciccerelli, Nicholas Cicco, Thomas Cifelli, Angelo Cifelli, Dom and Edith Cinelli, Dominick Cinelli, Daniel Cilino, Mrs. Mafalda Cinelli, Patricia Lea Cinotti, Gregg Cinnella, Dr. William R. Cinotti, Bernice Cioffi, Patrick (Barky) Cioffi, Louise Cioffi, Simone Ciriera, John Clancy, Debra Clark, Francis Clark, James Clark, Pat Clark, Pablo Clausell, Larry Clayton, Rosemary Cleary, Lou Cocca, Louis J. Coccaro, William Cochrane, Mr. and Mrs. Gene Cody, James Cody, Rose Cogan, Albert Cohen, Dorothea (Dotty) Cohen, Libby Cohen, Mrs. Manvin Cohen, "Quinny" Cohen, Sam Colacurcio, Carmela Colao, Ralphael Cole, Ronald and Helen Cole, Anthony Colello, Anthony Colello, Edward and Maureen Coleman, John Coleman, R. O. Coleman, M.D., Reginald Coleman, Frank Colletta, Sam Colleta, John E. Collier, Stephen and Joyce Collier, John J. Collins, Fernando Colon, Maria Colon, Rose Collins, B Collone, Angel and Moses Comacho, Angelo Commandore, Anthony Comandatore, Emanuel Commandatore, Frank Comes, Joseph and Mary Conklin, Vera Conklin, Bob and Marie Conlin, Elsie Connelly, Joseph Connelly, Michael E. Connelly, Raymond J. and Catherine D., Connelly, George Connolly, Thomas Connolly, M.D., Joe Consoni, Frank Constantinople, Severio (Sam) Constantino, Anne Constos, George Contey, Carole and Anthony Conte, Robert Conte, Carmine Conti, Joseph Cooney, Samuel and Jennie Cooper, Charles Cooper, Ralph Cooper, Jr., Kathleen Coppinger, Catherine Corcia, Steve Cornin, Patricia Coroccia, Bea Corry, Les Cosgrove, Anthony M. Costa, Nicholas Costanzo, Adeline Costello, Tony Costello, Frank Cottman, Marion Cottmon, Roy Couser, Thomas Cowan, Sr., James Cowan, John and Eleanor Cox, Elaine Cozzarelli, Salvatore Cozzetta, James Cranga, Robert D. Crawford, Samuel Crawford, Joan Crawley, Domenick Crincoli, Gennaro Crincoli, Italo Crincoli, Mayor Donald Cresitello, Vincent L. Crooks, Dennis Crowley, Mae A. Crudup, David Cruz, Julio Cruz, Howard Cubberly, Anthony Cucci, Ollie Culbreth, Richard J. Cullen, Audrey Culley, Thomas Cullinane, Bill Cullinane, Mort Cullity, Joseph Cullity, Thomas Cunninghan, John Cupo, Tony Cupo, Paul Cuprowski, Angela Curcio, John F. Curran, Beatrice Curry, Tim Curtin, Warren H. Curtis, Michael Cusack, Lorraine Cuthbert

Donald Daly, Domenick D'Alessandro, Rosario and Loretta D'Amato, S. D'Amico, Joan D'Angelico, August D'Aquilla, Gene and Gene D'Aquilla, Jr., Dorothy Dandridge, Alan Danese, Mary Dapoz, Ron Dario, Joe Davenport, Robert N. Davenport, Jr., Bruce Davis, Edward Davin, Charles Davis, William Davis, William Davis, Edward Deak, Dom De Asio, Mable Debbins, Frances J. De Cesare, Susan De Bauer, Christine and Nicholas DeBello, Charles C. Deberry, Thomas De Carlo, William De Carlo, Gertrude Dechert, Dominick De Clesis, Gus De Cottis, Albert Decresce, Lee Dedousis, Walter Deegan, Ann De Fazio, James D'Elia, Mayor Anthony De Fino, Arthur Delo, Samuel De Luca, Thomas DeLuca, Dominick DeLucia, Joseph and Cathy De Marco, Louis DeMarco, Mike DeMarco, Nick DeMarco, Joseph A. De Martino, Louis De Mascio, Ann DeLeva, Catherine and Joan Deloughery, Gerard Delpiano, Daniel Dennehy, John T. Dennis, Marianne DePalmer, Ralph De Rose, Peter Derchia, John DeSalvo, Neil De Sena, Marion and Francis DeSilvio, Sonny De Simon, Judy De Stefano, Robert Del Fino, Joe Del Monte, John Delmonte, Emil Del Prete, Jean Del Rio, Marie Della Corte, Gerald Deutch, James R. Devone Dom Di Asio, Luis Diaz, Wilfredo Diaz, Willie Diaz, Charles Di Buono, Franco Di Domenica, Diane Di Fabio, Joseph Di Fabio, Sam Di Feo, Rose DiGiancito, Antoinette and Marie Frances Di Giola, Joseph Diglio, Angelo Di Gregorio, Ken Dilks, Edmond Dillon, Evelyn Dillon, Martin Dillon, Louis

DiMascio, Dennis Di Mascio, Peter and Antoinette Di Mascio, Veronica A. Di Mascio, Gabriel Di Matteo, James Di Nardo, Genevieve Di Nardo, Margaret Di Nardo, Mike Di Nardo, Peter Di Nardo, Tom Di Nardo, Alvin Dingle, John Di Salvo, Richard Disbrow, Vincent and Viola Disbrow, Amity Di Toro, Anthony Di Vincent, Edith Dixon, Esther M. Doctor, Walter Dodd, George Doelger, Dr. Hugh Doherty, Joseph Doherty, Lawrence Doherty, George Dolan, Joanne Doherty, Frances Doherty, Joseph Doherty, Robert Doherty, Marte Dolan, Joseph Domin, Harry Donahue, Michael Donahue, Angelina Donahue, Owen A. and Margaret Donahue, Herman Donchin, Marie Donefria, Anna Donnellan, John Donnellan, Edward Donnelly, John J. Donnelly, Thomas and Barbara Donnelly, Michael Doolan, Milton B. Dorison, Ronnie Douglas, Alice Dougherty, Marie Dowd, Jack Doyle, Mark Doyle, James J. Doyle, Ken Drennan, Kenneth Drennan, Thomas Drennan, Anthony Drozdowski, Judy Dudik, Ann M. Dudik, Paul Dudick, Joseph Duffy, Hugh A. Duffy, Eleanor Dugan, James P. Dugan, Joseph Dugan, Mary Dugan, Mae Duggan, Patrick Dundee, Mayor Thomas Dunn, Mary Ann Dunoutt, Annette Dupuis, Kenneth Dutton, Irene Dwulet, Walter Dzemba, Tony Dzidual

Al Eaddy, Elvin Eady, Joan Earls, Eleanor E. Early, Father George Economous, Alan P. Edwards, Carla Edwards, Gerry Eglantowitz, Kantrow and Leff Eichenbaum, Marion El, Robert Elden, Anna Ellerson, Brian Ellerson, Glenn S. Ellerson, Mark Ellerson, Robett Ellerson, Lester Ellington, Lorraine Ellington, Carrie Ellis, Marjorie Ellis, Mohammed Emara, Barbara Engasser, John F. Engeldrecht, Herbert Enix, William Enright, Charles Epps, Jr., Rev. Charles Epps, Sr., Madelina Erifante, Gail Ernst, Ken Ernst, Patricia Ernst, Frank Esposito, Gloria Esposito, Margaret Esposito, Mary Ann Esposito, Michael P. Esposito, Theresa Esposito, Thomas Esposito, Douglas Evan, Bob Evans, D. and J. Evans, Jack Evans, Loretta Evans

Ed Faber, M.D., Margaret Fabian, Vinny Faccone, Anthony S. Faccone, Thomas P. Faccone, Francis X. Fahy, Gregory Fakrian, Linda Fakrian, Frank and Lucy T. Falco, Nino Falcone, Joseph Falco, Ellen Faleska, James Fallon, John J. Famularo, Mary and Nellie Farmer, John W. and Florence T. Farrell, Robert Farrell, Edward M. Farrelly, Edward M. Farynyk, Hector Favio, Epifiaixo Feliciano, William Fell, Carl Feltz, John Feltz, Frank Femise, Andy Ferguson, Joseph Fernandez, Marco Fernando, M.D., John Ferraiola, Joseph Ferrante, Joseph Ferrara, Salvatore Ferrigini, Vincent Ferro, Kathleen Field, Carmen Figueroa, Jennifer Figurelli, Rose Figurelli, Everett Filghman, Charles V. Finch, Charlotte Fince, Rick Fince, Howard Fink, Michael Finker, Joseph Finnerty, Mike Fiore, Michael Fiore, Bernard Fishelman, Bruce Fishelman, George Fisher, Judy Fisher, Wm. J. Fisher, Grady Fitzgerald, Kevin Fitzgerald, Bill F. Fitzgibbons, Francis G. Fitzpatrick, Joan Krute Fitzsimmons, Paul Fiume, John (Chalky) Flanagan, Thomas Flanagan, William J. Flanagan, William Flannery, Margie Flint, Jim Flood, Linda Flores, Andy Flynn, Frank Flynn, George Flynn, Richard Flynn, Ed Flynn, Robert Fogari, M.D., Pat and Ken Fogarty, Patricia Fogerty, Ann Foley, Eileen Foley, Joseph Foley, Kathleen Foley, Matthew Foley, Michael Forbanci, Al Force, Charlotte Ford, Dorothy Ford, Frank Ford, Michael Formisano, Michele Formisano, Alexander Forsythe, Dominick F. Forte, Sonny Fortunato, Anthony Foti, Bruce Fox, Ed Franco, M. J. Frank, Vincent Frank, Aaron Frankel, Sadie Frankel, John Fraraccio, Dominick Frasco, Joe Fraser, Kenneth Frawley, Madlyn Frazier, Bob Free, Charles Free, Dorothy Free, Florence Free, Millie A. Free, Gerard D. Freese, Jr., Bray and Adelaide French, A. J. Frenkeldie, Thomas Fricchione, David Friedland, Doris Frindak, John Fritz, Fuchs and Altschul, Joseph Fugel, Steven Furka

Felix Gabrush, Ann Gacina, John E. Gacina, Vincent Gadzinski, Pat and Mary Gagliardi, George Gaines, Gordon Gaines, Dr. James Y. Gaines, Carmine Gaita, Joe and Carmela

Galano, Millie and Pat Galasso, James and Marie Galderi, Joseph Gallagher, Kathleen Gallagher, Leo, Helen and Rose Gallagher, Anthony Gallo, Francis Gallo, Hank Gallo, Louis Gallo, Selma Gallo, Eugene G. and Julia Galvin, Pasquale and Michelina Gamarello, Thomas Gangemi, Marie J. Garahan, Andrea and Audrey Gardner, Louis Garguilo, William Gargiulo, Lester Garo, Emanuel Garshofsky, Connie Garzilli, Frank Gasser, Margaret Gasser, John Gaynor, Thomas Gaynor, Bob Gemma, Dominick R. Gemma, John Gemma, Gina Gentile, Angie and Ann Gentile, Joseph Georgia, Bobby Georgian, Dr. Deutsch J. Geraghty, Walter Gerardino, William Gerrity, Joel Gersten, Charles Geter, Ken Gewertz, Catherine Gfroehrer, Elaine Giaquinta, Bonnie and Cindy Giaquinto, Jonathan Gibbs, M.D., Elizabeth Gilcher, Jerry Gilday, Joseph Gilday, John Gillen, John and Pat Gillen, Jr., Joseph Gillen, Joseph Gillen, Gloria Gillespie, Jack Gillick, Francis X. Gillmore, Hattie Gilmore, Louise Gimbert, Robert and Andrea Gimbert, Barbara and Michael Giordano, Carmine P. Giordano, Joseph and Carol Giorgio, Ceala Givens, Herb Gleason, Mary Glenton, Richard Glover, Father Edward Glynn, Bill Goble, Dominick Godino, Maedell Goggans, Mary Goggins, Arthur Abba Goldberg, Jack Geddy Goldberg, Louis Goldberg, Thomas Goldsberg, Jr., Bess Gollin, Ann Gronsewski, Arsenio and Joe Gonzalez, Phylliss Gonzales, Jeanette Goodall, Robert Goodall, Jane and Robert Goodheart, Donald Gordon, Martha Gordon, Charles Gore, James and Eileen Gorman, Joseph and John Gornicz, Chet Grabowski, Joseph (Ziggy) Grabowski, Bill Graham, John Graham, Mayor Raymond Graham, Josephine Granderson, Louis (Bunchy) Grant, Gloria Graves, Theresa Greaves, Ray Greaves, Anthony Greco, Richard Greczlo, Horatius Green, Sr., Carl Greene, "Buddy" Green, Charles Greene, Mayor John T. Gregorio, Mike Gregory, Lenny Greiner, Anthony Grieco, Walter and Angela Griffith, Chuck and Phyllis Griffiths, Joseph Griglio, Angela Grilletti, Catherine Grimm, Frank Grisi, Kevin and Annette Grom. Anna M. Grompone, Peter Grompone, Joe Grossi, Tim Grossi, Mary E. Grubie, J. Owen Grundy, Louis Guanci, Frank J. Guarini, Jr., William Guarini, John Guerra, James Guida, Charles Gumina, Albert E. Gunnell, Rose Guorini, Nancy Gurczeski, Beverly Gurtenstein, Sol and Laurie Gurtenstein, Frank Gustaferro, Douglas Gutch, Edward Gutch

Morris Haber, Robert Hackel, Patricia Hadden, Peggy Hagan, Charlotte Haley, Alvin Hall, Patricia Hall, Wesley and Gail Hall, Julia Hamalaimen, Joe Hamelin, Gladys Hamilton, Karen Hamilton, Edward and Francis Hammill, Johnny and Winifred Hampton, Margaret Hand, Raymond P. Haney, Charles Hannon, Lillian A. Hanser, Brian Harding, David Hardy, Frank Harnett, Carol B. Harrell, Richard Harrison, Edward and Peg Hart, Mrs. Eleanor Hart, Morris Hart, Thomas Hart, Joseph Hartman, Charles Harvey, Lowell Harwood, Darlene Haslebush, Mary Haslebush, Jerry Haskins, Mendell and Dianne Hatcher, Tim Hawkes, Callie Hayes, Francis X. Hayes, Neil Hayes, Irving Haynes, Janet Haynes, Wayne Hayes, Francis X. Hayes, Ronald T. Hazzard, Pat Healy, Carl Heard, Claire Heath, August W. Heckman, Bernard Heckman, Marylou Heim, Ralph Heins, Henry Helstoski, Rev. Elijah M. Hendon, George Henne, Lorraine Hennessy. Delores Herelihy, Albin Herman, Mario Hernandez, George Heser, George Hettesheimer, William Higgins, Maureen and John Hill, John E. Hoffman, Annette and John Hogan, Ellen Hogan, Margaret G. Hogan, Mary Hogan, Mary Hoggarty, James Holmes, Henry Holtzmann, Robert A. Holzschuh, Eleanor Hopt, Domingo Hornilla, Jr., Purita D. Hornilla, Isadore Hornstein, Louis Horowitz, Kelly Hoskins, Catherine Hottendorf, Corine Howard, Donald Howard, William F.X. and Gertrude Howe, Sr., Tommie and Gertrude Howell, Jr., Frank Hughes, James Hughes, James F. Hughes, Irene Hughes, Lenore Hulton, Bill Humer, James Humphrey, Edward Hunter, Kathleen Hunter, Robert and Carol Hussey, Jack Hynes

Anthony Iazzetti, Vic Illonardo, Joan Introcaso, Nicholas Introcaso, Mary Intromasso,

Joseph Ioffredo, Anthony Ippolito, Frank Italiano, John A. Iungerman, Gertrude Izarehski Carl Jacob, Ann M. Jacobs, Dave Jacobs, Kay E. Jacobs, Sam Jacobsen, Chris Jackman, Charles Jackson, Sr., David Lee Jackson, Emily Jackson, Robert E. Jackson, Andrew Jamba, Gloria James, Jack James, Gerard Jamison, Nellie Janiszewski, Robert Janiszewski, Anthony Jannuzzu, Catherine Jarvis, Robert Jastrebski, Margaret Jeffers, Wayne Jeffrey, Bill Jelm, Louis W. Jenkins, Donald Jengo, Aretha and Viola Jessie, Joe Job, James Johnson, Lenore Johnson, Mark and Estelle Johnson, Richard Johnson, Rosemary Johnson, Willie L. Johnson, George Jones, David Jones, Gertrude Jones, Margaret Jones, Michael F. Jones, Pringle A. and Lucy Jones, Sandra Jones, William Jones, Willie S. and Eula Jones, Thomas Jones, Albert Jordan, Pamela Jordan, Dermat Joy, Janet Joyner, Mary Julian, Stanley Jurusz

D. and P. Kabitis, Gene Kacperowski, Raymond Kacperowski, Florence Kacprowicz, Harry Kacprowicz, Jerome T. Kacprowicz, Richard J. Kacprowicz, Marie Kacot, Robert W. Kalb, Ceslaus Kaminski, Julia Kaminski, Silvana and Chester Kaminski, Gale Kane, Robert Kane, Arthur Kaplan, Lena Karlson, Thornsten Karlson, Joseph Karpiak, Abbie Lynn Kattner, Mrs. Emily Katz, Catherine A. Kavanaugh, Alice and William Kavanagh, Joseph Kavanaugh, Joseph Kavanaugh, Jr., Joseph Kealy, Jr., Edward Keany, Raymond Kearns, Carol and Sharon Keating, Katherine Keelan, Raymond G. Keeley, Al Keenan, Monica Keenan, Wendell (Wimpy) Keenan, Helen Kelaher, Ann Kelly, Ellen Kelly, Frank (Buck) Kelly, George Kelly, Hugh Kelly, Loretta Kelly, Mike Kelly, Vincent Kelly, Jr., Thomas H. Kelly, James Kelton, Bernard Kennedy, Don Kennedy, Jim Kennedy, Jim (Ace) Kennedy, Thomas Kennedy, Lorryn Keogh, Charles "Buddy" Kerr, Gladys J. Kestner, Isabelle and Peter Kierce, Raymond Kierce, Walter Kierce, Claire Kierman, Jack Kikon, Thelma Kilby, Jerome Killeen, Kathleen D. Killeen, Richard Killeen, Daniel Killmer, James King, June King, Mildred King, Virginia Kirwan, Andrew Kizman, Chester Klejmont, Tom Klimkiewicz, Ralph Klopper, Alberta Knight, Larry Knights, Eleanor Knueppel, Charlie Koch, Charlie Koch, Sr., Robert L. Koenigsberg, Ed. Kolodziew, Dorothy Komar, Helen Kopycinski, Helen J. Kopycinski, Steve Kopycinski, Theresa A. Kopycinski, Peter Kordulak, Rose Kowalski, Chester Koyzeniewski, Helen Kozma, Ted Kozma, Joseph Krajnik, Hilda S. Kramer, Sol Kramer, Marjorie Krasko, Ray Krasner, Dr. Vincent Krasnica, Joseph Kraus, Linda Kraus, Rita Kraus, Charles K. Krieger, Maurice Krivit, Steven Krohn, Marjorie Krueger, Felix S. and Eva S. Kryscia, B. Kubicki, Linda Kufka, Walter and Alfreda Kurylo, John Kurzinka, Arlene Kysel

Rose La Bella, John La Bruno, Joseph Lafer, Thomas O. P. Lally, Christopher D. Lamb, Jane Lambert, Pat Lambert, Louise Lambides, Ralph Lambiase, Francis Lamonica, Salvatore and Bernadette Lando, Jacob Landau, Rose Landry, Beverly Lane, Francis Lane, Maggie Ann Lane, Bert Lanigan, Francis X. and Carol Lane, George La Porte, Vincent La Raia, Danny Larkin, Pete Larocca, Peter Larocco, William Lau, Bernie Laufgas, Harry Laurie, Harriet Lawless, Arnold Lazarus, Beverly Lazzara, Joe Leach, Joseph P. Lecowitch, John Leddy, Dominick Lefante, John Lefante, Michael Le Fante, Raymond Le Fante, David Leff, Fran Legraros, John Lekos, Noemi Lekos, Susan Lelenski, Frank Lemise, George Lemons, Jr., Dominick and Lucy Leone, Gross Leone, Joseph Lepis, Leon Lerner, Janet Leshynski, Diane Letizia, Jerry Letizia, Joan Letizia, Silvio Letizia, Marilyn Levin, Joe F. Levine, Peter Levine, Gert Lewis, Mildred Lewis, Moses Lewis, Walter Lezynski, Judge Abraham Lieberman, Janet Gaita Lisco, Edward and Alice Litke, Geneva R. Lockerman, Florence Lockheed, Donald Loehwing, Kathleen Logan, Al Lombardi, Edward Lombardi, Floyd Lombardi, Anthony E. Lombardi, Madeline and Anthony Lombardi, Jr., Grace M. Lombardo, Patrick and Alice Long, Morris T. Longo, John R. Longo, Antonia Lopez,

Maureen Lorancio, Jerome Lord, Rudy Loreca, Estelle Lorraine, Mary L Louf, Ray Louf, Mary LuBrowski, Albert E. Lucas, Dr. Estellita Lucas, John Luciani, Joe and Julie Luciano, Zaida Luciano, Anthony Lupino, Donald Lynch, Joe Lynch, James F. Lynch, Claire Lying, Dr. Irving Lynn, Frances Lyons, Kevin Lystak
   Anthony and Joann Macagnano, Dr. Michael Macaluso, Bill Maccarelli, Rose Macchia, Walter Macchia, James Macci, Francis MacDonald, Isidoro Machado, Patrick Mack, Robert Mack, Dorothy Mackenzie, Paul W. Mackey, Esq., Joe Macula, Michael Madden, Ed Madsen, Genaro Maffia, Edward T. Magee. Barbara Maggio, Irene Mahoney, Jack Mailly, Tom Mailly, Mrs. Victoria Maio. Carmela Maiolino, Diane Maisonet, Chester Majewski, Chester Major, Ceil Makowski, Naomi S. Malachi, William Malachi, George J. Malfetti, Mrs. Malinowski, Matty Malone, Alice Maloney, Francis Maloney, Helen Maloney, Jeanne Maloney, John, Eilleen and Nora Maloney, Mary Ellen Maloney, Raymond Maloney, Thomas Maloney, John Malta, Nick Malta, Joseph F. Maltaliano, Milton Mandel, John Manella, Albert and Lois Mann, Allen Manzo, Frank Manzo, Ronald Manzo, Sam Manzo, John J. Marchese, George Marchitto, Jeffrey Marciniak, Alexander Marino, Linda Markiewicz, Joe and Bob Markowski, Stanley Marney, Henry and Annette Marquand, Anthony Marra, Charles Marrow, Charles Marsella, Jr., Joseph Marsella, Maureen Marshall, Amelia G. Martin, C. Martin, Harry Martin, John Martin, William Martin, Francis R. Martineau, Manuel Martinez, Steve Marusak, Michael Marzitello, Michael Masacci, Robert Mason, William A. Massa, Ann Massett, Charles D. Massett, Jr., Harry W. Massey, Nick Mastorelli, Louis Mastramonico, James Mastres, James Mastria, Louis Mastromonica, Tom Mastropietro, Michael Masucci, Ciro Matarazzo, Angelina Matrachia, Leboria Matrachia, Lee Matrachia, Terence Matthews, Carmine Matticola, Dominick Matticola, Theresa Matulewicz, John Mauro, Paul Max, Deborah Maxwell, Ernest and Helen Maxwell, Kevin Mayer, Dolores Mayo, Leonard Mayo, Charles Mays, Clifton Mays, Dave and Ollie Mays, Lewis Mays, Walter Mays, Jack Mazer, Al Mazza, Angelo Mazzeo, Charles McAllister, Jr., Frank McCabe, Marguerite McCabe, Henry McCall, Elizabeth McCann, Maureen and Jerry McCann, Tony McCann, James McCarthy Mayor John J. McCarthy, Ken McCarthy, Brenda McClery, Mary L. McConville, John McCormick, Shelly McCrohan, Harold McCullers, Henry McCullers, Sandra McCullers, Carolyn McCuthchen, Pierce McDaniel, David McDonald, James McDonald, Thomas McDonough, Sr., Thomas McDonough, Jr., Joan McDonough, Izetter McDuffy, Michael McFaul, Edward McGovern, Helen McGovern, John McGovern, Dr. Patrick McGovern, Philip McGovern, Thomas McGovern, Robert D. McGowan, Ron McGowan, Tom McGrannahan, Edward McGrath Sr., John M. McGrath, John P. McGrath, Mary Ann McGrath, Patrick J. McGrath, Nora McGreeny, Vincent McGuckin, Hugh McGuire, Warren McHale, Ann F. McInery, Gary McKinnon, William McKinnon, Augustus and Dorothy McKnight, Eugene McKnight, Loretta McKnight, John McLaughlan, John McLaughlin, Mary McLaughlin, William V. McLaughlin, Newell McLeod, Addison McLeon, Elaine McMahon, Gertrude F. McMahon, Melvin G. McMahon, Tom MacMahon, Catherine McMichael, Joe McNally, Bob McNamara, John McNamara, Peter J. McNamara, Audrey and Gail McNaught, Fannie McPheason, Kenneth McPherson, Margaret McShane, William Meagher, Dorothea Means, Harvey Means, Ray Means, Sean Means, Lou Mecka, Claudette Meegan, Edward Meehan, Kenneth and Rose Ann Meeney, Christine Megargel, Chuck Melly. Ralph Melocco, Louis Meloro, Rufus Meloro, Allen W. Melvin, William and Virginia Melvin, Aida Mendez, Juan A. Mendoza, M.D., James Menge, Eugene Menter, Heidi Meola, Mary and Harry Meola, Lydia Mercadefe, Gloria Mercer, Edward Mesa, Ralph Messano, Charles D. Meyer, Robert Meyer,

J. Mezukiewiz, Israel E. Mi, Shirley Michalski, John Miele, Robert Migliaro, Beverly Migliozzi, Ernest Migliozzi, Terry Migliozzi, Joseph Miksza, Jean D. Miller, Richard Miller, Stanley Miller, Steve Miller, C. Milson, Nick Mina, Peggy Minan, John Vincent Minella, Anne Minervini, Hector and Mandee Miranda, George Mirsky, Julio Mistral, Alina Miszkiewicz, Peter Mocco, Jerry Molloy, Frank S. Monaco, Joan Monahan, Frank Mongelluzzo, Charles Montalbano, Edith Montalbano, Edmond Monti, Camille Mooney, Lorraine Moore, William Moore, Willie and Wyniana Moore, Sylviea Moose, Carmen Morales, Florence Morales, Robert and Janet Morales, Francis Moran, Francis and Mary Ann Moran, James Moran, Frank Morganti, Cornelius Moriarity, Carmen D. Mormandia, Bill Morton, Anthony Mosca, Ronald Mount, Sal Mosca, James Moyer, Larry Mullane, Sr., Doris Muller, Lorraine Mullin, Bob Mullins, John T. Mullins, John and Dorothy Mulrooney, Felicita Mundz , Richard Munoz, Mayor Frank Murphy, Jim Murphy, John and Margaret Murphy, Violet and Richie Murphy, Deborah M. Murray, Diane Murray, Angelo Mureo, Bill Murtha, Thom as and Ann Murtha, Joseph A. and Alfred Muscolino, Mayor William Musto, Ruby and Ri chard Mylak, James Myron

Anna Nacheczewski, Robert Nachezewski, R. Nalts, Catherine Naples , Frank Narcisso, Pat Nardolilli, Leonard and Norma Narushinsky, Joe Nass, Louis Nastasi, Norm Naviskinski, Danny Nazario, Isaac Nazario, Joseph Nazzaro, Josephine Nazzaro, Louis N egron, Mary Negron, Pedro L. Negron, Patrick Nelan, Jr., William Nelson, Paul Nemes, John Nero, Robert Netchert, Rick Newman, William C. Newton, Donald Nicholas, Ken Ni ckens, Mary Nickerson, Raymond and Mary L. Nickerson, Angel Nieves, Frank Nieves, Mi chael Nimbley, Dr. Joe Nixon, Joseph Nobile, Pauline Nolan, Tom Nolan, Jane No rcia, Jerry Norcia, Bernie and Alice Nordquist, Carmen Normandia, Peter and Helen No wak, Fred Nugent, Lucille Nuher, Carlos Nunez, Marvin Nusbaum

Dick O'Brien, John O'Brien, Katherine O'Brien, Robert O'Brien, An drew O'Connor, Daniel O'Connor, James O'Donnell, Kathleen O'Donnell, Robert and Maureen O'Donnell, Martin O'Gava, Harold O'Grady, Ed O'Haire, Charles O'Keefe, Cindy O'Keef e, Clarinda Okeefe, John O'Keefe, Mike O'Keefe, Colean Ognissanti, John Olama, Robert P. Oliva, Lee Oliver, Louie L. Oliver, Ann O'Malley, Dave O'Malley, Joan O'Malley, Ron O'Malley, Eileen and Bill O'Mara, John O'Mara, Brian O'Melia, Meta O'Neil, Jose O'Neill, Joseph Orchowski, Patrick Orrani, Marie Orrico, Cildimarra Ortega, Margarita Ortiz, Thomas Osborne, Robert Osterbrink, Edward Outwater, Vale Outwater, Perfecto Oyola

Louis Pacheco, Mayor Chris Paci, Gertrude Padalla, Robert and Joa n Padgett, Frank and Ann Pagano, Joseph Pagano, Gloria and Russell Pagliughi, Mr. Thomas Pakidis, Peter Paladino, Joseph J. Panepinto, Joseph Panepinto, Esq., Victor Paone, Jr., Phillip Papalardo, Jerry Papick, Lou Parisi, John and Mary Parke, Cornelius R. Parker, Jessie Parker, Joanna Parker, Marie Parker, John Pascale, Pat Pasculli, Edward Paterson, Doug Patterson, John Patterson, Robert Patterson, Dorothy Paugh, Donald Paulsen, Barbara E. Payne, James Payton, William Pearl, Mr. Jackie Pearson, Neil Pecoraro, Rufino Peglaspi, John Pehanic, Mary Pehanich, "Lucky" Pellagatti, Joe and Elizabeth Pellagatti, Vincent Pellecchio, Joseph Pellegrino, Mary Ann Pellegrino, Francis Peluso, Dorothea Penin, Ira M. Penn, Joe Pennullo, Gonzeles Perez, Cathy D. Perna, Agnes and Nancy Perri, Joseph Perricone, James Perry, Morris Pesin, Nathaniel Peterson, William Peterz, Keith Petrofsky, Susan and John Petrowski, Linda Pharmes, Charles Pheribo, Cathy Phillips, Joan Phillips, Raymond Phillips, Susan Phillips, Richard Piatkowski, Matty Piccillo, Ronald Piccillo, Thomas Pickett, Alexander Pierce, Carmine Pierro, Dr. Alfred Pignataro, Christine Pignatello, Ralph Pinelli, Nick Piombino, John Pipi, Pat Pipi, Sonny Piscitello, Mary Piscotta, Josephine Piszel, Robert L. Pittman, Joe Pizzelanto, Oscar Plotnik, Carroll Polakoski, Raymond Polakoski,

Ann Politano, Mary Polites, Ann Pollaro, Erwin E. Pollock, Joseph Pompeo, Gene Presscott, Edward Pulver, Walter Popyer, Al Poreda, Catherine Powanda, Mrs. Frank Prekop, Ronald Prekop, Emily Price, William Price, Anthony Prinzo, Jr., Nicholas P. Protomastro, John Prout, Jr., Hank Przystup, Andrew Puff, Felicia Pugliese, George Purcell, Walter Puriven, E. Pusaver, George Puterbaugh

Joseph Quail, Kenneth M. Queary, Karen Quinn, Ken and Regina Quinn, Kenneth Quinn, Mae Quinn, Raymond Quinn, Raymond W. Quinn, Ramond Quinones, Dottie Quinto, Mr. and Mrs. Edward Quirk, Edward P. Quirk, Irene Quirk, Maryann Quirk, Richard Quirk

E. Perry Rabbino, Herbert Rabbino, Beatrice Radozycki, Mayor Dom Raffa, Jan Ragni, Frances Ragno, Chick Raimondo, Casimir Rakowski, Joe Rakowski, Charles and Marie Ralph, Margaret Ranson, Arnold and Ceil Raphael, Edwin Rapp, Mary Ratyniak, Susan Ratyniak, Mary Ann Raymond, Emil Razzoli, Angelo Reale, Isabel Reardon, Francis X. Reddington, Pat Reed, Conrad Reehill, Jack Reehill, Natalie Reehill, Doris Regal, James Regal, Jr., "Duke" Regan, Mike Regan, Patricia Regan, Mary Rehbelin, Ed Reibasell, Albert F. and Mary Reicherz, Kenneth Reidinger, John Reilly, Peter Reilly, Elizabeth G. Reiser, Helen Rembizewski, Ruth Renevick, Harry Renner, Gwendolyn and Arnette Reynolds, Robert Reynolds, Mary Riccardi, Rosemarie, Carmela and Catherine Riccardi, August Ricciardi, Charles Ricciardi, Charles Ricciardi, Jr., Bernie Richardson, James Richardson, Theodore Richardson, Yetta Rickter, Gary and Carol Ann Riebesell, Edward Riebesell, Frank Rienzo, M.D., George Rienzo, M.D., Paul Riepe, William and Gloria Riepe, Robert J. Rigby, John and Ann Ripke, Estelle Ristaina, Frances Ristaino, Ralph Ristaino, Ronald Ristaino, Edwardo Rivera, Gil Rivera, Leonides Rivera, Ruth Rivera, Willie Rivera, Frank and Elena Roberts, Keith Roberts, Muriel Roberts, Valerie Robertson, Dr. Jerene Robbins, Harry Robinson, Julian Robinson, Lester Robinson, Patrick K. Rochford, Frank Rodgers, Rose Rodio, Andres Rodriquez, Ben Rodriguez, Emma Rodriguez, Louie Rodriguez, Louis Rodriguez, Lucy Rodriguez, Luis Rodriquez, Ann Rogalski, Arlene Rogalski, Diane Rogalski, Paul E. Rogalski, Fred Rolon, Noel Roman, Councilman Anthony Romano, Armand Romano, Alan Romanowski, John Romanowski, Josephine Romanowski, Julio and Frank Rosa, Joseph Roselle, Marvin Roseman, Howard T. Rosen. Janet Rosenberg, Philip Rosenbloom, Luis and Visitocin Rosca, Spencer Rose, Mary Ann Ross, Christine Rotily, Martin Ruby, Richard Ruggierio, Vincent Ruggerio, Anthony L. Ruocco, Marie Rush, Tom Rush, John P. Russell, Frank Russello, Peter Russillo, Michael Russomiello, Elizabeth Russum, Hank Rustic, Harold Ruvolt, Jr., Harold Ruvolt, Sr., Camilla Ryan, Margaret Ryan, Joseph T. Ryan, Kenneth and Joan Ryan, Michael G. Ryan, Joseph Rybakowski, Chester Rydwin, M.D., Ryglicki & Pompliano, John J. and Anna L. Ryska

Robert Sabello, Lou Sabbers, James and Ann Saccone, Ray Sadowski, Butch Sailer, Dennis M. Salerno, Frank Salerno, Joseph Sally, Julie Salmon, Joseph C. Saltarelli, Victor Samara, Julia Samman, Adela Sanchez, Jose A. Sanchez, Tony Sanchez, Tony Sanchez, Jr., Harry Sandwith, Jim Sansome, Louis F. X. Santangelo, Victor Santasieri, Eulodio Santiago, Evelyn Santiago, Carmello Santini, Jane Santollo, Dorothy Santora, Joseph A. Santora, Flora Santora, Andrew Santore, Frank Sapone, Nicholas Sardella, John Sardona, Charlie Sarno, Jacqueline Sarpa, James V. Sarpa, James Sarpa, Jr., Viola Sargent, Anthony and Fanny Sarno, Ann Marie Satero, John Saueracker, Rev. Kenneth Saunders, Stacey Sava, John Sawicki, Ann Sazalecki, John Scafidi, Ed Scala, Edward Scala, Robert Scala, Frank Scalafani, Jean Scalise, Patricia Scanlon, Eleanor Scappaticcio, Al Scerbo, Anthony Scerbo, Frank Scerbo, Fred Scerbo, Robert Schenker, Annette Schillari, Charles Schimenti, Connie Schimenti, Dorothy Schmidt, Angela F. Schmitt, William Schroeder, Seymour Schulman,

Louis Scialli, A. F. and Josephine Schifano, Josephine Schifano, Dr. S. Schlussel, Cohen and Solomon Schneider, Peter Schreiber, Aaron Schulman, Charlotte Schumann, Lou Scialli, Joseph Scibetta, Peter Scibetta, Jr., Frank Sclafani, Frank A. Scott, Joseph Scott, Joseph Scribellito, Marion Scuzzese, Pat Scuzzese, Pamela and Nantexter Sebron, Martin and Mildred Seel, Murray Seiden, Patricia Selvaggio, Mono Sen, Louis Serterides, Aurdra Sevano, Bernice Severini, Dr. John J. Seyler, Jack Seymor, Joseph Shaara, Desmond Shanley, Mike Shanley, Ray Shanley, Francis Shannon, Veronica Shannon, John Shapiro, Arthur F. Sharpe, Lois and Stanley Shaw, Robert W. Shaw, Maureen, Mary and Kathleen Sheehan, Alice Sheil, Anne Sheil, Carol Sheil, David Sheil, Frances Sheil, James A. Sheil, James P. Sheil, Katherine Sheil, Patrick Sheil, Thomas Sheil, Walter Sheil, David Shellman, Bucky Sherman, Jack Sherry, Joseph M. Shine, Phyllis R. Shootsky, Robert Shortell, Irving Shulman, M.D., Steve and Rita Sidor, Murray Siegel, Frank G. and Helen Sielski, Gary Sielski, Harriet Sigelkow, Vincent Signorile, Stephen J. Sikely, Mark Silver, Simon and Hortense Silver, Arsenio Silvestri, Michael Silvestri, Robert A. Silvestri, Joseph Simonovich, Frances Simmons, Paul Sinclair, M.D., John J. Sinisi, Carmelo Sita, Jean Sita, Nick Sita, John Sizzelkow, John Skevin, Howard Sklower, Frederick Skop, Joseph Skrypski, M.D., Charles B. Slade, John Sledzikowski, Earl Slocum, George Smaldone, Henry Small, Frances and Michael Smarro, Vic Smarro, Anne M. Smith, Carol Smith, Charles Smith, Charles R. Smith, Sr., Christina Smith, Florence Smith, Gloria Smith, James Smith, Kevin Smith, Mary Smith, Meyer Smith, M.D., Mollie Smith, Norman Smith, Regina and Carol Smith, Roxie Smith, Thornton Smith, Tina Smith, Rhudell Snelling, Rita Snyder, Agnes Sobczuk, Ralph Sodano, Peter Sommers, Marie Sorentino, Pat Sorentino, Joseph Sorino, Theresa Sorino, Joseph Sorrentino, Patricia Soto, Lucy Spaltro, Leo Spangenberg, Jack Spector, Joe Spector, Raymond Spellmeyer, Donald and Isabel Spence, B. Sperling, Mary Ann Spina, Edward Spinello, Edward J. Spinello, John Spinello, Carol and Joann Spink, Edwin H. Spitznas, George Staley, Gloria and Stephen Stallworth, John Stallworth, George Stampoulos, Thomas Stanaway, Andy Stanfield, Dr. Chris Stanley, Dolores and Gene Stanley, Lorraine Stanley, Florence Stanton, Thomas Stanton, Natalie Stapleton, Marie Stefanchik, Margaret Steinhauser, Eddie Stephens, Eddie Stephens, Jr., Mitchell Stepuch, Fred Stevens, Edward Stewart, Joseph G. Stewart, Stanely Stine, Isabelle Stisi, Elmer Stobe, Anthony Strangia, John M. Strichek, Gertrude Strunk, Jamie Suarez, Frank Sudia, Steven Sudia, Dot Sullivan, Estelle Sullivan, Fran Sullivan, Joe Sullivan, Joseph Sullivan, Willie Sullivan, Samuel Summers, Ray Sushko, Natalie Sussello, Nathan Susskind, James F. Sutcliff, Samuel Sutphen, Daniel Sweeney, Hildred Sweeney, Joe Sweeney, Joseph Sweeney, Kay Sweeney, Claire Swidryk, Thecla Switag, Edward Switas, Sr., John Sydor, Selener Sydor, Steven Sydor, Helen Symanski, Alex Szabo

Max Tabacchi, Irene Tafuri, Joseph Talafous, Guiseppe Tambone, David Taradash, Harold Tassi, William Tate, George Taylor, Peggy Taylor, Ralph Taylor, Thomas Taylor, Mae Tedeschi, Vincent F. and Rachel J. Tedeschi, Stanley Telkowski, Al Tentoni, Joseph Terpak, Eugene Terry, Catherine Teselli, Rodney M. Thomaier, Albert Thomas, Josephine Thomas, Florence Thompson, Jack Thompson, Lovett A. Thompson, William Thornley, Sr., Barbara Thornton, Elizabeth Thornton, Winifred Thurston, John Tierney, Barry Tikirian, Benny Tillman, Elizabeth Tinsley, Nick and Judy Tirone, Leo Tluchowski, John Tomaras, John Tomasin, Irene Tomaszewski, William Tomazewski, William and Anne Tomaszewski, Anna and Mary Tomeo, Fred Tomkins, Henry V. Topoleski, Andeen Tormey, Miguel Torres, John and Maureen Toth, Marion Tozzi, John Trafficante, John Train, M.D., Charles D. Travis, John and Joy Tredy, Marleen Tredy, William Tremper, Rosalia Trinidad, Guy

Trisolini, Tom Troy, Gary Tullock, William and Walter R. Tunnell, Dan and Ann Turco, Fred Turco, Richard Tylender, Chester Tyskewicz, John Tyskewicz, Paul Tyskewicz

Hyman Umansky, Joseph Urban, Dorothy Urbanski, Joseph and Leonard J. Urbanski, Raymond W. Urbanski, Thomas and Pat Urgo, Ronald Uttariello

Robert M. Valvano, Jackie and Virginia Van Wie, Carmine Varano, Anthony Varsalone, Jaime Vasquez, Fred Vassallo, Carlos Vequilla, Charles Velli, Ernie Veltre, Marie Venner, Anthony Venutolo, Antonio, Susan, Elizabeth, Tim, and Mike Venutolo, Florence Venutolo, Michael Venutolo, Bob Verbist, M. Verdi, Frank J. Verga, Joseph S. E. Verga, Hugo Vicari, Joseph Vicari, Frank Viggiani, Victor Villafane, Michael Viola, John Vitale, D.M.D., John Vizzacchiero, Joseph T. Vogellus, Joe Volpe, Sr., Joseph Volpe, Marilyn Volpe, Mark Volpe, Conrad Vuocolo

Daniel Waddleton, Bruce Wade, Fred Wager, George Walcott, Kent Walcott, Mary, Catherine and Henry Walker, Sol and Helen Walkes, Frank Wall, Helen Wall, Donald Walrod, Joan Walrod, Kathleen and Donald Walrod, Lee and Babs Walsky, David Walther, Jayne Walther, Joan W. Walther, Norman Walther, Burnett C. Walton, George and Sallie Walton, J. Walton, Charles Walty, Ann Wanca, Helen Wanca, Josephine Wandell, John Wanser, Elsie Ward, Joe Ward, Marilyn E. Ward, William F. Ward, Nancy Warlikowski, Pauline S. Warms, Everett Warner, Shirley Warnir, Helen Warrea, Bruenig Warzecha, Eddie Warzecha, Phyllis Washington, Nicholas Wasko, Joanne Wately, Ruth Watley, Elenora Watson, Robert Watson, Curtis Webb, Rev. Ercel Webb, Elnardo Webster, Paul Weiner, Wayne H. Weiner, Lester Weinmann, Harold Weinstein, Margaret Weinstein, Nancy Weinstein, Virginia Weinstein, Fanney Weisberger, George Weisenfeld, Debra Welty, Angela Wendolowski, Peter A. Wermert, Michael Wesco, Thomas Wheatley, Mary White, William White, Dennis Whitehead, Joseph Whitehead, Bobbie Whyn, Juanita Widejko, Florence Wieckowski, Brian Wiggins, Dock Williams, Martha Wiggs, Charles Williams, Franklin Williams, Janice Williams, Lillian Williams, Mamie Williams, Morris Williams, Henrietta Wilkins, Francis Wilmot, Dr. Arthur Wilson, Daniel G. Wilson, Raymond A. Wilson, Rose Marie Wilson, Susan Wilson, Marion Winds, Bruce Winn, Dennis and Patricia Winn, Mickey Winograd, Morris Winograd, Edna Winston, Merle and Olga Wise, Edward Wisniewski, Harry Witt, Rosemary Wodzanowski, Marshall J. Wofsy, William Wolfe, Wally Wolfe, Joseph Woodard, Eluie Woods, William Woods, James Wolleon, D. Wollrecht, Cecil T. Woolsey, Barbara Woote, Bernadine Wright, Constance Wright, Mary Wright

Leon Yablon, Phil and Ruth Yablon, Father Victor Yanitelli, George Yanuzzi, Rosemary Yawdozy, John Yeager, Robert Yeo, Margaret Youmans, James Young, Marie Young, M. E. Young

Anthony Zacche, Leo Zacharow, George Zadroga, Alfred Zampella, Andrew Zampella, Edward Zampella, Edward R. Zampella, Peter J. Zampella, Alexander Zapar, Warren and Audrey Zapp, Peter Zapple, Stanley Zaremba, Jean Zawistowski, Catherine Zdichocki, Joan and Robert Zdichocki, Charles Zelinski, Edward Zelinski, Ted Zelinski, Theresa Zelinski, Anthony Zeszotrski, Walter Ziemba, John Zjawin, Charles Zuppa, Jennie Zuppa, John Zuppa

And finally, John and Betty Betlow, Eddie (Shannon) Eckert, Lea Gutman, Walter Hudzin